Making Movies with Final Cut Express

Peachpit Press
Berkeley, California

Making Movies with Final Cut Express
A Self-paced Guide to Editing Digital Video
Michael Rubin
Copyright ©2004 by Michael Rubin

Peachpit Press
1249 Eighth Street
Berkeley, CA 94710
(510) 524-2178
(510) 524-2221 (fax)

Find us on the World Wide Web at www.peachpit.com
To report errors, please send a note to errata@peachpit.com
Peachpit Press is a division of Pearson Education

©2001 "Song of Santa Cruz" mural by James Carl Aschbacher
©2000 "David (151)" written and performed by Suzanne Brewer. Used with permission.
Still images from Seagate corporate videos © 2002 Seagate Technology. Used with permission.
Excerpts in Appendix from *Nonlinear: A Field Guide to Digital Video and Film Editing*, 4th edition, Triad Publishing Co., ©2000 Michael Rubin. Used with permission.

Editor: Nancy Peterson
Production coordinators: Myrna Vladic, Becky Winter
Copyeditor: Elissa Rabellino
Compositor: Christi Payne, Book Arts
Indexer: FireCrystal Communications
Cover design: TMA Ted Mayer + Associates
Chapter opening photos: Michael Rubin
Cover photos: Digital Vision (left) and Vicky Kasala/Getty Images (right)

ISBN 0 321 19777 1
9 8 7 6 5 4 3 2 1
Printed and bound in the United States of America.

Acknowledgments

This book derives from a successful and efficient method I developed to train professionals in how to use computers to make movies and television. They didn't care about computers or software, but they did care about editing. My method covered exactly what they needed to know to get their work done, and little more. My deepest thanks to the great editors whom I trained and who trained me, in particular my mentor, Gabriella Cristiani.

This book, like most of my works, relied on the trust and cooperation of my friends and family. A hearty thanks to Chris and Kirsten Mehl for starring in Chocoluv, our tutorial movie; Chris Bryant for his BMX excellence and video enthusiasm; Lisa Strong-Aufhauser for her valuable production contributions; Suzanne Brewer for her fine music; and Seagate Technology and Petroglyph Ceramic Lounge for access to their corporate videos. Thanks also to Lisa Jensen and James Carl Aschbacher; Danny, Louise, Maida, and Asa Rubin; Chris Breen, Cathy and Marty Newman (*we'll miss Griselda*), Hilary Bryant, Winston Whittaker, and Gina Katz. A sincere toast to the many professionals and visionaries who make up my *Nonlinear* brain trust— Ron Diamond, Dean Godshall, Ken Yas, and Lisa Brenneis. And, as always, thank you to Mary Sauer and Steve Arnold, who brought me to Lucasfilm in the first place and whom I can never thank enough.

Thanks to the team at Peachpit Press, who manage to tolerate my unorthodox visions and yet guide me through the process of producing acceptably professional books: my second-edition editor, Nancy Peterson, and original editor, Kate McKinley; and in particular Marjorie Baer, for her focus and vision. Also a hearty thank you to the rest of the book team at Peachpit: Nancy Ruenzel, Gary-Paul Prince, Scott Cowlin, Mimi Heft, Lisa Brazieal, and Nikki Echler McDonald, and Kim Lombardi, and all the rest.

A quick hug and kiss to the extended Rubin family—in Toronto, Santa Fe, Gainesville, Sedona, New York, and wherever they roam. I want to specially send love to my parents (happy 50th anniversary!) for their ongoing enthusiasm and interest in my disparate ventures.

Finally, the true source and inspiration for this book—Jennifer, Jonah, and Alina, whose lives are so much a part of my own that any work of mine necessitates their profound tolerance and unwavering support. Jen, my love, thank you for being my gentle reminder that at the end of the day, none of this technology means squat.

—Michael Rubin

Table of Contents

Acknowledgments iv

Introduction xi

Chapter 1 First Things First   1

A Place to Work 2
   The FireWire Connection 3
   A Video Monitor 5
A Quick Tour Through the Final Cut Interface 11
   Launching Final Cut Express 11
   The Browser 13
   The Viewer 17
   The Canvas 17
   The Timeline 18
   Workflow 20
Preparing for the Tutorials 24
   Saving Your Tutorial Project 24
   Loading the DVD Files into Your Mac 25
   Importing Video Clips 27
Playtime: Mastering the Video Controls 28
   Method 1: One Hand on the Mouse 29
   Method 2: One Hand on the Keyboard 36
   Going on a Scavenger Hunt 40

Chapter 2 Basic Editing   49

Familiarize Yourself with the Scene 50
   Shot Vocabulary Cheat Sheet 52
   Reviewing Your Coverage 53
Editing Your First Shots 59
Understanding Inserts 61
   The Insert Concept 65
   The Ripple Concept 66
   Two More Inserts 67
Timeline Features 73
   Time Scale 73
   Track Height 75
   Scrolling the Timeline 76
   Adjusting Shot Volume Levels 77
Adjusting Your Shots 78
   The Trim Concept 79
   The Delete Concept 90
Creating Multiple Versions 95
Review of Final Cut Express Editing Tools 97

Chapter 3 Less Basic Editing   101

Track Controls 102
   Locking vs. Linking 105
The Overlap 107
   Roll Edit (Non-Rippling Trim) in Picture Only 109
   A Rolling Shortcut 112
The Insert 115
   Three- and Four-Point Editing 116
   Overwrite (Non-Rippling Insert) in Picture Only 117
   Overwrite (Non-Rippling Insert) in Sound Only 122
Adjusting Your One-Track Shots 128
   Roll Edit, Part 2 (Trimming an Insert) 129
   Lift (Non-Ripple Delete) 129
   Slide 130
   Slip 133
Moving Shots Around 136
Life In and Out of Sync 141
   Putting It All Together 147

Chapter 4 Getting Fancy with More Tracks   149

Adding More Tracks 150
Sound 151
   Adding Music Tracks 152
   The Sound Mix 159
Titles and Text 165
   Creating Title Text 165
   Adding a Title to V1 170
   Adding Titles Using New Picture Tracks 175
   Adding a Drop Shadow 178
Basic Transition Effects 184
   Fade In, Fade Out Dissolve 185
   Cross Dissolve 189
   How to Add a Transition 190
   Other Transitions 194
Keyframes and Compositing 196
   Compositing: What It Is and Why We Aren't
      Doing It Here 197
Filter Effects 200
Basic Speed Effects 204
Putting It All Together:
   A Title Sequence 208
Adjusting the Final Cut Interface 210
   Formats for Editing 211
   Custom Formats 214

Chapter 5 Becoming Your Own Assistant   217

Managing Video Projects 218
   Continuous Timecode on Videotapes 219
   Labeling Videotape Cassettes 222
   Creating Log Sheets 223
   Shot Names in Scripted and Unscripted Projects 224
   Managing Disk Space 226
   Creating New Projects 230
Input: Capturing Video 234
   The Capture Window 235
   Loading a Tape and Entering Information 239
   Capturing Options 240

Naming and Saving Clips 245
Importing Music from CDs 248
Output: Finishing Up 252
The Master Tape 253
What to Record 257
Exporting 258
Backing Up 270
Putting It All Together 271

Chapter 6 Your Video Projects   273

What's in Your Camera Now? 274
Culling It 275
Compilation Videos: A Moving Slide Show 276
New Projects 279
Your Unscripted Projects 280
Your Scripted Projects 286
You Made It! 299

Appendix   301

Technical Issues 301
Storage 302
Bandwidth 304
FireWire 305
Timecode Basics 306
Answers to Chapter 1 Scavenger Hunt 309

Introduction

The moment Apple announced Final Cut Express, a little tear welled up in my eye—soppy sentimentalist that I am—for your good fortune. I was thrilled that such a wonderful product had been made available to the public.

The ability to edit video with ease and confidence is crucial for success in this media-rich world; and for users such as kids, families, small-business owners, hobbyists, and entertainers, Final Cut Express delivers perhaps the finest video tool ever created for the money. While the price tag for Final Cut Express might seem a bit stiff, it's important to realize that editing tools as powerful as this one have dropped in price over the past 20 years from hundreds of thousands of dollars to, well, a few hundred dollars. This product is a bargain. And while it's technically a "light" version of the more professional Final Cut Pro, make no mistake about it, there's nothing light about it: It is robust enough to manage enormously complicated feature films, professional commercials, music videos, wedding videos, corporate training materials, extreme-sports videos, travelogues, and even casual videos of your everyday life at home. One tool—a thousand and one household uses.

What Is Editing?

Editing is the process of taking the raw video from a camcorder and extracting pieces of it; arranging those pieces—bits of sound as well as picture; and constructing a new video from them. Editing allows you to be concise, and it also allows you to make a video that has a point of view, that tells a story, that is persuasive, or that stimulates whatever feelings you want the viewer to experience. It allows video to communicate not just information but emotion.

Once you master the fundamentals of editing video, you'll find more and more applications for your skills. Even if you don't intend to become a professional filmmaker or videographer, basic video literacy will benefit you in ways you may not yet imagine. (Chapter 6 outlines real-world applications for your newfound skills.)

Today, the number of people who shoot video and edit bits into projects for fun is small. But it will grow—because this *is* fun, because it appeals to people with many different kinds of interests, and because the technology that makes this easy and affordable has finally arrived. I believe the revolution that's brewing is not about encouraging everyone to make Hollywood movies (although that's pretty exciting) but rather about giving the skills of shooting and editing video to a wide range of people who can apply them in unique and personal ways, for work or for play.

This book is designed to help you get comfortable manipulating moving pictures and sound. Along the way you'll pick up some of the essential terms and techniques taught in film school, but mostly the book will introduce you to the basic features of Final Cut Express in a useful and pragmatic way. The goal is not to show you all the bells and whistles in the software (there will be plenty of time for fancy stuff once you see how much fun you can have editing video) but instead to familiarize you with the most basic (but critically important) tools.

Why Edit?

The most obvious reason to consider editing is that currently when you watch your own videotapes, you're not enjoying them enough. A sure sign is that you're tired of the tedious skimming through long bad parts, looking for good parts. If you're bored with your footage, there's a good bet your audience will be. True, editing tools will let you address this problem.

But editing is more than taking out bad parts. It's about making something interesting (or useful) out of the video you have. It might mean cutting out bad material, but it will also mean leaving out good material. I like to think of editing as building a model from a kit (or to be more accurate, building a model from two or three kits all mixed together). You open the box, dump the bits on the table, and put something together from them. If you're like me, you'll find that editing is an art and a craft you can lose yourself in, just as you might with photography, sewing, or, heck, maybe paleontology—hunting for raw materials from the world, picking through the scraps you've gathered up to find the gems you want to use, and then putting them together in a satisfying arrangement.

Up until now, video is likely to have been the stuff you shot with your video camera. You could watch the tapes (often long, and perhaps painful to watch without your finger on Fast Forward), but you didn't really *do* much to them after you shot them. This needs to change.

Welcome to Post-Production

There is a world of activities that only begin after the shooting of the video is over. In Hollywood, the shooting is called *production*. Consequently, the stuff that goes on after is called *post-production*. The principal aspects of post-production include three steps:

- Getting raw *source* video into your computer (capturing it)
- Editing the video
- Outputting the finished cut sequence to a *master* videotape

While *post-production* is the appropriate term for this range of activities it's convenient to generalize and refer to it by the dominant activity, *editing*.

Generally, you think of shooting and editing as distinct tasks, although in truth they often blur. I like to think of the combination as "holistic video." No matter how good an editor you are or how skilled you are with editing software, it's almost impossible to have a positive editing experience with poorly shot video. And even if you're the best videographer in the world, all that matters in the end is the product edited from your raw material.

Shooting (production) and editing (post-production) are yin and yang: independent and yet intertwined. (Forgive me—I moved to California a number of years ago, and this kind of New Age metaphor has finally lodged itself in my thinking.)

Many people I meet think that shooting video is pretty easy but editing is complicated (what could be more complex, you'd imagine, than making a movie?). Let me be the one to break this to you: Editing isn't complicated. In Hollywood, movies have been edited for 100 years with a little tool called a *cutting block*. The cutting block holds film in position while a razor blade swings down and neatly chops the thing in two. There's also a little roll of tape there to reconnect film after a bit has been snipped out. At its essence, that's editing—cutting and taping. You can do it with a blade and tape, or you can do it with most any reasonable modern computer. You don't need an advanced degree or a gigaflop CPU to edit.

The cutting block—a couple of moving parts, never crashes, responsible for a century of great movies.

Editing will fundamentally change your relationship to the video you shoot (and watch). It's also worth noting that even once you know all about video editing, you won't edit all the video you shoot. The material may not demand it, or you won't have the right pieces to make a cohesive project, or, most likely, you won't have the time. There's nothing wrong with being selective about what you edit.

Why Edit with Final Cut Express?

Final Cut Express rocks.

Final Cut Express is a video organizational tool, a piece of software that lets you edit digital video with professional ease and sophistication. You can also use it to add titles, special effects, and multiple sound tracks. When you're finished with your video, Final Cut Express can generate QuickTime output (or export in an assortment of other pic-

Final Cut Express was built on the foundation of Apple's well-regarded professional editing application. Final Cut Pro version 3, with all its features and versatility, is also remarkably easy to learn and use.

ture and sound formats, such as AIFF sound files, JPEG still images, and MPEG-4 supercompressed video). What's more, using Final Cut Express with Apple's iDVD makes it easy to generate DVDs of your finished videos.

Moving from iMovie

If you've been introduced to video editing in the form of iMovie, you may not be aware of iMovie's limitations. It's a fine product—simple to learn and a great introduction to video editing—but Apple's goal in creating it was to produce something really friendly looking and easy to use. To do that, its designers opted to limit its users to just a few critical editing tasks.

Where Final Cut Express has controls for watching and playing video that are essential to making critical frame decisions about your project, iMovie is very limited in the ways it lets you move video around. For instance, iMovie lets you shuffle shots around easily, but it doesn't enable you to easily use a bunch of video moments from a single clip. Because it treats the picture and its synchronized sound as a single unit (which is good), making adjustments to the picture or sound in one track independently of the other track can be confusing and sometimes impossible. To fully realize what editing can do, you need to be facile with your control of picture and sound tracks together or separately.

Final Cut Express can open projects you've started in iMovie (version 3 and up), and it can share projects and video transparently with Final Cut Pro. Consequently, if you're a novice, it's a perfect bridge to take you from iMovie to the basics of "real" video software and still give you room to grow.

Final Cut Express is a powerful video tool, well designed and affordable. Because it has a professional logic and tool set, you can fairly easily move from Final Cut Express to other professional video tools if you ever need to, in particular, Final Cut Pro. But the best thing about Final Cut Express is that you'll probably never need another piece of software to manage and edit your video. It's a fully functional personal editing system.

Learning to Edit—Rubin's Way

Most software training (particularly in books) takes you methodically through all of the product's features and introduces you to the myriad ways they can be executed. This book offers a wholly different approach. I try to keep you focused on the video material itself and what you're going to do with it.

The language I use and the concepts you'll be learning come predominantly from the film world (movies) and the videotape world (television)—two parallel universes that have merged over the past decade or so. Sprinkle in a little practical language from the computer world (we are, after all, doing all this on computers) and you'll understand a bit of the challenge here. My approach is adapted from the methods I used to teach new technology to nontechnical-but-professional filmmakers, using tools pretty similar to Final Cut Express.

I provide only the briefest explanations (sometimes none at all) of many *seemingly* important Final Cut Express features to make it easier for you to concentrate on the more important concept or tool at hand. For instance, you won't hear much about keyboard equivalents, you'll read little about timecode stuff, and you'll learn the *conceptual* names of certain features and not just their (sometimes arbitrary) Final Cut Express User's Manual names. It may even seem that I present functions out of order. You'll edit in Chapter 2, but you won't learn about media files or getting video into your Macintosh until Chapter 5—completely the reverse of virtually every other curriculum.

Trust me, I have my reasons. I believe you'll learn faster this way and ultimately have a deeper understanding of Final Cut Express and all editing in the end.

Final Cut Express vs. Final Cut Pro

Final Cut Express is the so-called light version of Final Cut Pro. It was designed by modifying a couple of features from version 3 of the professional product to streamline it for consumers. Meanwhile, Apple upgraded Final Cut Pro to include hundreds of new advanced features and tools—version 4 has modules for working with film, for using 3D titles, and for generating music tracks. It works better with high definition video and has additional intelligence concerning real time effects. *Are these things great?* Of course. *Do you need them right now?* Probably not.

Honestly, there was nothing wrong with Final Cut Pro version 3—it was good enough to win an Emmy and become adopted by thousands of pros. Apple just upgraded it to make it more attractive to people who earn a living by editing.

Final Cut Pro (v.3) on the left, Final Cut Express (v.1) on the right. Need I say more? Now that Final Cut Pro has moved on to version 4, it's probably useful to think of Final Cut Express as an old version of Final Cut Pro, rather than a light version.

As far as this book is concerned, *almost* everything you'll learn about Final Cut Express also applies to Final Cut Pro. Once you've mastered the contents of this book, you will be well situated to edit basic projects on either product. (In fact, in this book I sometimes refer to Final Cut without "Pro" or "Express" to highlight the notion that I'm talking about either product.) You've got a great bargain on a powerful product in your hands.

What You Need to Use This Book

All you really need to use this book is Final Cut Express software (probably any version, or even Final Cut Pro versions 1, 2, or 3), a Mac that will run it, and some footage to play with. That's it.

You'll be learning the very core fundamentals of Final Cut—Express or Pro. The great thing about fundamentals is that they're so . . . *fundamental*. They don't change much (or at all) over time, and consequently the contents here transcend the variations between these products or versions.

If you don't already have Final Cut Express up and running, your first assignment is to make sure the software can run on your Mac (check the current version's memory and hardware requirements if you have questions) and then install it.

Footage

This book is about video, so to follow along you're going to need some footage to play with. Normally, if you were going to edit, you'd need a digital video camera (either DV or Digital8 format) and some footage of your own. But for using this book, you need only a DVD drive on your Mac so you can work with the tutorial footage that comes on the enclosed DVD. Still, get a digital camcorder—it is, after all, the whole point.

You may feel a certain longing, an urge, to jump right into these editing tools using your *own* video, ignoring the typically dull tutorial content provided on the DVD. I feel your pain. But you need to play around with certain kinds of material to properly understand many of these tools and editing concepts.

What I Used

I illustrated this book using a dual 1 GHz G4 with Mac OS X (10.2.4) and 1 GB of RAM, but I also own a 500 MHz G3 iBook laptop (with 256 MB of RAM), which I use to edit for classes and on the road. Using the iBook and not the top-of-the-line PowerBook dramatically makes the point to beginning editors that you don't need the most expensive computer or the newest, fastest CPU. Today every new Mac is plenty good to edit with Final Cut Express.

The most important reason to use a high-end Mac with video editing software has mostly to do with speed—that is, how fast these computers can render complex special effects (which I hardly ever need) and how quickly they can burn DVDs (which I admittedly need to do occasionally). These are reasons to consider using Macs at the higher end of the food chain, but editing isn't. Also, a nice big hard drive is important (and two can improve performance), but you're fine if you have more than 20 GB—and I doubt you can even get a Mac today with less than 40 GB.

I first learned about editing by playing with 20 minutes of video from Scene 50 of *Return of the Jedi*. That just happened to be the material that Lucasfilm Ltd. chose in 1984 to illustrate the power of its groundbreaking EditDroid nonlinear editing system (I had been hired to teach editors and demonstrate the product). No lightsabers or X-wing fighters. In fact, no fancy special effects at all. A simple back-and-forth dialog scene between Yoda and Luke Skywalker.

I provide about 20 minutes of video clips on the enclosed DVD-R. Sorry, no Yoda. But while the scene I created doesn't have the hip cachet of something from *Star Wars*, structurally it's similar to the classic footage I learned on, providing the most common editing situations and requiring all the essential editing tools. Your own video projects may be unscripted and perhaps wholly unlike this material, but these scripted scenes make all the subtleties of editing easily visible. You'll learn more than you'd imagine about shooting your videos and telling a story through editing.

Where We're Headed

The editing skills you'll learn here apply equally to either professional or personal video. When we're done, you will

- Understand the basic technical workings of video and your computer
- Know how to capture video quickly
- Know how to organize your video materials efficiently
- Be able to insert, arrange, and trim your clips into a story line
- Be able to add a touch of polish, such as transition effects, music, and titles
- Know how to output your final movie to videotape, the Web, and DVD

So roll up your sleeves, pull up a chair, and get ready to learn how to use the most powerful business media tool ever made, Final Cut Express—even if you never cut anything more professional than a baby video. Let's get started.

First Things First 1

Before you start playing with Final Cut Express, you have a little housekeeping to take care of. You'll need to set up your Macintosh in a video-friendly way, and you may need some additional equipment. Once you're situated, I want to take you on my personal tour of Final Cut Express, breaking down the program into understandable components. (It can look kinda alien at first glance, especially when compared with iMovie—Final Cut Express has lots of small onscreen boxes of images and numbers . . . numbers with lots of digits.)

Finally, because the most critical aspect of using any editing tool is *having control over how you move and play the video,* before you start to edit, I'll present some exercises I've designed (which you'll use with some tutorial materials from the enclosed DVD) to help you master that control. I promise that the greater your comfort with all the ways you can move video around, the easier everything else related to editing will be.

By the end of this chapter, your hardware and software will be set up to edit, the files you need for the tutorial will be in place, your video muscles will be limber, you'll be on a first-name basis with the Final Cut Express interface, and you'll be ready to learn how to edit.

A Place to Work

With little more than a Mac and a DV camera, you can pretty much edit anywhere—I've edited in airport terminals, in hotel rooms, and sitting in my car waiting for meetings. In this section you'll get an overview of the primary components you need to start working and the basics of how to connect them all together.

Let's begin with your physical location. An *edit bay* is the professional term for a place set up to facilitate editing. Your edit bay primarily includes three items:

- A Mac
- A digital camcorder
- A FireWire cable

It might also include

- A video monitor (or TV)
- A comfy chair
- A box of DV videotapes
- A log book
- A set of headphones

Later, when you're souping up your edit bay, you might add

- External FireWire hard-disk storage (at least 80 GB)
- A set of external speakers
- A dedicated physical video console
- A digital video cassette player

But we're going to start simple: camcorder, cable, Mac, and Final Cut Express. Minimum configuration. Before you start working, figure out a quiet and maybe secluded spot to set up. You'll probably have some kind of desk or table, but a specially designed video countertop might be overkill. Ideally, an edit bay should be temperature-controlled (basic air conditioning is good; computers, cameras, and monitors may function less than perfectly if they get too warm). It should also be light-controlled, meaning that a cool view of the beach is going to be wasted. A room with no windows will work fine, and if there are windows, good shades will keep nasty glare off of monitors. If that sounds like a cozy air-conditioned closet, that wouldn't be a far cry from the professional edit bays of the world. They often have carpeting and sometimes noise-reducing padding on walls (like a sound studio), and nice ones have a sofa in the back so you can kick back and watch versions of your edits in comfort. Unfortunately, this doesn't sound much like my edit bay at home. I just work on my Macintosh in my office and keep the blinds pulled while I'm editing. This works fine, too.

The FireWire Connection

From a technical standpoint, there is one apparently simple invention that makes editing possible: the FireWire cable connecting your Macintosh and DV camera. You won't capture video this early in the book, so when you launch Final Cut Express, you can do it with or without your camera connected. Still, since it's an important part of setting up your equipment, let's go through the steps to hook up your camera and Mac. You'll need a 4-pin to 6-pin FireWire cable.

The smaller side (the 4-pin side) slides into your camera.

The larger side (the 6-pin "D") plugs into the Mac.

Unlike hooking up car battery jumper cables, it doesn't matter which end of the FireWire cable you plug in first. What's more, FireWire is designed to be *hot swappable,* which means you can plug in external devices even when your computer is running (in the old days of SCSI cables and connectors, you had to turn everything off before messing with the cabling; this is a fine advancement).

Be careful when you're hot-swapping devices not to zap your connectors with static electricity. Specifically, make sure you don't put the 6-pin connector in upside down—although this seems impossible it is a surprisingly common mistake.

While Final Cut Express can be made to *look around* anytime to see if you've plugged in any new hot-swapped devices, it's my habit to plug in hardware before I launch the application. It seems to cut down on problems.

This is what it looks like as you hook up your camera to your computer:

Plug the small end of your FireWire cable into your camera.

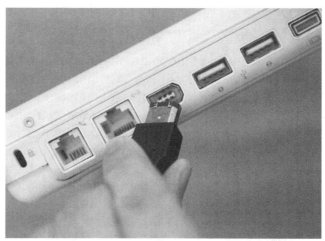

Plug the larger end of the FireWire cable into your Mac.

With your camera and Mac connected, and your camera turned on (and set to VCR mode), you're ready to launch your application and get down to biz. (If you're hungry for a little more technical and historical background on FireWire, check out the portion of the appendix on that topic.)

When your camcorder is in VCR mode, you will invariably light up those familiar VCR-control arrow buttons (such as Play and Rewind) somewhere on the camera body or LCD display. VTR (short for videotape recorder*), by the way, is the same as VCR (*videocassette recorder*).*

A Video Monitor

For all but the most basic setup, a video monitor is essential. You can certainly edit without one, and if you want the smallest possible setup, by all means skip it. But in no time you'll realize that video doesn't look "right" on a computer display. In general, it simply *can't*. Video plays on TVs in completely different ways than it does on computers. Without getting overly technical, let's just agree that Final Cut can't play your video smoothly and sharply in its interface, and even when it's playing as well as it can, it's still playing in a little window.

In this aerial view you can see the Mac display on the right and an old television displaying the video on the left. More important is my camcorder connecting the two. This principle works in Final Cut Express, Final Cut Pro, and even iMovie (shown here).

And thus the problem: To make good editing decisions, you really need to see video *in the way your audience will ultimately view it*. If something is shot for the big screen of a movie theater, you ideally need to see it played in a theater. Same with home video. While it's easy to watch your video on the Mac display or even mirrored on the LCD display of your (connected) DV camera, the best way to edit is to take the video signal from Final Cut Express right out of your Mac and pump it to a television set. This allows you to see the motion, the size, the colors, and the framing as they will look once translated from digital video signal to analog signal—the way they will be when played on a typical television.

Connecting this up is easy, even for me.

Monitors and TVs

To be fair, a television is not really the same thing as a video monitor, although I tend to use the terms interchangeably. And while we're on the topic, a video monitor is not interchangeable with a computer monitor. For those who are getting started with video editing, the most important difference concerns the available plugs on the back (or maybe front) of the display. Monitors designed to display video have an array of input/output plugs ("analog" [composite], S-Video, and so forth); televisions do not, and they sometimes sport only a single RF (coaxial) knobby for connecting up the cable. Unless you spend a lot of time editing video, I wouldn't bother purchasing a dedicated monitor; you can get by with an old TV set, which you can often find for cheap or even free.

HOW TO HOOK UP A TV

Since I usually have my camera hooked up to my computer with the FireWire cable, all I do to see my video on a TV is take the analog output of my camera (using either the S-Video plug or the simple composite analog video/audio plug) and jack those into any regular TV.

Hooked up to
a TV (analog in/out)

Going to a pair of
headphones (mini
headphone jack)

Plugged into
the wall for
power (AC)

Connected to the
Mac (FireWire)

Once your camera is completely cabled up, it might have a tendency to look like a hospital patient hooked up to various support mechanisms. In the middle of editing a full-length feature film, my camera looked like this—same as it does when I'm making a quick birthday party video.

Types of Video Signals

There are three flavors of video: component, S-Video, and composite. Most consumer electronics, from camcorders to VCRs, use the simplest video variation—*composite*. In composite video all the electronic elements of video are mixed together into a single signal ("composited") and can be hooked up with a single cable. The most professional variation is *component* video. With this type, the video elements are maintained as three separate components and require three cables and special equipment. Only professionals spend the time and money to work in component video. A good compromise of the two is technically called *Y/C video* but is commonly called *S-Video*. It maintains the signal as two elements.

While digital camcorders have a number of analog connectors, the S-Video plug is generally labeled "S-Video," but the composite plug is labeled "Audio/Video" or "Analog in/out" (even though S-Video is both video and analog). Because of the odd convention in the labeling on consumer cameras, I will refer to the composite audio/video as "analog."

By the way, many camcorders have a plug labeled "Digital I/O," which is really confusing. It is more appropriately labeled "LANC" (sometimes) or sports the LANC logo (shown here), and it provides for a remote cable controller for the camera in professional productions.

Many cameras have both the S-Video and analog connectors, and of the two, S-Video gives you better quality. But not all TV sets have S-Video inputs; consequently, I end up using the analog connection more often. Frankly, most people would be hard-pressed to notice the difference in image quality between the two connection methods, particularly when the original DV source material in either case is of high quality—higher than either can fully reveal.

Method 1: Analog AV Cable

Using the analog AV cable (that probably came with your camera) gives you both video (the yellow plug) and stereo audio (the red and white plugs for left and right). Like FireWire, it doesn't matter which end you plug in first:

I'm about to insert the all-important AV cable into the analog jack on the camera. The label may vary from camera to camera—"Audio/Video" is a poor description for "Analog audio/video input/output," but it is certainly more concise.

1. Plug the special RCA miniplug (the 1/2-inch plug with three stripes) into the audio/video jack on your camera. The jack may or may not be labeled "Analog input or output of sound and picture," but that is what it is. One of these specialized RCA AV cables probably came with your camcorder and may still be in a box some-

where. (If your camcorder sports a different type of analog connector, which is possible but not that common, the end that is a little different is this one.)

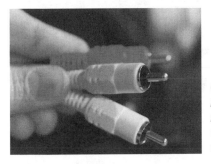

On the opposite end from the single miniplug is this get-up with three heads—yellow, red, and white. Other than in their colors, these three are visually identical.

2. Plug the three RCA plugs into your video monitor.

The jacks on your monitor are likely to be labeled "Video" and "Audio L, R." The problem is figuring out which cable plugs into which jack on the TV. I've found it pretty easy to remember that yellow is for video and red is for right audio (*R* for red, *R* for right), and therefore, through process of elimination, white is for left audio.

On many monitors video is the top jack and audio is below, although they tend to be pretty clearly labeled. On this TV there are three input channels, and I've hooked my camera to input 1.

Some TVs have only a mono input for audio—one plug—and so you must either (1) plug in only one of the two stereo inputs (the red or the white); or (2) get a stereo-to-mono adapter (sometimes called a *Y-cord*) that will let you push the red and white plugs into one side and then connect the single plug on the other side to your TV.

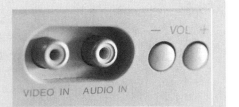

Method 2: S-Video Cable

If you have a really high-quality monitor, you may want to use the (higher quality) S-Video signal for the picture. This is easy: Plug an S-Video cable into the camera and into the S-Video input on your monitor (note: Not all monitors have an S-Video input). S-Video cables only carry video—and not audio—so you'll still need some audio from the AV jack. After going through the steps outlined above for connecting analog cables, simply unplug the (yellow) video plug, but leave the (red and white) audio cables connected. It looks weird, but it's OK to have the video cable hanging there.

The S-Video jack is probably the largest jack on your camera. Since it doesn't carry audio, you still need to hook up the analog audio output (the red and white strands of the AV cable)—and since my monitor is not top of the line, I tend to skip this extra step and skip S-Video. But that's just me.

1. Plug the S-Video cable into the camera.
2. Plug the other end into the monitor (both ends are the same, so it doesn't matter which way the cable goes).
3. Remove the video plug from the analog setup and leave it dangling.

Method 3: With a VCR

There are a few reasons why you might want to insert a regular old VCR (probably VHS) in the middle of all this TV cabling.

First, your TV may not have the S-Video or analog RCA connectors we've been talking about. But even the cheapest old television has a plug for cable service. (This type of plug is known as an *RF* type, and the cable is called *coaxial cable.*) An easy way to get from the camera to the TV with only an RF connector is to put a VCR in the middle.

1. Plug your camera into the VCR as if it were the TV in methods 1 and 2.

2. Run a coaxial cable from the VCR output to the TV.

The second reason you might want to do this—even if your TV can be connected to the camera—is so that you can make VHS dubs of material on your DV camera.

A Quick Tour Through the Final Cut Interface

Your computer screen, whether 12 or 20 inches across, must contain all of Final Cut Express's various windows and icons required to edit. Can it be done? Certainly. Some windows must be visible pretty much all the time; others you only need to check out once in awhile, so you'll tuck them away neatly and get back to them when the mood strikes.

Launching Final Cut Express

It's time to launch the application and see what's what. If you're having problems installing the software, get some help (try Apple Technical Support, for starters, or Apple's online Knowledge Base). Once the software is on your Mac, hopefully nested in your Applications folder, double-click the application icon and follow along.

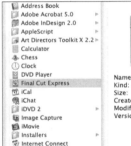

If you haven't yet hooked up your camera, or if your camera is turned off (or if the software simply doesn't see it for some reason), you'll get the following notice:

Don't worry for now if you get this message; you don't need the camera. Just click Continue, and let's get going.

One of the nifty features of Final Cut Express is that the screen, while cohesive and tight, is composed of a handful of distinct elements that can be moved around and resized to your personal preference. Of course, if you're new to Final Cut Express, you probably don't have much of a preference, so let's begin with *my* personal preference.

When you launch Final Cut Express for the first time, a new project opens—an empty, unnamed, and as-yet-unsaved project—where you can work. This blank work space probably looks like this on your display.

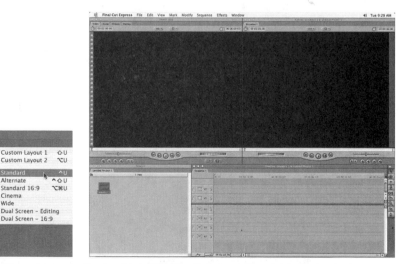

Let's make your display look like the figure on the right. Just select Window > Arrange > Standard. This moves elements around nicely to the format we'll use for the remainder of this book.

There are four sections of the display (plus a tool palette). Here they are disassembled.

Viewer

Canvas

Browser

Timeline

Once you're sure you've got the right layout onscreen, you may notice that what you've got is a screen full of black squares, odd rectangles, buttons, and icons. This is a traditional display for video editing (although the big black holes need to get filled with some video pretty soon).

The Browser

Your source material, which is the raw footage captured from your camera (or, in the case of the upcoming tutorial, imported from a DVD), stacks up in the Browser, a box that will contain all the materials of your project. You can display the contents of the Browser in a variety of views, such as text lists or icons of various sizes. If you've used iMovie, the default format with icons might be familiar, but as you work with Final Cut you'll find that the Browser is more efficient in list view.

A Browser in icon view and list view. When just a handful of items are in the Browser, icons are very nice looking. But as you add more elements, a list view makes navigation and organization easier. Items neatly stack up in the alphabetized pile, and you can see a lot of clips at a glance.

As this book goes on, I'll show the Browser only in list view.

When you start out, there's nothing in the Browser but an empty sequence labeled *Sequence 1*. But there are a handful of different "kinds" of source-material clips that can appear here, and each has its own distinguishing icon. When you capture videotape from your camera (or import QuickTime video), what you'll see are *clips*. Like the videotape they came from, clips are usually combinations of video and audio, but they can also be strictly video. Either way, the icon that represents video clips looks like this:

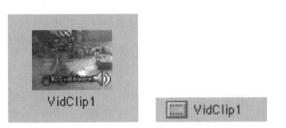

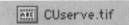

A clip is perhaps the most fundamental item in a project. On the left is a clip in icon view (the small speaker at the lower-right corner denotes that it includes sound); on the right is the clip in list view.

The icon that represents audio-only files (such as music taken from a CD or a voice-over you create from within Final Cut Express) looks like this:

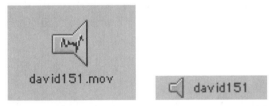

Similarly, audio is represented by a small speaker—on the left in icon view and on the right in list view.

You can also import still images in a variety of still-image formats (such as JPEG, GIF, and TIFF), which show up like this:

In icon view (left), image files look pretty much like clips (although there's no audio graphic on the bottom), but in list view (right) you can clearly see the unique icon representing the single-frame file.

When you begin editing, you generally start with raw clips and build them into sequences. You create a sequence through a series of *edit decisions.* When you open a project for the first time, there's always one empty sequence in the Browser already.

And as you edit more, you add new sequences as necessary. Here's the icon for a sequence:

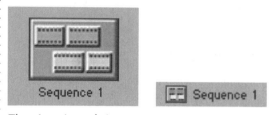

There's not much to see in a sequence icon (left); sequence information such as title, description, duration, and date created is far more useful than an icon in distinguishing between sequences, and you only get it in the list view (right).

Whenever you open a project, the Browser displays a list of all the elements it already contains, usually a mixture of clips and sequences. To work efficiently, it's important to be able to distinguish them at a glance.

Some History

Before editing was sucked into a desktop computer, it was done in the real world using a very large collection of objects. Two of those objects were television sets *(monitors)* positioned next to each other like this:

The two most central elements to an editing setup are the all-important monitors for the source material (on the left) and for the edited material (on the right). The Viewer and Canvas mirror that original architecture.

The Viewer

The Viewer is where you watch your raw material; it's where you mark the frames at which shots begin and end as you select bits of video to move into your sequence. It's the jumping-off point for editing. The lowest part of the Viewer window contains an assortment of play controls and functions. We'll investigate these controls later in this chapter.

The Viewer is where you screen raw (source) video material. It's where editing begins.

The Canvas

If the Viewer is for watching and marking raw source material, then the Canvas is for watching and marking the cut material. For the moment, think of editing as finding bits of video in the Viewer and dragging those bits into the Canvas to arrange them. While the Canvas has many special properties, it works pretty much the same way as the Viewer. These small TV sets are the same *type* of device, although each has special features. If you're ever unsure of which you're looking at, you'll find a small, faint label at the top of each window that gives the window name and, in the Canvas, the sequence names.

The Canvas looks pretty much like the Viewer, but the cosmetic similarities belie how important it is to distinguish them. Being able to watch and compare material in the Viewer and Canvas is an evolutionary leap from the one-display method of iMovie (see the sidebar "iMovie Rosetta Stone").

The Timeline

The Timeline is a classic graphical interface for editing that represents pieces of picture and sound cut together. It was designed as a kind of visual metaphor for lengths of cut film taped together, running in synchronization with reels of cut sound. Among its strengths are these:

- It shows clips in lengths relative to each other, so at a glance you know a lengthy shot is going to take more time to play than a shorter shot.
- It shows you where edits between shots happen relative to other edits in other tracks.
- It shows you where any frame, or edit, is relative to a fixed absolute time scale (a running duration).

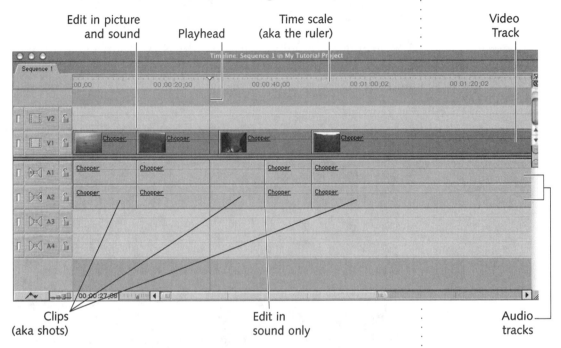

Once something is cut into the Canvas, it's also cut into the Timeline. The Canvas and the Timeline are two views of the same object—the cut material. The distinction is that the Timeline lets you see the relationships of the discrete clips that come together to form the apparently cohesive whole that plays in your Canvas. Dragging the playhead around on the Timeline will show you the video in the Canvas that corresponds to the playhead's position. Add a transition in the Canvas, and you'll see the graphical display of the transition in the Timeline. Like I said, they go together.

Once you can recognize each individual window, you'll notice that some functions and menu options are available from only one window or another. Which window is selected (called *window activation*) dictates what tools and options you can access. To make a window the active one, simply click anywhere in the window or frame. If you can't perform an action—say, controlling the Viewer or importing a clip—it may be because the wrong window is active. When in doubt, click the appropriate window before working.

Workflow

It's useful to imagine these windows as forming a kind of cycle—to visualize material entering the wheel at bottom left and then moving up, to the right, and down:

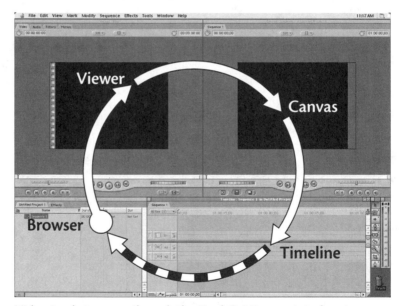

Video tends to move through the Final Cut Express interface in a great cycle—from the Browser list to being watched in the Viewer, cut into the Canvas, and visualized in the Timeline.

While there are notable exceptions to this flow, it's one way of looking at how these discrete windows work together. Another way is to think of the windows at the bottom of the screen as the *data* and the windows up top as the *media*, so editing is the process of moving material from the left side of the screen to the right. Either way, it amounts to about the same thing.

iMovie Rosetta Stone

iMovie is easy and powerful. It's great for beginners who want to become familiar with manipulating video and learn some basic editing concepts. Although iMovie is similar to other video editing software in many ways, iMovie isn't Final Cut Express. Apple has left a number of important features out of iMovie in order to make the product particularly friendly.

The first difference worth noting is that Final Cut Express is nondestructive, but iMovie is not—that is, with iMovie, cutting, breaking, and cropping shots actually changes the source media. It's as if the source material you input into iMovie is a hunk of clay that you modify, shape, and use or discard. Crop out a moment of video, and it ends up in the Trash. Final Cut Express doesn't make changes to source material and it doesn't throw anything out. If you input 15 minutes of video and edit it down to a 1-minute sequence, the whole 15 minutes of source video is still there, unaffected by your work. All your edits, trims, and deletions are made (for all intents and purposes) on *copies,* and your original material is never touched. Consequently, it's easy to try out a bunch of versions of your video or use different pieces of the same clips over and over. *This difference manifests itself through the entire editing process.*

Here's a quick translation that may help you move from iMovie to Final Cut Express with ease. (The comparable Final Cut Express features are in parentheses.)

A. Clip pane (Browser)

This is where you organize your source clips. You can set up Final Cut Express to look a lot like iMovie and show source clips as picture icons, but only in Final Cut Express can you choose to show them as text and associated data (which is surprisingly useful).

Another difference between the two programs is that Final Cut Express doesn't pull a clip out of this pane when you use any or all of it in the Timeline. In fact, much of the time you don't treat whole clips like immutable solid objects, dragging them around from Clip pane to Timeline as you do in iMovie; there's almost always a step in the middle that requires you to mark what *part* of the clip you want to use.

continues on next page

iMovie Rosetta Stone *(continued)*

B. iMovie monitor (Viewer and Canvas)

In iMovie this display plays whatever type of material you select, whether it's source material from the Clip pane or shots in your Timeline. Final Cut Express, on the other hand, uses two displays—one for raw material (the Viewer) and one for the clips in the Timeline (the Canvas). Having two screens gives you a great advantage: Sometimes you'll want to see raw materials or clips without moving the other, or compare two shots at once when you're making decisions about what images to keep and where to make cuts. This pair of displays is essential for the interim step you need when you move material from Browser to Timeline.

C. The video track in the timeline viewer (Timeline)

iMovie offers two views of an edited sequence: clip view and timeline view. Final Cut Express uses only the Timeline view, although its Timeline is a little more functional. While you might miss the clip view, that kind of presentation is designed for a certain kind of editing: using clips once and simply shuffling their order, like playing cards in your hand. The editing in Final Cut isn't generally about shuffling clips' order but rather about fine-tuning the durations of clips and the ways they connect to other clips. It's also often about deciding where picture edits happen, as opposed to where sound edits happen.

In iMovie, you view source material (picture and sound together) as a single object, unless you specifically split them apart. Final Cut Express always recognizes the separation of picture and sound tracks, although they can easily be treated as a single object. For these (and other) reasons, the clip view is deemed unnecessary and the Timeline view mission critical.

D. Scrubber bar (scrubber bar! Yeah!)

These are *sort of* the same in both applications. This representation of a clip, regardless of the clip's duration, allows you to move around in your video easily and shows you where you are. In this way they're identical. In iMovie you do the actual editing (called *cropping*) in this zone (Final Cut Express doesn't let you *crop* clips, per se). Final Cut Express lets you cut parts out of a clip, use any portion of a clip, and "trim" the beginning and end points of any edited shot anytime. This is a key functional difference between the products. So while you don't "crop" in the Final Cut Express scrubber bar, you'll still see important information there relating to your editing decisions.

E. Clip viewer and timeline viewer (Timeline)

There's really no clip view in Final Cut Express; everything is Timeline view, all the time. You can, however, show picture icons in the Timeline to help you identify what shots you see in that graphical display. It won't look like the clip view, but you can set preferences to give you pretty much the same information.

F. Zoom (zoom controls)

In timeline displays, it's critical to see detail and structure in your edits from a variety of vantage points—very close up to remarkably far away. Final Cut Express offers the same tools, and more, for this function. Embedded in the frame of the Final Cut Express Timeline are many tools for changing the magnification of the Timeline; the zoom controls include a magnifying glass (in the Tool palette), a zoom bar (onscreen), and some preset magnifications (onscreen). It's important when editing using a timeline to be able to quickly adjust the time span it presents to fit the part of your edits that you need to see.

iMovie Rosetta Stone *(continued)*

G. Tracks on/off (Track Selection tools)
On the far left side of the Final Cut Express Timeline are toggles much like these (which, oddly, are on the far right in iMovie). You can turn tracks on or off, make them invisible, and perform other track functions with these important tools.

H. Various libraries (tabs)
Some of the iMovie libraries (called *panes*) are functionally equivalent to tabs in the Browser and Viewer windows. Comparable menus for Clips and Photos have analogs in the Final Cut Express Browser; Trans and Effects analogs are both on the Final Cut Express Effects tab. Titles are created in Final Cut Express in the Viewer, under a small button, and Audio is on a Viewer tab. There is nothing in Final Cut Express as direct as iMovie's iDVD button. I have to say, the iMovie libraries are remarkable, simple, and sorely missed in the more professional products.

I. Camera/edit toggle (Capture mode)
At the beginning of a project when you bring in raw source material, Final Cut Express requires you go to a menu to find Capture mode, which lets you control a camera and get new video into your Mac. Most of the time, however, you're editing, so there's no onscreen toggle between these states. I like the iMovie toggle, and it makes going into "Capture mode" seem like an entirely separate operation. On the other hand, going into Capture mode *is* an entirely separate operation—one you'll get comfortable with the more you edit.

J. Disk space indicator (Capture mode)
In Final Cut Express, you can see how much free disk space you have available for importing new video only from within Capture mode. When you're about to input new video is really the only time you care about that kind of information, and it makes sense to keep it as part of the capture process. Because you never delete source material while working in Final Cut Express, you don't need to have it on the main screen—the amount of available disk space doesn't change nearly as fluidly as it does in iMovie. In Final Cut Express you don't throw out bad footage, you simply don't use it.

K. Clip speed (Motion Effects in a menu)
It's a few steps further from the top layer in Final Cut Express, since it's a less common function, relative to other tasks you need to perform all the time. I find the iMovie version far easier to manage and like having it up on top of the screen. But of course if you put everything in the main display, it would get pretty complicated, and you don't need this feature often.

L. Shuttle controls (a smattering of cue/play tools)
For precision editing and fine-tuning of clips, you need more control than you get with iMovie. It provides three transport buttons (play speed, cue back to the head of the clip, and play full screen) along with the ability to drag the playhead around in the scrubber. Final Cut Express offers a professional assortment of tools for watching and moving through your video. They're located in about the same place on the screen as they are in iMovie: beneath the particular monitor (Viewer or Canvas) in which you want to shuttle around. The entire region under the Viewer and Canvas is devoted to creative and functional ways to pop around in a clip and play it at different speeds. The arrow keys on the keyboard in both products will give you frame-by-frame play control.

Preparing for the Tutorials

Traditionally, video material comes from a video shoot—in your case, from your digital camcorder. But as we delve into the basics of Final Cut Express in this book, you'll use video that I'm providing explicitly for this purpose. This material is the patient and you are the doctor. (OK, well, maybe the material is the cadaver, and you're the medical student . . . *whatever*.) You're going to learn about editing, the tools you need, and the nuances of the art, using standard, simple material. That's much of what's on the DVD enclosed with this book.

First you need to get all the supplied tutorial files in place. If you're particularly comfortable with your Mac, with file organization, and with new applications, I suppose you might skip this section and see if you can do it on your own. That would mean copying the files off the DVD and onto your Mac, launching Final Cut Express, and importing the video clips you need for the first tutorial of the project. I'd still recommend skimming through these instructions so that you don't risk wasting time trying to find misplaced files when you'd rather be playing with your video.

Saving Your Tutorial Project

Before loading in files, save and quit out of the project you have open. It is important to do this so you don't confuse loading the DVD files onto your Mac with some Final Cut Express functions (like importing or opening).

1. Choose File > Save Project As.

   The Save dialog appears, asking for a name for this project.

File	
New Project	⌘E
New	▶
Open...	⌘O
Close Window	⌘W
Close Tab	^W
Close Project	
Save Project	⌘S
Save Project As...	⇧⌘S
Save All	⌥⌘S
Revert Project	
Restore Project...	
Import	▶
Export	▶
Capture...	⌘8
Reconnect Media...	
Voice Over	
Capture Project...	^C
Print to Video...	^M
1 Sketchwork	
2 Rubin Cuts	

Save

Save As: Untitled Project 1

Where: Documents

Format: Project File

Cancel   Save

2. Type a name in the highlighted box. Might I suggest "My Tutorial Project"? (Feel free to improvise here.)

Before you click Save, decide where you want to place this project on your Mac. Eventually you may want to have these kinds of files in a special folder—perhaps one for your videos—but for now I suggest you leave them on the Desktop so they're easy to find if you get disoriented.

Once you've saved the project with a name, the interface changes ever so slightly: All those places that used to say Untitled Project have been replaced with My Tutorial Project.

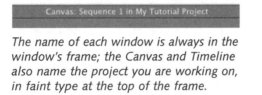

The name of each window is always in the window's frame; the Canvas and Timeline also name the project you are working on, in faint type at the top of the frame.

Now go ahead and quit. (Note: If you try to quit before saving your project, Final Cut Express will still stop to ask if you want to save, which you can. Most of the above steps still apply in that case.)

Loading the DVD Files into Your Mac

Let's begin by getting the video (and other materials) from the DVD into your Mac.

1. Insert the DVD that came with this book.

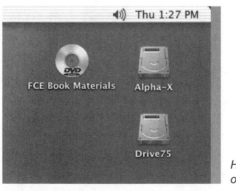

Here's the DVD as it shows up on my Desktop.

2. Double-click the DVD icon on your Desktop to open the DVD.

Inside is a single folder labeled Making Movies with Mike.

3. Drag the entire folder to your hard disk, but don't bother opening it yet.

This copies the entire contents (about 4.3 GB of data) to your Mac. Once that's done, you can take out the DVD and put it away for safekeeping. It doesn't matter where you put the folder on your hard disk; just be sure to remember where you dropped it. Since it won't be on your drive forever, I'd put it right on the Desktop, where it's easy to find and delete.

If you're interested at this point, feel free to open the folder Making Movies with Mike to see what's in there. Nothing much. Folders with video clips for all of the chapters. The ~Extras folder contains some PDF files I discuss later on, and the project files you'll need are in the FCE Project Files folder.

Now you have a folder (labeled Making Movies with Mike) somewhere on your hard drive, such as the Desktop. This folder is identical to the folder on the DVD, but more accessible.

Relaunch Final Cut Express. If all goes according to plan, the interface should open in the format you used for the tour, with the Browser in the lower-left corner and the Viewer and Canvas spanning the top of the screen.

Final Cut Express-land is made up of *projects*. Every video you make will be part of one project, but a single project might yield a bunch of related videos. Said another way, a project is composed of all the material you need to make a single video, or all the videos you can make from one body of source material. Projects consist of two fundamental types of elements: clips (raw material) and sequences (edited material).

Since we aren't using a digital camcorder yet, you need some video clips.

Importing Video Clips

Let's go get two clips from the Chapter 1 tutorial folder and put them into this new project. Leave the rest of the files for now.

1. Choose File > Import > Files. Locate the Chapter 1 folder in the Making Movies with Mike folder.

2. Select VidClip1 and click Choose.

3. Repeat these steps for VidClip2. Now two clips should be in the Browser.

In Final Cut Express, "importing" clips has nothing to do with capturing video from a camera (even though in iMovie importing and capturing are equivalent). In fact, once you start working with your own shots, you'll usually capture video rather than import clips to get material into Final Cut Express. Importing the tutorial video is more like importing still images from other folders on your Mac or moving clips from one project into another. You can read all about importing files in a good reference guide, but for now what's important is that you import the clips that you need for the tutorial.

Playtime: Mastering the Video Controls

You could jump into the tutorials now that you have the software on your Mac and have a sense about the geography, but I want to pause for a few moments to give you a chance to get very comfortable with video. This may be even more important than all the shortcuts and tricks you'll ever learn about this software.

Good editing is often the result of one simple skill: the ability to control precisely the place where you stop in a clip of video. Determining the right place to make a cut (for instance, between two words, just a moment after someone exits the frame, when her hand touches the glass) requires being comfortable moving backward and forward through the video clip, sometimes quickly and sometimes very slowly while you look at each frame. A frame of video is only on the screen for 1/30 of a second, faster even than human reaction time (how quickly your body can respond after your eyes are presented with a visual stimulus), so good editing demands good tools for playing the video clips.

Much of the Final Cut Express interface is covered with tools, knobs, and buttons for moving the video around, so you know this kind of functionality has to be important. And each onscreen controller has a keyboard equivalent so that you can choose whether to manipulate it with your mouse (or other input device) or the keyboard, whichever is more comfortable.

Much of the apparent complexity of the interface comes from having many somewhat redundant play controls. Learn them, and the screen becomes a lot less threatening.

If you use a mouse with great dexterity, you could use the mouse to do *everything*—open files, play video, shuttle around, grab tools, and make edits. This is a good way for a beginner to first experience many of the editing tools. But even die-hard mouse (or trackball) fans will, from time to time, still want to hunt and peck for an odd keyboard item.

And as time goes on, you'll realize that some tasks are easier (or more logical) to perform with your fingers on the keys, and some are perfectly easy with a mouse. There's no right or wrong here. I'll show you both and my personal preferences.

Playspeed vs. Non-Playspeed

Press Play on any VCR, CD deck, or other audio or video device, and the machine runs at *playspeed*. Fast forward and fast reverse are examples of *non–playspeeds*, as they are moving the media in unusual directions and velocities. When you edit, you will learn to live with video and audio played at many non–playspeeds (from very slow creeping or stepping, to high-speed scanning), all of which are important depending on what you are doing. Playspeed reverse, a special case in which the video moves in normal playspeed but backward, provides almost as much information to the editor as the more familiar forward direction.

Method 1: One Hand on the Mouse

Let's start with the mouse (or other input device, depending on your setup). Use one hand (your mouse hand), and let's do it *all* this way.

First, double-click VidClip1 in the Browser to open it into the Viewer. At the bottom of the Viewer you'll see a row of controls for playing the video. (The bottom of the Canvas has the same controls, and they work just the same.)

The Play button. Simple. Seems obvious. I use it far less than you'd imagine.

PLAY

Click the Play button in the Viewer, and your video will start to move forward, in playspeed. Notice that once you've clicked Play, if you click the button again, the video stops. (In that sense, it's really a play/stop button, but it looks like a play button.) Start and stop your video a few times.

You may find that video plays in your Viewer (or Canvas) a little more choppily than you're used to seeing video play. This is possibly a function of your Mac (not having a very fast hard drive, for instance), but more likely it's just the way video looks when playing on a computer. If you watch the video on your (connected) monitor, it will look natural and smooth even when it looks jumpy on the Mac.

Even though using the Play button seems as though it would be the most common way to view video, it's actually not. There are other ways to do it that are more useful. In fact, I don't use the Play button all that often.

The shuttle knob (which Apple calls the shuttle control) is a cool little device, designed to work like similar-looking knobs on professional videotape decks. It's my third-favorite motion controller in Final Cut Express.

SHUTTLE KNOB

Click and hold any point and drag a little bit left and right, and you'll go forward or backward, slow or fast. This control is forgiving—if you're sloppy and your hand strays a little high or low in one direction or another, as long as you still have the click-and-hold secure, you'll pull that shot along in the appropriate direction. This is good. It gives a feeling of acceleration as you head in one direction or another, and yet the video plays smoothly enough at higher speeds to let you skim the footage. The knob is scaled to speed, which means that the farther you move it in any direction, the faster you move your material.

The nice thing about the shuttle knob is that it moves the video around quickly, but not too quickly. When editing, it helps to be reasonably familiar with your footage. Linearly shuttling through tapes or captured footage as you do with the shuttle knob—even at high speeds—allows you to find on-camera events that you didn't know you were going to be looking for. That's one of the special aspects of editing: As you work, you may realize that you need some certain shot to solve a problem, and now you know how to get that shot quickly to see if your instinct was right, to see if the shot works.

Perhaps the best thing about shuttling is that the audio pitch increases or decreases with speed; the material you're watching *sounds* slower or faster. It's nice feedback about speed and direction and can be useful in the rhythmic motions that are part of selecting a frame to edit.

The shuttle knob, while cool, is only so fast. In fact, at full crank it moves at about 20× playspeed. It skips frames to move this fast, but you still see much of the action on the tape. (Most cameras, by the way, can only shuttle at 10× speed and still let you watch the video.)

Audio Scrub

There are two ways to hear sound moving at non–play speed, called *scrubbing* audio. The first is with the pitch changing as the speed changes (a familiar sound from old analog editing days—one you might think of when you recall the Chipmunks singing silly songs). The second (a nifty modern invention) holds the pitch constant regardless of the speed—which leaves audio clearer, particularly at very slow speeds. You can hear sound in both of these ways in Final Cut Express, depending on which tool you use to move the video around. The shuttle knob allows for the pitch change; moving slowly with the jog wheel (another Final Cut Express control) holds the pitch constant.

When you're really racing around linearly, this next control is the one to use.

SCRUBBER BAR

Under each video image (in the Viewer or Canvas) there is a horizontal bar—a graphical representation of the duration of the entire clip of video you're watching. It works in much the same way as the shuttle knob: click, hold, drag left or right (you can also just click somewhere within the length of the bar to move to a specific point in the video). The difference is that the bar is not scaled to speed, but scaled to length (position). Click all the way to the left and you're at the beginning of the clip. Click all the way to the right and bam, you're at the end. It could be a 5-second clip or a 50-minute clip; you

The scrubber bar. I really like this device as a shuttle tool, although it has other uses.

can zoom from the beginning to the end just by clicking, or clicking and dragging.

Thus, the longer the clip, the faster you move with this control (and the harder it is to hit any exact spot). When you start to use your own video clips, you'll recognize the trade-off between long clips (which are convenient for efficiency in capturing, for instance) and short clips (which are more accurately navigated in the scrubber). For beginners, it's usually more difficult to negotiate the scrubber bar with long clips of, say, 10–20 minutes (clicking and dragging and stopping must be much more tightly coordinated); anything under 10 minutes is pretty basic to control, but if that's still too much, try less. The more skilled you are with this click-hold-drag motion, the longer your clip can be and still be manageable in the scrubber bar. Keeping clips to between 2 and 10 minutes is a very functional compromise in terms of capturing video. And it makes the scrubber bar pretty easy to use and thus a powerful ally.

Head/Tail

In the editing world, the beginning of something, be it a clip or a shot as edited into a sequence, is called the *head*. Similarly, the *tail* is the end. If you move headward through a series of edits, you're moving toward the beginning of the sequence. Technically, the head of the shot is only its first frame, but it's fair to generalize and use the term *head* to refer to the beginning zone of whatever material you're editing.

With this tool and the shuttle knob, you can pop around in a clip and scan at super high speed looking for a specific moment in the video. When you're near what you're looking for, switch to the shuttle knob and use it to do finer searching. When you edit, finding a bit of video you like requires not only finding *it* but finding the *first frame* of it and the *last frame* of it. Those are not approximations; those are precise decisions and they matter. Being able to hit a particular frame is critical.

Ah, but even these three methods—play, shuttle, and zoom-in-the-scrubber—are all too *macro*. What you always need is some *micro* manipulation. And thus, we come to . . .

THE JOG WHEEL

The jog wheel (which Apple calls the *jog control*) is another device borrowed from professional videotape machines, where the wheel doesn't quite play the videotape so much as nudge it forward or backward a bit at a time. This is called *jogging*, and it lets you move video with precision. The jog wheel is open-ended and loose; it rolls and rolls in whatever direction you click and drag. In some respects, it's like a fine-tuned shuttle knob. If you pull far from the center point, it will jog faster; small pulls from the center will move you a gentle frame or two at a time.

I don't use the jog wheel all that often (and I'll explain why after you've played with it).

Now you are ready to combine these onscreen play controls.

> There actually is a fourth excellent onscreen navigation tool. Once you've edited material into a sequence, simply grab the playhead in the Timeline and drag it around—it works like the scrubber bar in the Canvas (but you can see where the edits are). In fact, this is my favorite method for bouncing through material onscreen, but it only works in the Timeline. I won't use it in this exercise, but we will use it as we get deeper into editing.

TARGET PRACTICE

Let's see how good your video control is, and start to practice using the onscreen controls you've just learned about.

If you haven't done so already, double-click the VidClip1 icon in the Browser. This opens it in the Viewer window right above the Browser. You should now be looking at the first frame of this clip. If you've been playing around in this clip already, use the scrubber bar to move to the first frame.

Here's the jog wheel. I don't think I've used this much in years. Once you try it, maybe you'll see why.

This is the first frame of VidClip1. You should be staring at it in the Viewer window. The big black bar in the middle of the frame with numbers (and beginning with "TCG") is part of the video itself and not coming from Final Cut Express.

Shuttle through the clip and stop on the frame with the small white circle (called a *punch* in film editing). Since there's only one frame with the punch, you may have to work a little to find it, and work harder to stop right on it. I could have made finding the punch harder by placing it randomly in the clip, but to be nice I placed it on the *clap*—on the one frame where the jaws of the slate are closed and there's a loud snap sound, which you can use as an audio clue.

Try to get to this frame in VidClip1. It's the first frame in which the slate is snapped shut, and also I put a punch here to make it easier to find. If all else fails, it is 6 seconds and 15 frames from the beginning of the clip, which you can tell from the big number in the middle of the screen.

Some Background About Slates

VidClip1 shows the action of a slate (often referred to as a *clapboard*), a typical Hollywood device that both labels a section of film and provides the ability to easily synchronize sound tracks with pictures. When a slate is snapped shut, the video shows one frame with the jaws open and the next frame with the jaws closed.

The effect on the sound track is to create a distinct spot that contains no sound, followed by the first frame of sound, like a spike.

When you line up these two events—the closed slate and the spike of sound, picture and sound are in sync. (Another way to think about this is that they are in sync to start with, and if they ever accidentally move out of sync through various procedures, they can be realigned.)

When someone working with the film identifies the first closed-jaws frame of picture, she typically marks it with a hole punch to make it easy to find again. This punch produces a kind of flash as you play through a reel of film. It is one frame long, which means that it flashes on the screen for 1/30 of a second—0.033 seconds, or 3.3 hundredths of a second. It sounds short, but you'd be surprised how long it can be.

Try different methods to find the punch frame, but at this point practice doing so using the mouse.

- The Play (and Stop) button
- The shuttle knob
- The scrubber bar
- The jog wheel
- A combination of them, as desired, for accuracy

When this seems easy enough, you might try again with the sound off (turning down the volume on your Mac is a fine way to do this), just to make sure you're using your eyes and not your ears. In real editing, sometimes you will use both, but just as often you'll search with only your eyes or only your ears. You won't go wrong practicing with each.

Of all these onscreen motion controls, the one I have the biggest problem with is the jog wheel. Sometimes you just need to move one frame, and it's actually a fair amount of work to do with the jog wheel. And so I end up heading for the keyboard. Once you have your fingers on the keyboard, a new horizon opens up in the land of video navigation.

Method 2: One Hand on the Keyboard

The keyboard gives you another way to shuttle and hunt through video—there are keyboard equivalents for almost all the onscreen controls. The keyboard utilizes different skills and provides slightly different control from that of the mouse. For instance, there is no dragging. You can hop around from control to control, but your hands are relatively fixed. Most keyboard controls for beginners are optimal for one hand, probably your right. When you get good and learn more keyboard functions, you'll find that you can edit with two hands, just as if you were typing. This book will not go into that. I suggest not trying to learn all the keyboard functions right away; add shortcuts only as your confidence grows.

SPACEBAR

The spacebar is perfect for playing and stopping video, particularly when you want to just get something rolling and lean back to watch it, or give the spacebar a quick slap to bring everything to a stop as you lean forward to get down to work.

The best control on the keyboard is that big ol' spacebar: It functions as play/stop. It takes up about eight times the space of any of the other keys, so you know it's got to be particularly important.

With the same VidClip1 in the Viewer, make sure the Viewer is active and press the spacebar to play, and press it again to stop.

Now let's learn how to move faster and how to back up, as you did with the shuttle knob.

J, K, L

Line up the J, K, and L keys under the first three fingers of your right hand, and use them like this:

J = play backward, K = stop, L = play forward. J, K, and L are like three keys on a piano that can play a tiny song. If you're going to use the keyboard at all, these are likely to be the most central of your controls.

By pressing the keys in a pattern—L . . . K . . . J . . . K . . . L—you rock and roll over a given spot. You could skip the K—there's no need to stop between going forward and backward—but sometimes the point is about trying to stop on a frame to look at it, so you roll back, stop, look at it, roll forward a bit, stop, look again, and so on. But yes, you could just go back and forth, back and forth (L, J, L, J).

These are nice controls for rockin' and rollin', but you can also increase the playspeed. The more times in a row you press the J or L keys, the more speed you gain: Press once and you go at playspeed, twice gives you 2× speed, three times gives you 4×, and four times gives you 8×.

I sometimes use these keys for their multi–hit speed shuttling, but if what I'm looking for isn't nearby, I tend to grab hold of the mouse and try to go faster, probably using the scrubber bar.

If you want to get even fancier, you can use the K (stop) at the *same time* as the J or L, to crawl in either direction. This requires holding one finger down while tapping or moving the adjacent finger, which takes a little more coordination. A nice feature of using K with J or L is that the audio pitch changes as you move. Again, there are times when you want to hear unaffected audio, and there are times when a pitch change is nice.

LEFT AND RIGHT ARROW KEYS

Arguably, the arrow keys provide the best way to move frame by frame forward or backward.

Many keyboards also have arrow keys for navigation. If yours has them, you'll probably find them useful in Final Cut Express. The left and right arrow keys serve to move a *step* forward and backward, in a single-frame movement. This is my favorite way to move frame by frame. I repeatedly press the arrow keys to move around when I'm close to where I think I need to be and want to examine the frames more closely. Playspeeds, and even slow crawls, are just too fast sometimes. They actually slow me down, making it difficult to hit the right spot. If you hold an arrow key down, the video will start jogging in that direction, slowly.

Repeatedly pressing a key, like the one-frame step arrows, may not always be the most efficient way to look around, but it's remarkably simple. And a side benefit is that it makes editing feel a bit like playing a video game—think a Fire/Shoot button in Asteroids (if you're over 30) or Tomb Raider (if you're not).

You can use other dedicated keys to pop from beginning to end of a clip, or between various marks that you can place within the clip—but let's skip placing marks for the moment and just work on keyboard target practice.

A Special Kind of Navigation

The up and down arrow keys perform a special kind of navigation in your material. They pop  you either toward the head of your clip (up) or toward the tail (down), stopping only at special points of interest along the way. In the Viewer, the arrows take you to the head or tail of the clip, stopping along the way at any special marks that you may have placed in your material. In the Canvas, where there are usually many more intermediary marks and edits, they move you edit-by-edit in whichever direction you're going (yes, they also stop at In and Out points). It's a terrific way to move quickly around in a sequence or clip.

The closest onscreen version is the buttons located near the Play button in both the Canvas and Viewer.

 These navigation tools are excellent for moving around in clips but aren't ideal for finding frames within a shot. We'll revisit these alternate forms of navigation later, when we get into editing.

TARGET PRACTICE

Here are a couple of exercises to help you gain the kind of control you need to edit comfortably. They'll help you test yourself on accuracy.

1. Double-click the VidClip1 icon in the Browser again to make sure this clip is the one in the Viewer window.

You can just click in the Viewer itself, if you know that the clip you want to play is there, but if you ever play more than one clip and get confused about which one is in the Viewer, this is a surefire way to establish that you're looking at (and controlling) the clip you think you are.

2. Go to the first frame of the clip.

Final Cut Express is smart. Smart enough to come back to a clip where you left it. If VidClip1 doesn't open in the Viewer at the first frame, it's because you moved it in the last exercise. To return to the head frame, press the up arrow.

3. Using the keyboard, try to stop on the flash frame again.

First use the spacebar.

Next use the J-K-L buttons.

Finally, play around with these in combination with the arrow keys, if you have them.

Going on a Scavenger Hunt

Once you've finished your target practice, it's time for the real (or almost real) deal. This scavenger hunt takes you on a romp through 3,000 or so frames of video, letting you use your new skills to locate hidden frame targets.

I edit primarily with one hand, the right one (since I'm right-handed). I mostly use a mouse (or trackball) to click buttons and clips on the screen, but I let go and switch to slamming the spacebar or settling into the J-K-L or arrow keys to do more detailed selecting and marking. Ultimately, I go back to the mouse to make the edits and move the Timeline around.

You'll find your own balance.

Now let's move on to VidClip2. It's been sitting in your Browser, abandoned until now. Double-click it and begin to play it in the Viewer. Use your thumb on the spacebar to start and stop the clip.

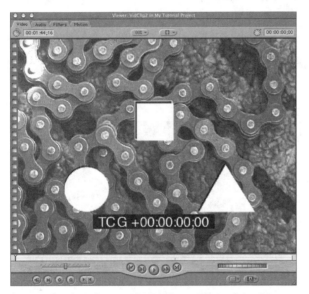

Here's the first frame of VidClip2. I'll explain the doodads on the screen in a bit. Those filmstrip graphics on the left side of the image are a helpful reminder that you're parked on the first frame of a clip.

MARKING IN AND OUT

Playing around through your video, and having fine control of that motion, is important for the editor, but the all-important moment of editing is when you "tell" the computer that you have found what you're looking for by *marking* a frame.

An In icon says, "This is the beginning."

An Out icon says, "This is the end."

When you edit, you mark the in and out of a segment of a clip, and move just that segment into your sequence. To mark an In point or Out point, you need to click a button on the screen or press one on the keyboard to tell Final Cut Express where to place the appropriate mark. On the screen, you look for those In and Out icons. The Mark In and Mark Out buttons are located adjacent to the shuttle controls at the lower portion of the Viewer and Canvas.

Marking In and Out points is so critical that you should be equally adept at doing it with the mouse and with hands on the keyboard.

This button marks an In point.

This button marks an Out point.

The I key marks In.   The O key marks Out.

Notice how conveniently close the I and O keys are to J, K, and L. (It's lucky that I and O are next to each other. It makes this all so much more logical.)

You won't do any editing right now, but you will practice using the Mark In and Mark Out buttons to mark the designated frames in VidClip2. Use mouse or keyboard or both to get to the desired frames and mark them. Most of what you do as an editor relates to your fluidity at performing this activity.

What Is This Weird "Mark" Symbol?

The symbol used to mark beginnings and ends is adapted from the film world. It's the head of an arrow running up against a line. Film editors would often mark places in their film with a grease pencil; they'd draw long horizontal lines down the center of the celluloid, and when they got to a place where some event would happen in the frame, they'd draw a line to mark the end, and put arrows on the ends, like this:

End of film   Beginning of film

Mark Out   Mark In

An aspect of this that may be confusing is that in film, the head of a shot or clip is on the *right;* in Final Cut the head of a shot is on the left (since we read from left to right, computer metaphors for video tend to run left to right, also—which is in fact pretty logical). If the beginning of a shot is on the right, the Mark In arrow will be the one on the right.

SCAVENGER HUNT INSTRUCTIONS

To practice this work, I've hidden a handful of geometric punches in the 100 seconds of VidClip2. These shapes will be the targets of your hunt. Play through the clip and you may notice them. The clip contains three punch shapes: circle, square, and triangle. There are two sizes: large and small. And there are three durations: one, two, and three frames. There are a total of nine targets, with combinations of these variables. The background video (of my friend Chris playing around in his yard) is designed to be somewhat distracting, although the targets aren't as invisible as they could be. All are readily locatable.

When you double-click VidClip2 in the Browser again, the first frame will pop up in the Viewer. If you've already been shuttling around in VidClip2, get back to the head:

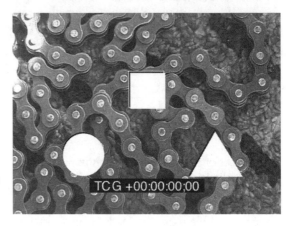

This first frame of VidClip2 has examples of the three shapes in their small size. Look for these flashes in the rest of the clip.

As you go through this obstacle course, take mental notes:

- How long does 1/30 of a second feel versus 2/30 (1/15) and 3/30 (1/10)? Savor this sensation.

- How quick is your reaction time using different methods of stopping the moving video? At playspeed, after a target first flashes, how many frames are you from it when you stop? It's not so important that you be able to stop on a target the moment you see it, but only that you can easily get back to it if you do.

- How good are you at noticing small targets versus large ones? Sometimes the thing you search for in your video is not a scene but something within the scene: an eye opening or a ball touching the floor. These can be subtle.

- How distracting is the background content? As an editor, you have to be able to turn on and off your attachment to what is going on in the narrative of your project in order to find things you are looking for in the shots.

THE HUNT IS ON

1. Play through the video, and mark an In point on the first frame of the two-frame small circle target.

2. Mark an Out point on the one-frame small triangle.

OK, I'm giving this one to you. But don't get cocky—we need to pause here and look around in the Viewer.

Easy?

This is a good time to look down at the bottom of the Viewer—at the scrubber bar. As we discussed earlier, the bar represents the entire duration of this 100-second video clip.

Mark	
Mark In	i
Mark Out	o
Mark Split	▶
Mark Clip	x
Mark to Markers	^A
Mark Selection	⇧A
Select In to Out	⌥A
Set Poster Frame	^P
Clear In and Out	⌥X
Clear In	⌥I
Clear Out	⌥O
Clear Split	▶
Clear Poster Frame	
Markers	▶
DV Start/Stop Detection...	
Play	▶
Go to	▶
Previous	▶
Next	▶

You may have already noticed that there are two marks within this bar, near the front. The first is the In mark you made at the circle target; the second is the Out mark you made at the triangle target. Marking specific frames—adding them (marking) and sometimes removing them (clearing)—is the essence of editing.

I want to point out something to you: the timecode numbers onscreen. Not the big one I burned into the picture (called a *burn-in window*—embedded permanently in the picture itself), but the small box at the top left of both the Viewer and the Canvas.

There is a pull-down menu dedicated to Mark stuff. Although we aren't going use the menu during this exercise, it's important to know that it's available.

These small boxes with timecode numbers are handy when you know what they do.

It's called the *Timecode Duration field,* and it provides a handy bit of information: the elapsed time between the In point and the Out point.

If you marked the In and Out points correctly on the first two targets, your Timecode Duration field should say 00:00:04;25.

The number itself isn't that important in editing, but being able to know a shot's duration is sometimes useful. Anyway, we're using the numbers here primarily to check that you landed on the right frames. That kind of accuracy is the critical thing in learning how to control video. You should be getting the feel of shuttling around, stopping, and moving to a specific frame. Since you'll do this all the time when you're editing, it's important to be very comfortable with it—more than any other single skill in editing.

But this isn't the only timecode box. At the top right of the Viewer (and Canvas, too) is a second box, called the *Current Timecode field.* This shows you the time elapsed from the start of your material. Since my burn-in window began at 00:00:00;00, it turns out that the number on the burn-in will match the small "live" calculation of elapsed time in the Current Timecode field.

In real life you won't have a burn-in window in your video, so don't get used to this elapsed time matching something "in" the video.

In the Canvas the Current Timecode field shows a time that is equivalent to the location in the timeline where the playhead is parked. Move your video around and be aware of these numbers—what changes and what remains the same when you play and when you mark things. Check to see that at the Out point the running time is 12 seconds, 22 frames. That's all you need to know at this point about the onscreen timecode windows.

To complete this scavenger hunt, follow the steps below and fill in the blanks with the last five digits of timecode as they appear in the burn-in window at the bottom center of the screen image.

1. The timecode for the large, one-frame circle: _____

Mark a new Out point here. (Look at the scrubber bar. Notice the Mark Out icon in the top-right corner of the video. This is one of a handful of little graphics called *overlays* that Final Cut Express superimposes on special frames for you.)

TCG +00:00

OK, this first one is pretty hard because the circle, while large, is tough to make out against the background. Here's a little hint.

2. Find the one-frame small square; enter the timecode here: _____

Mark a new In point on this frame.

Notice that when an In point falls after an Out point, the Out point disappears (the same thing happens if an Out point falls before an In point). Also be aware that you are only allowed one In point and one Out point per clip. Thus, every time you click Mark In or Mark Out, the location of this mark moves to the most recent spot.

While still on the small one-frame square, mark an Out point. There is now both an In point and an Out point here. Note that the two marks appear simultaneously on the screen (as well as in the scrubber bar).

3. The duration between these marks: _____

When you are parked on a single frame, it can be both the beginning and the end of a shot, and the shot is therefore one frame long.

Now, using the scrubber bar to navigate, go back toward the beginning of the video clip, back to the first target we found—to the first frame of the two-frame, small circle target. Mark a new In point here.

Why am I asking you to return to the first target? To learn one of the great advantages of using the scrubber bar to move around. You know sort of where you're looking, because we looked at the scrubber a few moments ago when you marked this target. So you're not randomly searching for it but have a general idea. Clicking in the scrubber bar pops you to that location without forcing you to scroll through a length of video. Then, once you're close, it's easier to shuttle around looking for the frame you want. This is more like the way you will look for bits of video in the "real world" than starting at the head of a clip and rolling straight through it, hunting as you go.

At any rate, if you did it right, the duration timecode should read 36;14.

Now go ahead and find (and write down the timecode for) the rest of these marks, listed here in no particular order:

4. The large one-frame square: _____

5. The large one-frame triangle: _____

6. The last frame of the small three-frame square:

_____

7. The middle frame of the small three-frame triangle:

_____

8. The small one-frame circle: _____

(Answers appear in the appendix.)

. . . .

Now that you've mastered moving your video around, been up and down the interface, and shuttled in every direction at every speed, with fine control, you are ready to cut some real video. As you edit more, without even trying you will rehearse the skills we focused on in this chapter.

Basic Editing 2

When you first look at any professional editing system (Final Cut Express included), you're assailed with buttons and windows and images and doohickeys . . . so of course it seems complicated. In truth, people have been editing film using some pretty primitive mechanical tools (for more than 100 years) and primitive computers (for the past few decades). From a technical standpoint, editing is not particularly difficult.

Most of the complexity in Final Cut Express comes from the fact that there are almost always two and often three or four ways to accomplish every kind of editing function. This is why the interface for editing can appear complicated. To see how simple editing can be, we're going to ignore many features of Final Cut Express. It's not that they're unnecessary; it's just that many perform functions that either don't come up that often or are particularly advanced.

To make it simple, we'll work tutorial-style with the material from the DVD rather than focus on particular Final Cut Express functions. We'll edit a basic scene together, exploring only the tools necessary to do the trick, and only as you need them. Your skills will build on each other and grow in power as they accumulate.

Familiarize Yourself with the Scene

```
LIVINGROOM -- DAY

CHRIS is sitting in a comfy overstuffed chair, reading a
magazine. KIRSTEN enters. She holds something in her hands,
but we can't see it at this point.

She stands before CHRIS, miffed perhaps, waiting for him to
take notice of her. In a moment, he does.
                    KIRSTEN
          Do you love me?

CHRIS looks up, perplexed by the question. He is certain in
his response.
                    CHRIS
          Yes.

KIRSTEN eyes him incredulously.

                    KIRSTEN
          I found these next to your bed. You
          could have told me about this... I
          don't understand why you felt you
          had to hide this stuff... Chris?
          You're supposed to be able to talk
          to me...

While she rants, she holds something we still can't see;
CHRIS slowly looks down to see what it is she has. His face
drops with his recognition of what she has found. His jaw
opens, grasping helplessly for some kind of explanation.

          ...So I'll ask you again... do you
          love me.
                    CHRIS
               (less sure this time,
               maybe convincing
               himself)
          Yes... yes...

                    KIRSTEN
          More than chocolate?

He is unable to answer... he looks from her face to the bag.
And back... silent... apologetic. She is incensed. Without
warning she throws the bag at him and storms out of the room.

CHRIS opens the bag to reveal a pile of imported dark
chocolate bars.

CUT TO BLACK

There is the sound of a candybar wrapper being torn open...
the sound of munching...
```

Here's our script (it's also in the ~ Extras folder in the Making Movies with Mike folder, in an Adobe Acrobat file called chocoluv.pdf). Print it out and have it nearby as we start to work on the scene. Also, take some time now to read it, and get your head around the characters and story line. You may even want to take some notes on it.

I shot this scene in my living room with a couple of friends. It's not part of a real movie, and these aren't actors. I used a slate at the beginning of most shots to make it easy to see where each starts and ends, and to provide a simple visual label. There's a punch on the first frame of each shot (not at the clap) to help delineate the clips.

To be practical, I designed a one-page script for our video. Granted, the story line is kind of dumb, but I assure you it will provide an excellent place to learn about editing and Final Cut Express.

Shots, Clips, and Scenes

There simply aren't enough interesting words to describe all the bits of material you need when working in film or video. Even though it might seem like there are dozens (in the same way Eskimos are said to have scores of words for *ice*), none are rigidly enforced in proper usage. Lacking a good alternative, I've even heard engineers call material "HOFs" (for "hunks of film").

A *scene* is a unit of a film as it is shot, generally from a single location. Everything in the living room scene you're about to use is Scene 1. Every time I move the camera around and shoot again, I am changing the *setup*. Filmmakers label setups with a letter after the scene number—thus, Scene 1A and Scene 1B. These sound like different scenes, but they're really both Scene 1. Every time I reshoot a setup, I'm shooting another *take*, and I will reshoot takes until everything is right. There could be dozens.

When you put all this material into a computer, Final Cut captures *clips*, which may be as short as a frame or as long as an entire videotape, and don't necessarily line up with the scenes and takes. *Shot* is slang for both *scene* and *take*, and for that matter, *clip*. The real meaning of shot is more about what the camera sees (such as close-up or wide), so a shot might *describe* each setup. For instance you might say, "Take 3 is a close-up shot."

When you start to edit, you are using a clip or a piece of a clip (which is probably a piece of a take) and cutting it into a sequence. What is this piece called? Well, it was a clip when it was in the Browser, but now that it's edited, it's fair to call it a shot. Final Cut Express tends to refer to these as clips. Both choices are fine.

Professionals spend an appropriately long time organizing these distinctly slated shots. Organization is fundamental in complex productions, and lack of organization will make even simple projects almost impossible to bring off. Eventually you'll look at how scripts, material, and editing software can be used to organize, but for now, just familiarize yourself with the script and shots we use to practice editing in the next three chapters.

Shot Vocabulary Cheat Sheet

TYPES OF SHOTS	SPECIAL SHOT RELATIONSHIPS

TYPES OF SHOTS

Close-up (CU or CLOSE)
Head alone
*A shot of one person is
called a single.*

Medium shot (MS or MED)
Head to waist
*A shot of two people is also
called a two-shot (2/s).*

Wide shot (WS or WIDE)
Head to toe
*This one is particularly far
away—referred to as an extreme
wide shot (EWS).*

SPECIAL SHOT RELATIONSHIPS

Shot ⟶ Reverse shot

Shot ⟶ Cutaway shot

Shot ⟶ Point of view (POV)

Shot ⟶ Establishing shot (ES)

> **Coverage** is all the footage that may be used to edit a given scene. If there's a dialog between you and me, and the director has only shot video of me, then there is incomplete coverage, and it would be challenging to edit a scene from the material. A director may use different camera angles (high angle, low angle), camera positions (setups for shot and reverse shot), and lenses (close, medium, and wide) to generate the coverage of a scene. Without good coverage, you can't really edit.

I filmed the scene in a traditional way: close, medium, and wide shots on the man (Chris), close and medium on the woman (Kirsten), and then a couple of close-up detail shots for use as *cut-aways* (detail shots that augment the main action of your scene).

Reviewing the Coverage

Among the tutorial files you copied onto your hard disk in Chapter 1 is a folder of FCE Project Files; inside that folder is a project called Chocoluv Tutorial.

When you open this project (double-click the project icon), the display will look mostly empty, but it does include the source-material clips I placed in the Browser. You may also notice a couple of sequences in the Browser as well. Double-click the Dailies Reel sequence to open it—you'll see it in the Timeline and Canvas.

Chocoluv Tutorial

This is the project you'll use for editing

Name	Duration	In	Out
1A-2 MS Chris	00:01:13;08	Not Set	Not Set
1B-1 CU Chris	00:01:12;16	Not Set	Not Set
1C-1 ECU Chris	00:02:15;11	Not Set	Not Set
1D-1 WS Chris	00:01:23;16	Not Set	Not Set
1E-1 ECU Chris/Ring	00:00:25;22	Not Set	Not Set
1F-4 MS Kirsten	00:00:45;28	Not Set	Not Set
1G-2 CU Kirsten	00:00:47;20	Not Set	Not Set
1G-5 CU Kirsten	00:00:41;26	Not Set	Not Set
1J-series CU BAG	00:00:54;10	Not Set	Not Set
1K-series CU Chocolate	00:01:25;27	Not Set	Not Set
Dailies Reel	00:11:06;12	Not Set	Not Set
Sequence 1	00:00:00;00	Not Set	Not Set

Here are the video clips, already labeled and broken down into individual takes. (Consequently, one take equals one clip.) Although it's common practice to capture videotapes as a single long clip (to save time in organization and preparation) for most personal projects, professionals need to see one take per clip.

Before editing, it's a good idea to watch your dailies and familiarize yourself with the footage. While it's easy enough to double-click each clip from the Browser and watch the material in the Viewer, another professional method is to assemble all the clips into a sequence and watch them end to end; I created the 11-minute Dailies Reel in just this way. Watching it is pretty much like watching the original videotape before I captured it into the computer.

For scripted projects, assembling all the source material end to end into Dailies Reel sequences makes for convenient reviewing before editing. Each clip is composed of a picture track (V1) and a stereo pair of sound tracks (A1 and A2).

Dailies is a Hollywood term for the raw film footage taken the previous day and delivered for viewing today. The British call them *rushes*. They're also generically referred to as *unedited source material*.

Let's examine the coverage for this scene and start to think about how to approach an edit.

This scene is shot with the most elemental (and kind of boring) shots—using some pretty uninspired staging. All the better to see how editing changes the material. On the following page are single frames (sometimes referred to as *poster frames*) with basic (traditional Hollywood) descriptions, illustrating each camera shot *(setup)*.

Scene 1A, Take 2
MED Chris

Scene 1B, Take 1
CU Chris

Scene 1C, Take 1
ECU Chris

Scene 1D, Take 1
WS Chris

Scene 1E, Take 1
ECU Chris hands

Scene 1F, Take 4
MS Kirsten

Scene 1G, Takes 2 and 5
CU Kirsten

Scene 1J, series of shots
CU Bag (Kirsten)

Scene 1K, series of shots
CU Bag (Chris)

If you haven't already, double-click the Dailies Reel. Play this sequence and get ready to take notes on your script. A script is more than lines of dialogue. For the editor, it's an organizational outline. Professionals take special notes on a script to facilitate finding shots and understanding the existing coverage. You don't need to do this yourself, but I hope that showing it to you will emphasize how important it is to know your material and coverage. My script notes about what was shot are on the following page.

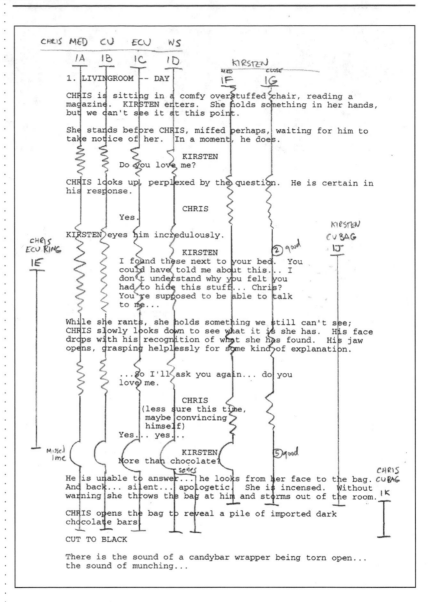

CHRIS   MED   CU   ECU   WS

1A   1B   1C   1D

KIRSTEN

1F   1G

MED   CLOSE

1. LIVINGROOM -- DAY

CHRIS is sitting in a comfy overstuffed chair, reading a
magazine. KIRSTEN enters. She holds something in her hands,
but we can't see it at this point.

She stands before CHRIS, miffed perhaps, waiting for him to
take notice of her. In a moment, he does.

                    KIRSTEN
          Do you love me?

CHRIS looks up, perplexed by the question. He is certain in
his response.

                    CHRIS
          Yes.

KIRSTEN eyes him incredulously.

CHRIS
ECU RING

1E

                    KIRSTEN
          I found these next to your bed.   You
          could have told me about this... I
          don't understand why you felt you
          had to hide this stuff... Chris?
          You're supposed to be able to talk
          to me...

②good

KIRSTEN
CU BAG

1J

While she rants, she holds something we still can't see;
CHRIS slowly looks down to see what it is she has. His face
drops with his recognition of what she has found. His jaw
opens, grasping helplessly for some kind of explanation.

          ...So I'll ask you again... do you
          love me.

                    CHRIS
          (less sure this time,
          maybe convincing
          himself)
          Yes... yes...

Missed
line

                    KIRSTEN
          More than chocolate?

⑤good

He is unable to answer... he looks from her face to the bag.
And back... silent... apologetic. She is incensed. Without
warning she throws the bag at him and storms out of the room.

CHRIS
CU BAG

1K

CHRIS opens the bag to reveal a pile of imported dark
chocolate bars.

CUT TO BLACK

There is the sound of a candybar wrapper being torn open...
the sound of munching...

Here's a professional method for annotating a script (on movie projects this is a task for the script supervisor, who records notes in this way and tracks continuity issues). A solid line means a character is speaking on camera, a wavy line means that character is not. At a glance, an editor can see which setups (1A, 1B, and so on) cover which parts of the scene. This is sometimes called a lined script.

After you've had a look at the Dailies Reel sequence, you're
ready to face the tutorials. You'll start by using Sequence 1
(the empty default sequence that Final Cut Express creates
when you first open the program—a convenient starting place).

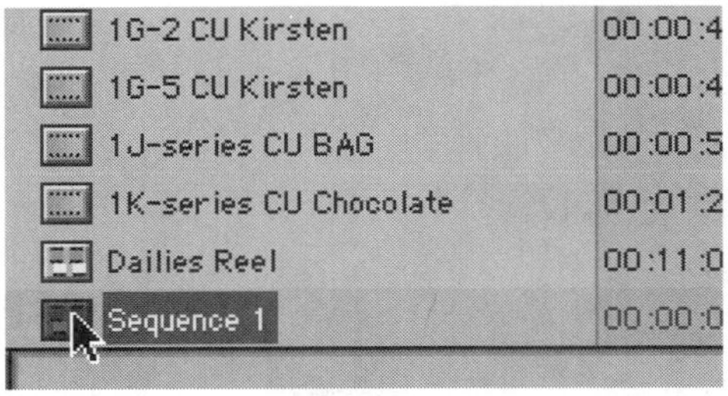

At the bottom of the Browser is a blank sequence where you'll start working.

Double-click Sequence 1 in the Browser. Notice that it opens a clean, empty Timeline. The Canvas, too, will be empty.

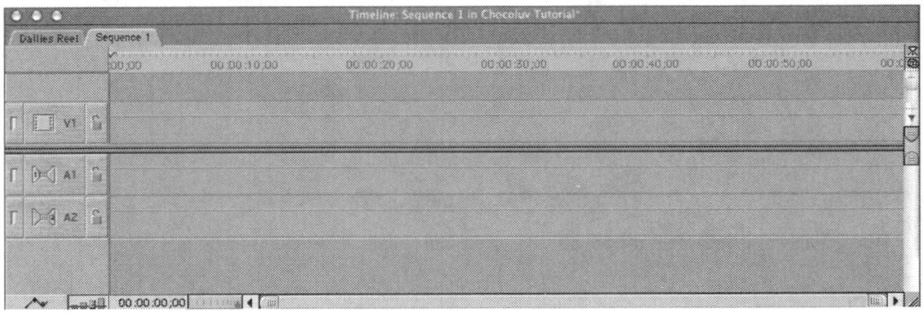

An empty Timeline. Nothing much to look at yet. But it's where all the action happens.

Once you double-click Sequence 1, a new tab appears above the Timeline. Now, in addition to a Dailies Reel tab, there's also one called Sequence 1. Tabs in the Timeline allow you to switch among different sequences that are open at the same time. These can even be sequences from different projects.

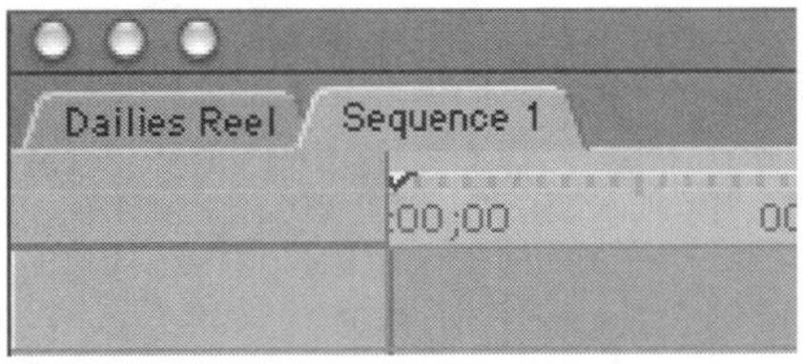

Two open sequences show up as two tabs in the Timeline window. Pop from sequence to sequence by clicking the tabs. If you rename an open sequence in the Browser, the name on all applicable tabs will get updated.

Using Tabs

Every window has tabs, and each has a slightly different purpose.

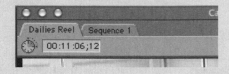

Tabs in the Canvas show the same sequences as shown in the Timeline. As in the Timeline, you can see any sequences that are presently open, even if you aren't watching them.

To *close* a sequence—thus putting away the Timeline and the associated Canvas—choose File > Close Tab.

Tabs in the Browser don't list sequences but instead let you access different projects that are open at the same time. Note: There is always one tab for your Effects tool set, but you can ignore it until Chapter 5. If you open a new project without closing the one you're currently in, you'll see them pack in among the Browser tabs.

Tabs in the Viewer let you view different "slices" through a clip. For now we only need to look at the Video slice. The Viewer display usually shows the picture of the selected source clip, but there is an Audio slice, which shows waveforms of the stereo sound tracks; a Filters slice, which outlines the filters you've applied to this video; and a Motion slice, for the motion effects you've applied. Viewer tabs are perhaps the most potentially complicated, so don't bother with these for the time being.

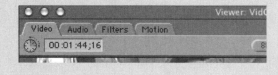

Editing Your First Shots

Time to make your first edit. Glancing at the script, you'll see that the scene begins with Kirsten asking Chris the question, "Do you love me?" You can see from my lined script that we have some options for this first line of dialogue.

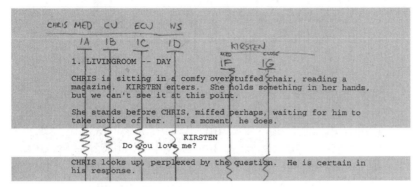

At each line of script dialogue, my "script lines" help me identify what setups cover it and which ones have the speaking character onscreen. To know which set up to use requires reviewing each clip at this line of dialogue.

There are two shots (but three takes) of Kirsten saying this line: two in close and one in medium. For the moment, we're not concentrating on the quality of her performance; we just want to get the line delivered on camera.

1. Select the clip labeled 1F-4 MS Kirsten in the Browser, and double-click it to open it in the Viewer.

2. Play the clip, using the spacebar or other controls. (If you have any trouble, go back to Chapter 1 and review the "Playtime: Mastering the Video Controls" section.)

3. Watch the shot until Kirsten utters her first word, then back up a little and mark an In point. When you click Play again, there should be a moment of silence (called a *beat*) before she starts talking. (Watch her eyes to help pick that starting frame.)

4. When she finishes her line, click Stop, look around a frame at a time in either direction to make sure you're on the precise frame, and mark an Out point. Make sure you aren't hearing any other audio at the point where you choose to mark an In or Out point. (Finding these In and Out points involves exactly the kind of precision shuttling with the jog wheel, J-K-L keys, and frame-by-frame stepping that you practiced in the last chapter.) Your Viewer should look approximately—although almost certainly not exactly—like this:

The duration of the shot is 3;20.

This particular frame is 12;09 from the start of the clip.

Here's the Mark Out icon ("Out point overlay").

The cut relative to the entire clip

Understanding Inserts

You've found the part of the clip you like. The next step in the editing process is to make some *inserts*, which is all about adding bits of source material to the edited sequence. The way you make inserts in Final Cut Express is by moving material from the Viewer to the Canvas.

If you click and hold a clip in the Viewer, you can drag it around. Drag it into the Canvas, but don't let go of it yet.

It looks as if you're dragging a small icon of the shot as you move the pointer, and when you reach the Canvas, a translucent menu (called the Edit Overlay) pops up with a handful of choices for putting this shot into the edited sequence.

Drag the clip to the big yellow Insert rectangle and drop it. Technically speaking, this rectangle is called the *Insert section of the Edit Overlay*, but I'm just going to call it the Insert button.

When you let go, you'll notice that the shot appears full frame in the Canvas and also below in the Timeline.

Congrats: You're editing.

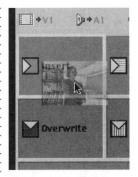

The Insert button is large and pretty easy to hit.

Duration of
the bit we liked   Watched clip here   Mark Out Icon

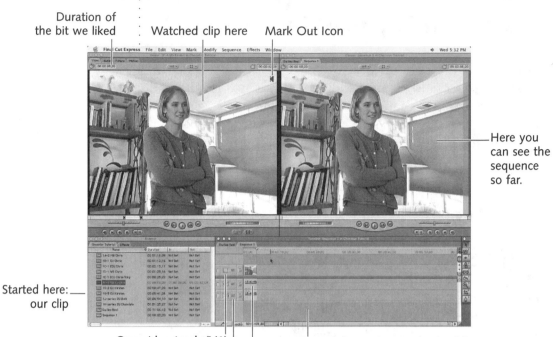

Here you
can see the
sequence
so far.

Started here:
our clip

One video track (V1)
Stereo audio tracks (A1 and A2)   These tracks all move together.
The Timeline: where our edited bit went

The editing you've just done demonstrates the essence of *non-destructive editing.* You chose a bit of video to put in your sequence, but you didn't move, change, or otherwise affect the video you started with. It's still in the Browser. It's still in the Viewer. But a bit of it has been copied into the Timeline, and you can see it in the Canvas.

This is significantly different from the way iMovie handles editing. iMovie moves shots into the Clip pane from the camcorder, but when you edit with them, it takes them out of the pane and places them in the Timeline. That can be a problem because a single clip may have many parts you want to use; when the clip is moved (and cropped) after you use it the first time, you're in trouble if you later decide you want to use another part. The Final Cut Express method is considerably more functional.

You can also see in the Timeline that the video track and stereo audio tracks are actually three separate items, even though they move as one. The little triangles between the audio tracks (called stereo pair indicators) show that the two tracks are not just any two tracks, but a left and right stereo pair.

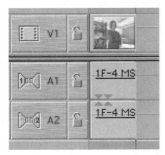

What began as one clip in the Browser, with a bit snipped out and inserted in the Viewer, can now be revealed as three items linked together—a bit of video and a pair of synchronous audio tracks. You can still think of this trio as a single unit.

Feeling OK? If you aren't truly comfortable with these events, don't keep going until you are. You'll need this solid foundation for digging into editing.

Let's break from the Insert to mess with the screen just a bit. Now that you're getting comfortable with the interface and have done some editing, it's time to make sure you feel comfortable using the tabs in the Viewer and Canvas.

Select the Dailies Reel tab (in either the Canvas or the Timeline, it doesn't matter).

When you select the Dailies Reel tab, the material switches in both the Timeline and the Canvas, but whatever was in the Viewer remains there. This kind of shift should not be jarring, as you might be doing this all the time when you're working.

Click back to Sequence 1; things should be just where you left them. You could go back and forth like this all day long.

Without watching the material you edited in Sequence 1, let's go get another shot to add on to the end of this one. (If you've already watched, make sure you're parked at the end of the first and only shot. If you aren't, the next few moments may get confusing.)

1. Go to the Browser and double-click shot 1A-2 MS Chris, the medium shot of Chris.

2. Scroll into the shot until you hear Kirsten's line finish and before Chris responds.

It's not right at the beginning of the clip, but you'll see Kirsten cross the frame just before Chris hears her line.

3. Mark an In point here, but do not mark an Out.

You've marked an In point here. See the Mark In icon (the In point overlay) in the top-left corner of the frame and the In mark in the scrubber? According to Final Cut Express, the duration of this clip is 34;23—the time from this point all the way to the end of the clip.

When you don't mark an In or an Out point, Final Cut Express makes some assumptions about what you're doing. If you don't mark an Out, Final Cut Express assumes the end of the clip is the Out, and if you don't mark an In point, it assumes the beginning of the clip is the In. Thus (until you are quite advanced), Final Cut Express sees every clip as having two and only two marks in it. You can move them around, but there are always only two.

4. As before, drag this shot over to the Canvas, and drop it on the Insert button.

After you let go, what has changed? You'll see in the Timeline a new, large clip that appears to be substantially longer than the first shot, and the playhead parked at the end.

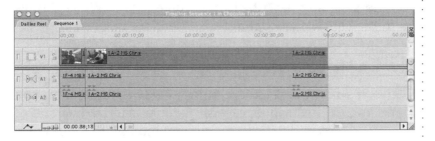

Final Cut Express cues up to the last frame of the shot you just edited, which in this case is the tail of 1A-2, and shows it to you in the Canvas.

The Insert Concept

While the generic term for what you've been doing is *editing* or maybe *splicing,* the actual term is *inserting*. In editing, inserting generally means adding new source material to an edited sequence. In practical Final Cut Express terms, it means moving material from the Viewer to the Canvas. This may not seem that different from the dictionary definition of the word *insert,* but it's special because simply inserting source material into the sequence is not enough; an editor needs to know *how* it

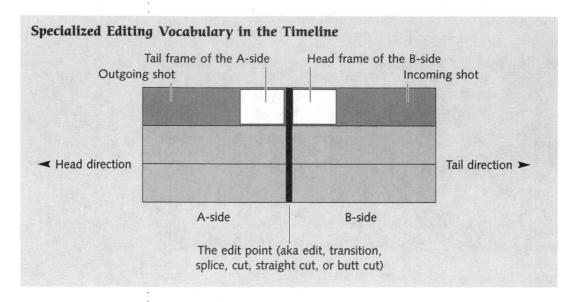

Specialized Editing Vocabulary in the Timeline

Tail frame of the A-side   Head frame of the B-side

Outgoing shot   Incoming shot

◄ Head direction   Tail direction ►

A-side   B-side

The edit point (aka edit, transition,
splice, cut, straight cut, or butt cut)

should be inserted. The function Final Cut Express calls *Insert* is more generally described as a *ripple insert*. Which brings us to the concept of *rippling*.

The Ripple Concept

Everything that happens in editing—every manipulation you make to an edited sequence—can be characterized as one of two types: a manipulation that *ripples* and one that does not. So what is rippling?

Imagine you're stacking toy blocks. When you insert a block into the middle of the stack, every block above the insertion point goes higher. When you pull a block out of the middle (if you're careful), all the blocks above it will drop down to fill the gap. The part of the stack above the change must move up or down every time you make a change to the blocks. This is rippling.

Turn the stack on its side (that is, line up the blocks on the floor), and you can now remove a block without moving the others. If you choose to close the gap, you're rippling the blocks. If you decide to leave the gap, you're not rippling them.

Similarly, as you make adjustments or add material to your edited video shots, it seems natural for the shots to ripple around, sliding back and forth to make room for the changes, but keeping all the individual shots themselves unchanged and connected. In fact, rippling is sometimes referred to as *film-style* editing, because film is edited with changes that push and pull all the other shots around.

If you're trying to keep different tracks (picture and sound, for instance) in sync with each other, a ripple in one track will invariably throw it *out of sync* with the others. This is why rippling is also sometimes considered dangerous (or advanced), and the icons for it in professional editing systems have historically been colored red. Final Cut Express colors them yellow, reminding you that while it could be dangerous, *you will never accidentally erase something by inserting*; proceed with caution.

The alternative to rippling is, of course, *not* rippling. In general (but not always), Final Cut Express refers to this as *rolling*. Whatever the function is called (not-rippling, rolling, or over-writing), it means that whatever modification you perform, the overall length of the edited sequence will not change.

So, if you add 2 seconds to something in the Timeline, 2 seconds are automatically removed from the material already in the Timeline. A zero-sum game, as they say. When you perform operations that don't ripple, you can never accidentally throw your tracks out of sync from each other, even if you're making changes to only one track. In that sense, a non-ripple modification is "safe." However, because you might inadvertently remove material, there is a more serious chance of ruining something in your sequence. For this reason, not rippling is considered more dangerous than rippling and thus is color-coded in red.

Two More Inserts

First, let's put a shot ahead of the one that's currently starting out the sequence. We'll use a shot of Chris before Kirsten enters, to help establish the scene.

1. Open clip 1A-2 MS Chris into the Viewer again. Notice that the part we used is still marked with an In point (we never marked an Out).

2. Drag the playhead across the scrubber to move ahead of the In point, and find Chris sipping his coffee, before Kirsten enters.

3. Mark a new In point, and you'll see the old one disappear and a new one appear at your new playhead location.

Find a nice, quiet part of Chris's wide shot before Kirsten enters, where he's minding his own business. After you mark an In point, you'll see the familiar In point overlay—this will be the new first frame of the sequence.

4. In the Viewer, scrub around to find the frame where you want this shot to end, and mark an Out.

It's not a great establishing shot, but as an editor your job is to work with what you've got. Just make sure you get out of this shot before Kirsten begins to enter the frame.

There's that Mark Out icon in the top-right corner of the Viewer. You need only a few calm seconds of him reading the paper. I tend to cut a little long at first and then tighten up shots later.

Now that you've marked clip 1-A2 MS Chris with two points—an In and an Out point—you need to tell Final Cut Express where to put the shot. *Final Cut Express inserts shots in the Canvas wherever the playhead is parked.* Since we want the video to begin with this establishing shot, move the playhead to the beginning of the sequence.

It may be a little hard to see in the Timeline, but the Canvas should be cued up to the first frame. How do you know it's the first *(head)* frame? Final Cut Express superimposes an L-shaped icon on Canvas images to indicate head and tail frames of shots. These icons indicate that your playhead is parked on a head or tail frame of a clip in the Timeline. Like I said, the Timeline and the Canvas go together.

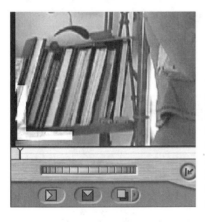

The translucent white L in the bottom-left corner of the Canvas indicates that this is the first frame of an edited shot. Final Cut Express puts a reverse L-shaped icon in the bottom-right corner at shot endings. If you move from shot to shot in the Timeline, you'll see these at the beginning and ending of each one.

With everything lined up properly, drag clip 1A-2 MS Chris from the Viewer to the Canvas, and insert it at the beginning of the sequence. This is what should happen:

Three shots in a row, from 1A to 1F and back to 1A. The playhead is resting at the end of the newly inserted shot, before the other two—just where it was before the insert.

Notice that when you inserted a shot at the beginning, it shoved the other two down to run a little later. You *rippled* them. Final Cut Express calls this simply an *insert edit*, but you should understand this as a ripple insert. Just to drive the point home, let's do one more.

Play the sequence from the beginning one more time, and be ready to hit the Stop button (any stop button will do). Play through the three shots and stop just after Chris finishes his line with "yes." He's kind of smirking in this take, anyway, so see if you can get the part of his performance where he's credible. It's short.

This is about where to park the playhead to prepare for inserting the next shot.

You've found the natural end of Chris's shot. The playhead is parked there. Now, leave the Timeline and Canvas for a moment. It's time to move back to the source material to find Kirsten's reaction.

Let's start with 1F-4 MS Kirsten again. We used it before. Maybe we'll use some more.

Double-click 1F-4 MS Kirsten in the Browser; it appears in the Viewer. Notice it's right where you left it. Click Play and see what Kirsten does next.

She says her line of dialogue, of course. Let's see what other coverage we have for this line, since there might be a particularly good delivery of the line in another take. (Having the discipline to check other takes for better performances is one of the tasks of an editor.) Double-click 1G-2 CU Kirsten in the Browser.

Since we've never used this clip before, you'll see it cue up to the head frame when it shows up in the Viewer. Besides the punch, how do you know for sure that this is the first frame of the shot? Final Cut Express superimposes sprocket holes on the left side of the frame to indicate that this is the beginning of a clip. (Sprocket holes will also be on the right at the end of the clip.) This is the third overlay we've seen that Final Cut Express superimposes over pictures to identify beginnings and ends, which include:

When there is lots of coverage, be prepared to spend a fair amount of time and energy searching each take for better performances. Cue up 1G-2 and see if you think the delivery is better here.

- Sprocket holes in the Viewer indicating clip beginning or end

- The white L-shaped icon in the Canvas indicating an edited shot's beginning or end

- The small Mark In and Mark Out icons (In point and Out point overlays), denoting a frame in the Viewer where a marked clip starts or stops

Play through this shot and mark In and Out points around Kirsten's response. Do the same thing with 1G-5 CU Kirsten. You can now directly compare her delivery of this line in the two takes.

You've now seen all the coverage you have of Kirsten; insert the take you like. I used 1G-5 CU Kirsten. Insert it as we practiced: Drag it into the Canvas and let go over the Insert button—this will stick it into the sequence right where the playhead was sitting.

When I drag shots over to the Insert button, I try to take one more moment before letting go to check the location of the playhead in the Timeline. It's going to break the sequence there and insert the shot.

Even though the playhead wasn't parked between two shots, when we indicated that we wanted to insert (and ripple) this new shot, Final Cut Express ripped open the sequence right where we were parked and dropped it in. Then it shoved the rest of 1A-2 MS Chris down (to the right). Play your sequence now, and you'll see what I mean. You'll see what you cut and then you'll see that it trails off into 1A-2 MS Chris material that you probably don't want.

After inserting the shot of Kirsten, its easy to see how shots before the insert point are untouched, but everything after the insert point has been rippled—pushed farther down in time. The playhead is now parked at the tail of the newly inserted shot.

The Match Frame Button

I can't even begin to describe the many interesting ways you'll use this simple little button in the lower-right corner of the Canvas, but I guarantee you'll come to love it. It really only does one thing, but that one thing is both subtle and powerful. Try this:

1. While you're watching video in the Canvas, click Stop.

2. Then click the *Match Frame button*. Final Cut Express finds the exact same frame from your source material and puts it in the Viewer.

At its simplest, this aids in clip navigation, particularly when you're continually moving back and forth between certain shots during editing (and, in particular, inserting). As you progress to more advanced editing tricks, the Match Frame button will repeatedly come into play.

Note: There's also a Match Frame button in the Viewer, which matches the Viewer's frame to the Timeline. But its use is more complicated and potentially confusing.

Timeline Features

The Timeline is its own little landscape in Final Cut Express. It graphically represents your cut as if you were connecting *real* objects. Now that you've had a chance to do a few inserts and see the Timeline in use, this is a good opportunity to take a break and investigate some of the many detailed Timeline features available to you.

Time Scale

The Timeline has a yardstick across the top, called the *ruler*, which represents the scale of time against which the clips are measured. Increasing the window width will, of course, show more of your sequence, but you can also accomplish this by changing the scale. As your sequences grow in length, you may want to see more at a time (say you want to move an entire scene or you want to see how long one area is compared with another). There are also more practical, functional reasons (say your shots are hard to grab, see, or work with).

There are lots of ways to adjust the scale and zoom in on the Timeline, such as these two examples:

1. The *Zoom control,* which is nestled in the lower frame of the Timeline window.

The Zoom control is a cryptic little tool that, once you get used to it, is actually pretty easy to use and powerful. Still, it's less intuitive than the comparable zoom slider in iMovie.

As you move the small center pointer left and right over the scale in this small box, you'll see the Timeline squeeze or stretch correspondingly.

When the scale lines draw closer together, so does the graphic representation of your cuts.

Notice the scale across the top. Here the Dailies Reel has been squished to fit—there are almost 12 minutes of video represented here.

Similarly, when the scale lines move wider apart, the Timeline expands, like an accordion, to display the shots larger, with more space between cuts.

When you zoom in tight, the Timeline represents only about a second of video. It's so close, in fact, that you can see the way Final Cut Express places the playhead at a single frame and highlights it in the Timeline.

2. You can also zoom using the magnifying glass with the plus sign (the *Zoom In* tool) from the Tool palette. With this tool, you can pinpoint a spot you want to see in detail and click repeatedly to zoom in to the scale that works for you (to zoom out, select the *Zoom Out* tool—the magnifying glass with the minus sign—or Option-click).

Once you venture away from the Timeline's Zoom control options, there's still the classic magnifying glass tool that you can get from the Tool palette. It works intuitively, zooming in when there's a plus in the circle and zooming out when there's a minus. Click and hold on it in the Tool palette and a couple of other interesting (but less useful) tools become available.

Final Cut Express Time

Video plays 30 frames every second. Thus, you can measure time by counting frames. The traditional *timecode* format is hours, minutes, seconds, and frames, each separated by a colon (00:00:00:00). A special kind of timecode, called *drop-frame timecode,* uses a semicolon rather than a colon between the seconds and frames. Because this is what is used in most DV camcorders, this is the notation you'll see in all the timecode and duration windows scattered across the Final Cut Express interface. For more about timecode, see the Appendix.

Track Height

Most of the time when you edit, you'll work with three tracks: one picture and two sound tracks. But Final Cut Express can have many more of either. The default configuration in Final Cut Express opens up two picture tracks and four sound tracks, for a total of six running along your Timeline. There may be times when you want to make each track thicker, and thus more visible (and manageable), or narrower, to see more at a time. You use the *Track Height control* for these adjustments.

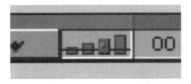

The track thickness can be managed from the Track Height control box. It's tiny, yes, but easy to use and understand.

I don't know why, but making tracks thin (or "short") like this makes editing feel more complicated to me. It's harder to see what shots you've selected, and it's a little harder to select them.

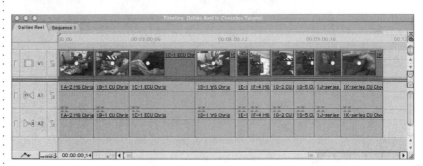

Making tracks thick (or "tall") makes them easier to see and work with, but it also kind of makes you feel like you're working on a baby toy (think Big Note Songbook) or kids' product. I tend to work in the middle range.

Scrolling the Timeline

You don't always want to see your sequence from the beginning. As your projects get longer, you may find yourself working with the Timeline set to about 20 seconds wide, but with your work space many minutes down into the sequence. You can move the active part of the Timeline by dragging the playhead toward either end of the Timeline for a quick (but not highly controlled) movement up- or downstream. (Of course, you can also move the Timeline by moving the playhead in the Canvas scrubber.)

There are also scrolling arrows in the bottom of the Timeline that provide a little more controlled scroll in one direction or the other.

Finally, there is a scroll bar (called the *Zoom slider*) between the arrows that you can drag left and right to move the Timeline. Interestingly enough, you can also grab the ends of this scroll bar to adjust the zoom in the Timeline.

> *Well, not really finally, as there are a variety of other methods scattered throughout Final Cut Express, but most require more keystrokes or are more buried and thus approach the "more trouble than they're worth" level.*

Playhead

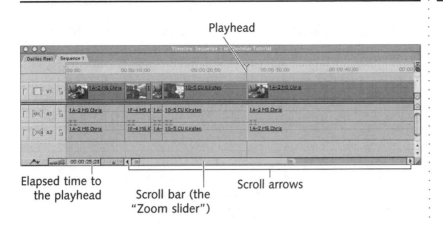

Elapsed time to
the playhead

Scroll bar (the
"Zoom slider")

Scroll arrows

Adjusting Shot Volume Levels

In Final Cut Express you can adjust the volume (actually the *power*) of any shot in the Timeline. It's called *adjusting audio levels,* and you use the *Clip Overlays control* to do it.

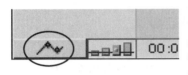

The Clip Overlays control, nestled in the lower-left corner of the Timeline frame, gives you access to the control for sound adjustment. Clicking this button doesn't change anything about the sound; it just makes it possible for you to adjust sound volume in the Timeline.

When you click this button, a red line down the middle of your audio tracks appears (called a *level overlay*). As your pointer moves over this red line, it changes into a strange-looking cursor (the Adjust Line Segment pointer)—raising or lowering this line as you click and drag.

Clip Overlays
control

Adjust Line
Segment pointer

Change in
volume

Level overlay
(the red line)

-3 dB

You can see the Adjust Line Segment pointer, but it's hard to see the red Level overlay line in black-and-white. Experiment on your own to see them clearly. The gain—how much louder or quieter your shot is in decibels—is the number in the small box that pops into the tracks as you start to move the line.

In the sound tracks, this level line is used to raise and lower the volume of the shot. (Oddly, there is a similar *black* line in the picture tracks, and moving it raises and lowers the opacity of a shot, but ignore that for now.) Drag the line in any clip to your desired level of loudness. Click the Clip Overlays control again to turn the lines off, if you want.

Volume

What we call *volume* is actually a function of acoustic or electrical power and is measured in decibels (abbreviated *dB*). Decibels are on a logarithmic scale, which simply means that a large degree of measurement (and user control) has been squeezed into a condensed range of numbers. Thus, it doesn't usually take an adjustment of too many decibels to even out the mix of different takes. One dB is about the smallest discernable change in volume. Making an adjustment to the decibel levels is sometimes called "adjusting the gain."

Adjusting Your Shots

When you realize that it is very easy to make changes to the In and Out points of any shot in your sequence any time the mood strikes you, you'll find that some of the stress that comes from making edit decisions will decrease, and some of the fun in *sculpting* a sequence will increase. I'm not saying that you'll cut sloppily and then fix mistakes later, but on the other hand, you can do just that if it's your preferred way to approach material.

Your sequence at this point is cut pretty simply, with a shot of either Chris or Kirsten for each line of dialogue. We paused after five shots (and the wide shot of Chris—1A-2—rolls along into material you aren't going to want), but you see how this works. It's OK to have material in your sequence that you know won't last. This shouldn't stress you out at all.

Now that you've made some edits, let's change them a little. There's an old adage (well, cliché, perhaps) that says that the secret to editing is *re-editing*. This is your chance. There are two primary ways to fix shots already cut into your sequence. The first is by trimming the transitions between shots in the sequence, and the second is by deleting material from anywhere in the sequence (not just near the edit points).

The Trim Concept

Trimming means changing the transition (called the *edit point* in Final Cut Express) where two shots are joined. It can mean subtracting or adding frames—to either side of the selected transition. The thing to remember about trims is that they are *always* about the two shots that are there now in the Timeline.

Let's take a close look at a trim. Move your pointer in the Timeline over any transition. The pointer changes. I'm going to demonstrate this over the first transition in the sequence, between Chris sitting on the couch and Kirsten entering.

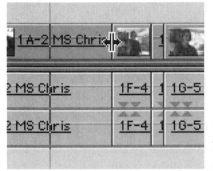

Move the pointer over an edit point and it changes, anticipating that you might want to select an edit as opposed to an entire shot.

If you click a transition once, you'll highlight that particular splice point.

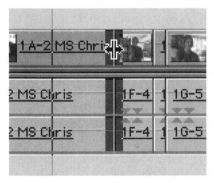

Select a splice point. If you look closely at this thick, dark-gray highlight, you can see it's actually highlighting a little on the tail of one shot and more on the head of the other. This isn't always the case. Keep this in mind as we dig deeper into trims.

Double-clicking the transition will break it open into a special trim workspace, called the *Trim Edit window*, which goes on top of the Viewer and Canvas.

The Trim Edit window is what you get when you double-click a transition; it's ready for you to adjust one or both sides of the edit. It's not the same as the Viewer and Canvas, although it does look very similar.

For any trim, you'll begin at the point where the tail of the outgoing shot is attached to the head of the incoming shot. Imagine that a piece of tape is holding these two shots together. A trim always takes place at the tape. Double-clicking the transition itself "rips the tape off" and displays both the outgoing and incoming frames *at the same time.* Now you can decide if you want to adjust one or both sides of the splice.

> *Editing software gives the impression that an edit is simply the point where one frame is taped to another frame. The Trim Edit window accentuates this notion because it shows you the two frames adjacent to the edit point. What you'll come to realize is that an edit isn't so much between two frames as between two shots. If you only look at the two frames at the edit point, you may never learn the art of playing with the way the shots move together and into each other.*

A RIPPLE TRIM

With a trim, it's important to decide whether you want to change both sides of the transition together or individually. Much of the time you'll want to make discrete decisions for each of the outgoing and incoming shots. You do this with the function called *Ripple Edit* in Final Cut Express.

As with any function that ripples, a ripple trim is likely to change the overall length of your edited sequence. To perform a ripple trim you must always choose one of the two shots that you wish to adjust. You adjust only one shot at a time, but you can still make independent modifications to both.

Let's do it in the Trim Edit window:

Selection bar   Mark Out icon   Mark In icon   Mark Out ("do it") button   Selection bar

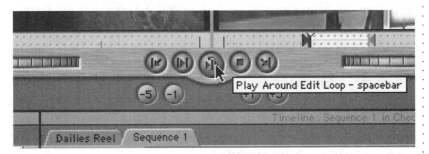

Mark In ("do it") button   Shuttle and position controls   White zone bounded with Mark In and Mark Out icons

Scrubber with odd little dots

Here's where we left our stars. If you haven't already, double-click on the first edit you made, between Chris sitting there and Kirsten entering the scene. If you want to see how this transition looks, press the Play Around Edit Loop button.

Play Around Edit Loop – spacebar

Dailies Reel   Sequence 1

In truth I don't use this feature all that much, but I can admit that it sometimes comes in handy. The Play Around Edit Loop button plays the last few moments before the cut and the next few moments after, to help you see the transition in context. It will keep doing so until you stop it (press the spacebar). Far more often I get out of the trim (by clicking the time-scale ruler in the Timeline), and then drag the playhead back a bit and slap the spacebar (to play).

Popping Headward

Often it's not enough to watch just the transition you're working on; most of the time it's imperative to see a cut in the context of the sequence. So, it's quite common to move headward one or two edits at a time, watch your edits (on the Canvas), and then back up to watch them again. Each edit you make represents a decision, and backing up two or three edits to watch your evolving sequence is largely a chance to see how your decisions are adding up.

Moving headward (or tailward) in your cut—in particular when your attention is on the Timeline—is such a convenient way to move around while editing that I think it merits a moment here.

While there are Previous Edit and Next Edit buttons among the transport controls in the Canvas (which cue to edits headward or tailward, respectively), my preferred method to back up a few cuts is to use the up arrow key and then hit the spacebar (for Play).

THE TRIM EDIT WINDOW

Let me point out a few of the more important elements of the Trim Edit window:

The *selection bars* (also called *green bars*) along the top are mission critical. You can't tell from the black-and-white photo, but they're bright green, and they indicate that both frames are currently locked together so that when you change one, you'll change the other. But if you want to adjust just one side, having green selection bars on both sides won't get you what you want. Both sides are green because when you selected and double-clicked the transition in the Timeline, both sides were highlighted. Green bars on both sides means that both sides change together. A green bar on one side means that only one side can be modified.

The *Mark In* and *Mark Out* buttons in the Trim Edit window are your "do it" buttons. They allow you to move the Out or In points to new locations before reattaching these shots. They are no different from the Mark Out ("o") and Mark In ("i") buttons on your keyboard (although personally I find executing trim changes on the keyboard more confusing than doing it onscreen).

> *Reminder: You can move around in the two shots with the shuttle controls all you want, but you won't be adjusting anything until you re-mark an In or Out point. A common beginner's problem is forgetting to re-mark after playing the shots in Trim Edit window.*

The *pointer*. Try this: Move the arrow cursor (called the *pointer*) back and forth across the two frames in the Trim Edit window and notice how it changes into one of two icons. When the pointer is on the left side of the edit point, it's a left-handed Ripple Edit icon; on the right, it's right-handed. (When it's over the middle, it's a different trim icon—but we'll get to that.)

No, the screen does not really look like this; I'm illustrating the changing icon as you move the pointer back and forth across the screen. These are strange-looking figures, I'll give you that—Ripple Edit icon on the left and right (for ripple trims), Roll Edit in the middle (for non-ripple trims).

When you click one shot or the other with the Ripple Edit icon, it lets you select, and thus alter, only one shot at a time. Click a frame with pointer in this form and notice what happens to the green bars above the window. Also notice what happens to the splice highlight in the Timeline. Everything shifts to only one side of the transition.

When the bar is over only one shot, you can change only that shot.

1. Click the outgoing shot of Chris on the left. The green bar will now be over 1A-2 MS Chris only.

If you ever go into the trim mode and don't see images in the left and right windows but instead see a big speaker icon, it means that you selected a sound edit to trim and not a picture and sound edit (or just a picture edit). It could also be that your picture track is locked. Check that you're selecting a picture and sound edit (which is all you have in your sequence at this point in the book) and try again.

2. Use the shuttle controls in the Trim Edit window to move this shot around. Just like in the Canvas or Viewer, you can play, shuttle, scrub, and use the J-K-L keys and other controls. (The forward and back arrows don't work to move one frame at a time in the Trim Edit window—which is a bummer—so I use the jog wheel to micro-adjust things.)

3. Adjust the outgoing shot of Chris so that it ends just as Kirsten is leaving the frame but is still visible. Make sure you click the Mark Out button again after you change the scrubber position in this shot.

4. Now, still in trim mode, click the other side of the transition so that the green bar is over clip 1F-4 MS Kirsten. Do the same adjustment, but this time back Kirsten up so that she is just entering frame on the left. Make sure you mark a new In point.

5. Now watch the transition by clicking the Play Around Edit Loop button.

When Final Cut Express loops the transition, the left side fades out a bit and the right side becomes the viewer for the video you're working on. This can be confusing at first.

Ugh!

Well, you did the trim correctly, but my problem is one of editing *aesthetics*. While Kirsten is in about the same position in both shots, and she's exiting the frame in one and entering the frame in the other, her *screen direction* is wrong. She's moving right to left in the first shot and left to right in the second, and the abrupt cut from one to the other doesn't work for me.

A better way to make this work is to let her leave the frame totally in the first shot and then let her enter the new shot. You're still in trim mode here, so repeat steps 3 and 4 to readjust the frames until the transition works better.

It's not perfect, but you can minimize the difficulty here by letting Kirsten fully exit the frame on the outgoing shot (left) and having the incoming shot begin just as she gets to the edge of the frame to enter. You can see the small Ripple Edit icon on the right side if you look carefully.

That's better. Anyway, that's the basis of ripple trimming.

When you're satisfied with your trim, you can click the Timeline to get out of this window.

Whenever I need to select the Timeline window, I click the time scale (ruler). It makes the window active but does not force a selection of one of the clips in the Timeline (which can be a tiny bit irritating).

A NON-RIPPLE TRIM

Before you leave the Trim Edit window, though, try a non-rippling trim, called a *Roll Edit* in Final Cut Express. Let's move to the next transition, where Chris says "yes."

Now we're at the tail of the short shot of Chris saying "yes." One click will select the transition here; double-click and you open it up ready for adjustment. Notice that the playhead is not parked at the edit—no problem. In trimming, it's about the edit you select, not the location of the playhead.

When you are in Roll Edit mode, no matter how many frames you add or subtract to one side of a transition, the exact same number of frames are added or subtracted from the other side of the transition to keep the overall duration the same.

Remember the green bar above the frames? In a Roll Edit you want that bar over both shots. If you only see one green bar, move the pointer toward the middle of the window until it turns into the Roll Edit cursor, and click.

Here's the icon for the Roll Edit

Same Trim Edit window as before, but now we want the green bars above both shots.

Now, let's adjust Kirsten's shot so that it starts after her line "I found these next to the bed ..." and before she says "I thought you could talk to me about stuff like this." (This requires clicking the Play button under Kirsten's shot on the right, and then stopping after her line.) Click the Mark In button to indicate a new In point.

Don't roll too far! When you're looking at the outgoing and incoming shots in the Trim Edit window, you can see them marked in their respective scrubber bars (the small dots in the scrubber remind you that this isn't an ordinary scrubber).

A trim is only an adjustment to the Out point of the outgoing shot (on the left) or the In point of the incoming shot (on the right). If you try to select a new Out point for the outgoing shot and you pick a location that comes before the point where that shot presently begins, uh...you can't do it.

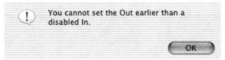

You'll get a warning because all that is outside the ends of the original clips is unavailable source material. It would be clearer if what you saw after rolling to far were black instead of more source material.

When you mark a new In point, watch what happens to Chris's shot, and notice the Timeline.

The entire sequence is the same in every way, except for this one transition, which has "rolled" to the right a little. Every frame added to one side was removed from the other for a net zero change. This will be of particular importance in the next chapter.

The transition moved, but none of the subsequent shots moved. It is as if the transition *slid* to the right. Also notice the *In Shift* and *Out Shift values* at the bottom of the Trim Edit window—both shifted exactly the same amount (+ 2:12).

Here's a case where the small numbers on the screen can be useful and important. The In and Out Shift values tell you how much you moved a cut, and in which direction. Plus (+) means the edit shifted to the right, minus (-) means it moved to the left.

Play the cut. Personally, I don't think this works. Even in material based on a script with multiple (similar) takes, it's still probably better to adjust each side of a transition independently, specifically to the right spot, and not together in this way. What you'll discover if you play with Chocoluv enough is that it doesn't present the best editing situation for using a Roll Edit, and I don't recommend using it right now.

Just undo the edit (Command-Z) to take it back to the way it was before we started this.

We'll come back to non-rippling trims when it makes more sense to use them.

The Delete Concept

While *trimming* certainly seems like it means *deleting*, as you have seen, it does not. Trimming can mean adding *or* removing frames. But there are times when you just want to take a knife and cut out something you don't like. There's no more fundamental way to do this than to delete it. And as with inserting and trimming, each time you remove material from a sequence, Final Cut Express must be told whether the delete ripples or doesn't ripple the following shots.

There are a few different ways to delete material from your sequence, but almost all center on the use of the Razor Blade tool.

RAZOR BLADE TOOL

We haven't spent too much time using the tools in the Tool palette. If you look in there, you'll see an arrow tool (the default Selection tool), some other tools we haven't discussed, an edit tool (you probably recognize the Ripple Edit and Roll Edit icons wherever you see them), and then there's a razor blade. Remember how all editing was done for years with little more than a razor blade? Here it is.

 When you click the *Razor Blade* tool, your pointer becomes a razor blade, and anyplace in the Timeline you click, you cut the sequence right there. Cutting doesn't affect your ability to move through a clip. You can cut it up into lots of bits, but you won't notice any change when you play through the chopped-up region. Cutting, however, creates bits that you can easily move or delete.

LIFT (A NON-RIPPLE DELETE)

Let's say you dislike the way this whole scene begins. It looks as if Chris is watching TV or something before Kirsten enters the frame. You could trim the head of his shot, but you could also just play the sequence until you see where you think it should start.

Notice as you move the Razor Blade tool into the Timeline that it's popping (like a magnet jumping to an iron bar) from transition to transition. When you get near the playhead, it pops there, and small triangular icons appear. Great. This is called *snapping*, and it gets you right to the spot where you want to cut this shot.

> *Snapping makes your pointer pop from key spot to key spot—edits, the playhead, other marks—in the Timeline. A number of Final Cut Express's tools, including the Razor Blade, have this important snapping feature. Make a point to experiment with snapping as you grow more comfortable with the basic editing features. Snapping is on by default; to turn it off (or back on), click the Snapping control, nestled in the frame of the Timeline window.*

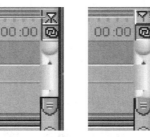

For ease with using the Razor Blade tool, keep snapping on. This allows you to watch video in the Canvas, and wherever you stop (the place where the playhead parks), it will be easy to snap the Razor Blade to that spot to make a cut.

Click the spot where the Razor Blade snapped, which is where you want the shot to start. Looking at the Timeline, you'll see that the Razor Blade cut the first shot in two. We like the second part, but not the first. The slowest but simplest way to get rid of the first part is to use the Selection tool to select this clip, and press Delete.

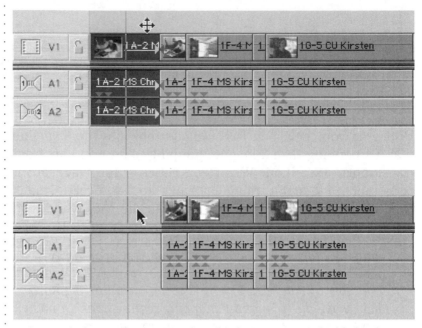

Before and after. In the top Timeline the first segment is highlighted. When you press Delete, the shot disappears, but the space is still there, as you see in the bottom Timeline.

Final Cut Express doesn't call this *deleting*, however; it calls this *lifting*.

All you need to know is that Lift (technically, "lift editing") is another way of describing a non-rippling delete. You removed something from the Timeline, but instead of everything sliding down into place, filling the gap created, Lift just leaves things where they were. This is good to know, but it's less important for you now than deleting and rippling the shots down to fill the gap.

So undo that Lift, and let's get to it.

Editing vs. Culling

Even if you don't have time to edit your personal video projects, a number of editing tools can be very handy to make your material more accessible. With only the Razor Blade tool and ripple delete, you can roll through your raw video footage and delete the really bad, unwatchable parts. Dropping weird camera moves, lens cap footage, shots of your feet as you walk, and moments when you didn't realize the camera was recording—all this cutting will make your videos more watchable, but it's not the same as editing. It's called *culling*. Culling is easy and fast, and even if you never want to (or get to) spend too much time in post-production, just culling your videos will make them much, much better.

1. Drop a long clip into the Timeline.
2. Use the Razor Blade tool to chop up the clip into good parts and bad parts.
3. Using ripple delete, remove the bad parts.

Unlike culling, editing is less about deleting bad parts than about building something interesting from the material you shot. Editing throws out bad video, but it also throws out good video— too much good material is still too much. In the editing process, you have to be a little detached from the production and use only the material you *need* to use.

But there are, of course, hybrids of these activities. Often you *want* to edit your video, but after culling it there simply isn't enough coverage to make a cohesive story. When your material is more like a series of disconnected moving snapshots, you don't have too many options. In this (common) case, it's enough to cull the video and use a few editing tricks to make the bits flow together, without worrying about story structure.

RIPPLE DELETE

Ripple delete is a powerful function. It can be faster than the trim mode, but more important, it can be the more efficient way to tighten shots as you work.

The only difference between performing a Lift and a Ripple delete is the Shift key—instead of just pressing Delete, press Shift-delete to ripple. This is not the only way to Ripple delete, but it's how we'll do it here.

1. Select the first part of the shot (the part we don't like).
2. Hold down the Shift key and press Delete.

   The shot disappears and the other shots slide down neatly.

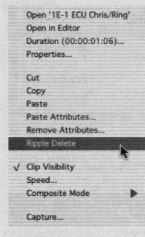

Before and after. In the left Timeline the first segment is highlighted, again. When you press Shift-Delete, the shot disappears and all the following shots slide down to fill the gap, as you see in the right Timeline.

Still comfortable? It may be dawning on you that the handful of functions you now know are both fundamental and enormously powerful. If you're flummoxed by any of these basic concepts, this is the time to go back and work through the tutorial more slowly, making sure you're OK with the language and concepts. We're in no rush.

Contextual Menus

Open '1E-1 ECU Chris/Ring'
Open in Editor
Duration (00:00:01:06)...
Properties...

Cut
Copy
Paste
Paste Attributes...
Remove Attributes...
Ripple Delete

√ Clip Visibility
Speed...
Composite Mode ▶

Capture...

As in most every Mac program, you can access contextual menus by holding down the Control key as you click an item or region of the interface. When you hold down the Control key, you'll see the pointer change into the Contextual Menu icon, which signals that something interesting may happen if you click (you'd have to be in a hot zone for a menu to pop up).

If you're feeling comfortable with the other features we've covered, these menus may quickly raise you up a notch in speed and efficiency. For the most part, I don't use them, but one tends to come in pretty handy:

- Control-click a clip in the Timeline for quick access to Cut, Copy, and—my favorite—Ripple Delete, among other things.

There are many contextual menus sprinkled around the Final Cut Express interface. Just start small and add them slowly, as you need them. Then when you're ready, spend an afternoon exploring and test them for yourself.

Creating Multiple Versions

Before we leave this chapter, I want to show you one more thing.

One of the great things about computerized editing is that, as with word processing, you can rough stuff together and then try risky approaches without undoing all the work you've completed. Yes, it's true that Final Cut Express has 32 levels of undo, which come in pretty handy (Final Cut Pro has 99!). But it's better to get your work to a place where you're satisfied, then make a copy of it, and keep going from there. If you don't like what you do, it is easy to go back to your sequence before the experiment. I make multiple versions all the time and keep them around throughout my work in a project.

Sometimes I start simply by culling my source material down to the parts I like (this would be Sequence 1), then I start editing from there (Sequence 2). I might have a couple of versions of that work (Sequence 3) but finish up the edit and keep it before I start adding fancy elements: effects, titles, music, that sort of thing. I just keep duplicating my latest sequence and start fresh in the new sequence. It's important, however, to keep the names of these versions similar—only differing by the version number ("v1" or v2"). That way they sort together, near each other, and there's little risk of not recognizing the latest version and working in the wrong sequence.

So let's create a new version. All the work we have been doing so far has been in Sequence 1.

Go back to the Browser and locate this sequence.

1. In the Browser, click the name of the sequence once to highlight it.
2. Click the highlighted name once more, and it changes color.

Name	Duration	In	Out
1A-2 MS Chris	00:00:08;12	01:00:20;28	01:00:29;09
1B-1 CU Chris	00:01:12;16	Not Set	Not Set
1C-1 ECU Chris	00:02:15;11	Not Set	Not Set
1D-1 WS Chris	00:01:23;16	Not Set	Not Set
1E-1 ECU Chris/Ring	00:00:25;22	Not Set	Not Set
1F-4 MS Kirsten	00:00:03;20	01:00:08;20	01:00:12;09
1G-2 CU Kirsten	00:00:02;29	01:00:30;14	01:00:33;12
1G-5 CU Kirsten	00:00:12;02	01:00:12;05	01:00:24;06
1J-series CU BAG	00:00:54;10	Not Set	Not Set
1K-series CU Chocolate	00:01:25;27	Not Set	Not Set
Dailies Reel	00:11:06;12	Not Set	Not Set
Sequence 1	00:01:04;01	Not Set	Not Set

As with any filename on a Mac, just click the name of a clip in the Browser and you can change it.

3. Type a new name for Sequence 1—I suggest My Cut v1.

Regardless of what you may think of My Cut v1, it's good organization and a safe working habit to make copies of your work periodically. Not just backups of data, but new sequences that let you keep old versions around in case you need them.

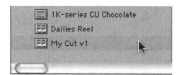

To make a copy of your sequence,

1. Highlight it in the Browser.

2. Select Edit > Duplicate.

This places a copy in your Browser, conveniently named My Cut v1 Copy.

Edit		
Undo	⌘Z	
Redo	⌘Y	
Cut	⌘X	
Copy	⌘C	
Paste	⌘V	
Paste Insert	⇧V	
Paste Attributes...	⌥V	
Remove Attributes...	⌥⌘V	
Clear	⌫	
Duplicate	⌥D	
Select All	⌘A	
Deselect All	⌘D	
Find...	⌘F	
Find Next	⌘G	
Item Properties...	⌘9	
Project Properties...		

> 1K-series CU Chocolate
> Dailies Reel
> My Cut v1
> My Cut v2

I create copies of sequences all the time, although it's important to be methodical in your naming. Creating duplicate sequences can be more convenient than backing up a project, and it's practical—it's easy to move parts of one old sequence into a newer one—like copying blocks of text in word-processing software.

3. Change the name of one of these to something else, I respectfully suggest My Cut v2.

You now have two identical sequences with different names. Going forward we will work on v2. Double-click My Cut v2 in the Browser (notice that it opens in the Timeline and Canvas, and also notice the new tabs in the Canvas and Timeline.)

Review of Final Cut Express Editing Tools

The cutting you have been doing in this chapter has been in both picture and sound together. These are known as *straight cuts,* because they all line up neatly in the Timeline across all tracks as you move through a sequence.

Although straight cuts are simple to do, they're still important. The first time I move through video material making edits, I do so with straight cuts (knowing I will be augmenting them later). I make my edits where there are pauses in dialogue. This way, I control the breaths between those lines, which goes very far toward setting the tone and emotion of a scene. (I almost never cut between words.)

This first pass is about building the timing and rhythm of the dialogue, and paying less attention to the picture. It's not that you won't change the timings later, but it's always easier to make changes to a scene with straight cuts than to a scene complicated with lots of split tracks.

It is through control and use of this timing that good editors start to rise above the pack. By making the moments between lines of dialogue short and fast, an editor can make a scene frantic or hostile, or perhaps give the impression that characters are flirting; long pauses often make characters seem more pensive, serious, and emotional. Lots of things are going on in a movie when words are not being spoken.

The tools we've used in this chapter are sufficient to do many important tasks. With rippling and non-rippling added to the basic editing functions of inserting, trimming, and deleting, you can see the breadth of editing you can accomplish.

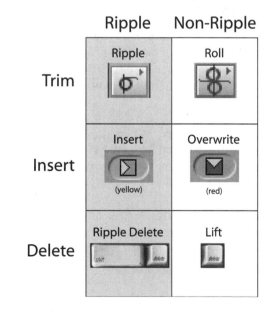

Now is a good time to practice the skills you've just learned. Delete shots you don't like, go through the source material and cut together better performances of each line of the script, and see if you can cut the entire scene using insert, trim, and delete functions.

No doubt there will be things you want to do that you won't be able to accomplish with the tools we've discussed. Don't do them. Just get a feeling for what you *can* do with these features and without messing with audio tracks. Also, make sure you limit yourself to using straight cuts before you attempt the significantly more complex variations in the next chapter.

When you're done cutting the scene, compare your edits with mine. My edit is in a different project in the tutorial folder, labeled Rubin Cuts. You can open this project without closing yours (File > Open), and use the project tabs in the Browser to move among them. Rubin Cuts contains a handful of sequences. Ignore most of them, but open my straight-cut version of this scene, called Rubin Cut 1; I'll eventually be using it as a starting place as we get to work in the next chapter.

Less Basic Editing

3

All of the edits we did in the last chapter were *straight cuts*—that is, cuts with picture and sound held inextricably in each other's arms. But what you will come to see is that one of the ways you hide edits in picture (and that is partly what editing is about) is by *burying* them in sound. Until you can split picture away from sound ("split the tracks") and manipulate each—separately as well as together—you will always be handicapped in your ability to edit.

I had trouble cutting the Kirsten-and-Chris scene using only straight cuts. Often I wanted the picture but not the sound, or I wanted to use Kirsten's off-camera line but to see Chris's face. Don't kid yourself, as much as this chapter is slightly more advanced than the last, being able to split tracks can make the process of editing easier.

There are dangers with splitting tracks, though. Principal among these is *going out of sync.* When picture and sound tracks slip apart from each other—by even a single frame—managing them gets difficult, even if the sync problem isn't obvious. When they go more than five frames out of sync, it becomes more and more visually irritating; in rare situations an audience has been known to lynch the projectionist.

Much of what you'll do in this chapter is about splitting tracks, but in a way that keeps picture and sound from ever moving out of sync in the first place. We'll build on the basics from Chapter 2, but by adding this dimension of manipulating tracks separately, everything gets a little less basic and a lot more interesting.

Track Controls

Here's your Timeline at this point in the edit:

Well, actually, this is my Timeline. This is Rubin Cut 1 (and should be pretty much like your "My Cut v2"), which I created at the end of the last chapter. Ignore the material; focus on the tracks and all the boxes and graphics on the left edge of the Timeline.

The Timeline comprises three tracks running together, locked in sync: one of picture and two of sound (the left and right channels of stereo audio). They may seem like one immutable whole, but they are three tracks. We're going to start to treat them as such. (Actually, we'll still manage the two sound tracks together more like one. But that's a minor detail.)

Perhaps the single most important ability you get in the Timeline is control over what tracks you watch and edit. The track controls are on the left side of the Timeline.

The columns in the track controls determine the track's state—any one of three. In order of importance to us right now, they are

- Can be edited (locked or unlocked)
- Can be seen (green light on or off)
- Targeted for editing (yellow highlight on or off)

In each of the following examples, I have modified the A1 track alone, so you can differentiate it from the other two.

Can be edited: the Lock Track control simply lets you lock down a track so that you can see (or hear) its contents but can't change it in any way. Until you've had more practice, this is the only track control I advise messing with.

Can be seen: the Track Visibility control, when green, means you are previewing the contents of that track in the Canvas. Turn it off and you won't hear the sound in a track, or the picture goes black. Until you are more advanced with lots of tracks, ignore this control.

		V1		1A-2 MS Chris		1	1G-5 CU Kirsten	1A-2 MS Chris	
		A1		1A-2 MS Chris	1F-4	1	1G-5 CU Kirsten	1A-2 MS Chris	
		A2		1A-2 MS Chris	1F-4	1	1G-5 CU Kirsten	1A-2 MS Chris	

Targeted for editing: This track has been selected as the target for placement of new material, such as an insert. When you're working with source material in just three tracks, as we are, you don't need to pay attention to the Target Track controls. That's because source material is at most one picture and two sound tracks, and the Final Cut Express default is to put these tracks in a logical place: Picture goes in the picture track, and so on. With advanced editing (which we'll do in Chapter 4), though, you have multiple picture and sound tracks, and it becomes important to specify the target track for a particular bit of source material. But not now.

The frame of the Timeline window has an array of embedded buttons and tools. They're interesting, and some are important, but none compare in importance to the track controls—which are, not coincidentally, larger.

Tracks in Final Cut Express are virtually the same as layers in any graphics application. The features I just described of the track controls are also pretty much standard in graphics applications and may be familiar. Though they sometimes have different names, in general you always have at least the same three options for any layer.

Here are some layer controls in Adobe Photoshop. Incidentally, when you import a Photoshop image with multiple layers into Final Cut, it will put each layer into its own track. See, kinda the same thing.

And here they are in Macromedia FreeHand. I'm sort of joking around by naming my layers "picture" and "sound."

Notice that the green light in Final Cut Express is akin to the eyeballs (signaling whether or not you see the layer); and Final Cut Express's locks translate into locks or chains (signaling whether you can modify the layer). But they all give the same types of options.

Locking vs. Linking

When you select a shot, you may notice that Final Cut Express is smart enough to select the *whole* shot—picture and sound tracks together. It does this because the separate tracks are *linked*. Because they are linked, you can't select just one track, you can't change just one track—which is great because much of the time, this is exactly what you want. It would be laborious if every time you wanted to delete a frame or trim a second, you had to do it three times, once in each track.

Tracks in Final Cut Pro 4

Wouldn't you know it, when Apple released Final Cut Pro 4, it introduced a streamlined design (and a tiny bit more functionality) for the track controls—which of course makes them slightly different from Final Cut Express's track controls.

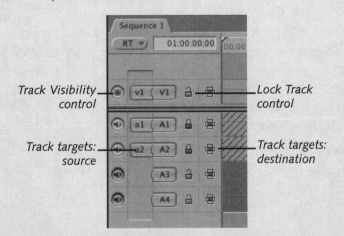

Track Visibility control — Lock Track control

Track targets: source — Track targets: destination

All the features we've gone over in Final Cut Express are present in Final Cut Pro 4, but the most significant functional difference is the way track targeting is done—it's a lot more intuitive in this new format, and with any luck, it will find its way into future versions of Final Cut Express.

These two Timelines are identical except for the linking selection. In the top Timeline, because the tracks are linked, selecting a shot selects all three tracks together. In the bottom Timeline, with the linking toggle off, clicking the Timeline selects only the track of the shot you clicked on. This would be bad in Chapter 2, but it's great in Chapter 3.

If you really do want to perform an action on only one track, you must be able to select it individually, without selecting the others. Now, there are tools that allow you to *permanently* unlink a picture track from its sound, but what you want here is something more temporary—to make Final Cut Express behave as if the clip were unlinked, but without losing that important link relationship. To select one track of a clip and not others, you need to change the link selection mode.

The button for changing this linking/unlinking mode (a toggle button called the *Linking control)* is very small, and it's nestled in the frame of the Timeline window just below the *Snapping control:*

The Linking control is a teeny button, hard to even notice, but extraordinarily important. What you're looking at are two rings, either interlocking or broken open.

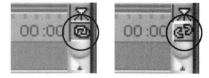

On the other hand, when you want to change only one track, it often makes more sense to *lock* the other tracks and *not* change the link mode. To change only picture, for instance, you just go over to the track controls and lock all the sound tracks. When you're done working on the picture, you turn them back on. Very easy.

I'm locking my soundtracks to keep them from being modified as I make changes—I'm over there in the track controls locking them right now.

In our work it doesn't really matter which you choose—unlinking or locking. I will use the track lock method in this chapter both because I prefer it and because it's easier in this book's Timeline illustrations to see when I have a track locked (as opposed to having changed the linked selection mode).

The Overlap

People unconsciously expect edits to happen in places where one person stops talking and another starts. And by placing edits in these pauses, you make your edits that much more obvious to the viewer. Remember that one component of editing is hiding edits—not letting the audience realize they are watching something with cuts. Now, you might want jarring and you might not. But if you don't, you'll often want to move the picture cut *away* from the sound cut.

In other words: You want to see people *not* talking for a little bit before or after they speak.

You do this by sliding the cut point between two pictures, while leaving the sound cut where it is: Slide it ahead of the sound cut, and you've created an L-cut (also called a *prelap*); slide it after the sound cut, and you've created a J-cut (*postlap*). The name (L or J, prelap or postlap) doesn't matter much. In either case, this kind of edit is called a *split edit* or *overlap*, and you do it with a non-rippling trim (a Roll edit) of the picture track alone.

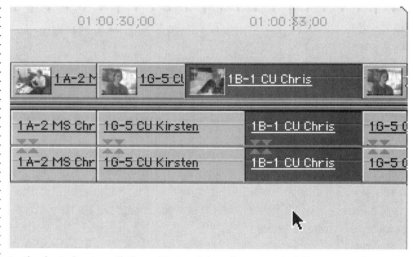

In the last chapter all the edits in picture happened at the same place as the edits in sound, making for vertical lines between shots. Here the picture has been trimmed to start before the sound in the highlighted shot. See how the outgoing shot (the one before the highlighted shot) takes on roughly the shape of an L.

There are many reasons to create overlaps. In the first place, they make a video more sophisticated. They make edit transitions subtler and give the editor an opportunity to sculpt a video that presents aesthetic nuances in greater detail.

It's said that in movies, it is often more important to see the person being spoken *to* than the person speaking; that you can determine more about a person's character watching him react to something than watching him move his lips. Overlaps not only are a good way to hide edits and soften transitions, but also let viewers see more character revealed.

3: LESS BASIC EDITING

There's a small downside to overlaps: They make re-editing a little more complicated. They take time, and time is one thing every editor must be careful not to squander. But in the end, overlaps are important tools for all but the least experienced of beginners, and becoming good at them is a worthy skill.

Roll Edit (Non-Rippling Trim) in Picture Only

Let's make a few overlaps in your sequence. There are many ways to directly execute a non-rippling trim, but let's do it in the most conservative way as a means of explanation.

Before you begin, open the Rubin Cuts project (you don't have to close the Chocoluv Tutorial to do this, and I suggest you don't). Inside you'll find a few sequences. Highlight Rubin Cut 1 and make a copy (Edit > Duplicate). Call it something different from My Cut, such as Ch3 Edit v1. You can work on this sequence even while accessing the raw material of Chocoluv Tutorial in the Browser.

Now, lock both sound tracks in the Timeline by clicking the Lock Track controls for A1 and A2. This prevents the audio from changing in any way when you do your adjustments.

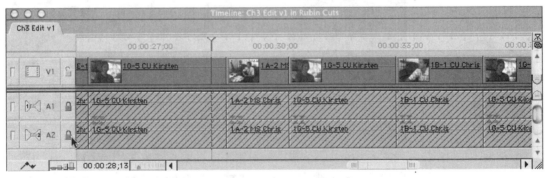

Before you do any trimming, make sure you've set yourself up for success: Check on those Lock Track controls to guarantee that you're about to modify only the picture track.

1. Double-click a transition you want to adjust.

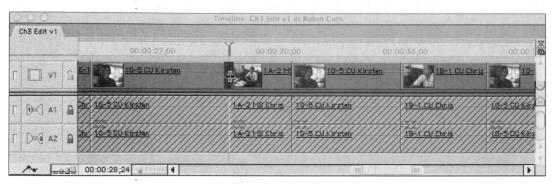

I'm demonstrating with a shot that comes between where Kirsten says, "I'll ask you again. Do you love me?" (1G-5) and Chris replies hesitantly, "Yeah" (1A-2). It's about 27 seconds into the sequence.

The only difference between the trim you're about to do and the one you did in the last chapter is that here it's critical you don't change the overall duration of the picture track while the sound is locked. Roll edit trims prevent such a change. Ripple trims (like those in Chapter 2) do not. *Look for those green bars on both sides.* Look for the Roll edit icon.

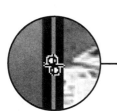

For a Roll edit, make sure the green bar appears over both sides of the Trim Edit window. The Roll edit icon is tiny and in between the outgoing and incoming shots.

2. Play either side of the cut; you'll see that you can select and shuttle each side independently.

3. Go to the shot of Kirsten on the A-side (the left side of the Trim Edit window), and adjust the Out point to start a second or so earlier. When you mark a new Out point,

the other shot moves automatically to correspond to the change in the shot you played. Notice that the Timeline representations also shift but still remain in sync.

Your first overlap! Because you're using a ripple trim (in the form of the Roll edit), no shots are affected but the two you're working on. A change of –27 frames (almost a second) to one, automatically changes the other to compensate.

Now let's see what Chris is doing on the B-side.

It looks as if he's listening to her speak. He seems serious. Good. The overlap works, and I think it improves this moment. This is a fine time to use the Play Around Edit button.

After you make the rolling trim, clip 1G-5 is L-shaped. It fits perfectly with clip 1A-2. And all the shots after this still have their straight cuts. This is a successful ripple trim execution.

A Rolling Shortcut

There's another way to execute a Roll edit; as we go over it, you can adjust the one you just made. This method doesn't use the Trim Edit window (and consequently can be a little fly-by-night), but I want to show it mostly so you can better visualize the rolling process.

To start out, play the part of the scene you've been working on, where Kirsten says, "I'll ask you again, do you love me?" and Chris says (more hesitantly), "Yeah." Stop the playhead in the middle of the B-side (the shot of Chris), after the overlap has occurred.

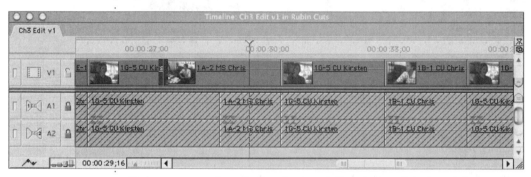

Make sure you stop playing (and park the playhead) just past the overlap.

Rather than double-clicking the edit to bring up the Trim Edit window (as before), go to the Tool palette and get the Roll Edit tool.

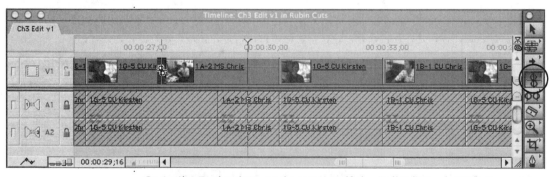

Go to the Tool palette and get yourself the Roll Edit tool. With it you can perform trims directly in the Timeline.

Now click and hold on the transition, and a different sort of trim window appears.

Yet another trim display for your convenience: the two-up display. See those familiar Mark In and Mark Out icons in the window? It all should be a comfortable presentation even though it's new to you.

This is the Canvas version of a trim window (called the *two-up display*). It's not as full-featured as the Trim Edit window, but it will show the net effect of the trim you're working on. Whenever you use the Roll edit tool, you execute the trim in the Timeline. You are likely to use the playhead to help identify the cut point—the spot you are trimming "to."

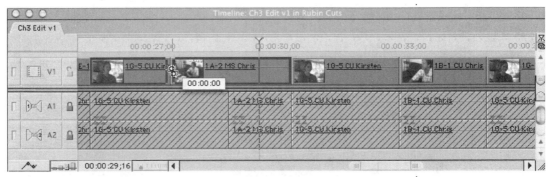

When you click and hold on a transition with the Roll edit tool, a black outline box appears around the pair of clips being affected, the Canvas window changes, and this tool tip pops up at the edit in question to tell you how far you've rolled this edit point.

While you continue to hold the mouse button down, you can drag the edit point back and forth (either with or without snapping). Notice that in the Timeline you can see the graphical representation of your moving the picture cut point back and forth to any location you like. This really drives home the "rolling" nature of the Roll edit. As you move left and right from the place where you started, a small box, called a *tooltip*, appears to show you the number of frames by which you've moved the cut point (plus to the right, minus to the left).

Watch out: You can roll a shot clear out of the Timeline. I like to choose one shot or the other and make that my main focus as I try an overlap. In this case, I know I want to choose the Out point based on Kirsten's line. I want her talking. I want her eyes open. And I don't want her shot made too short. When I mark a new Out after the first part of her line "I'll ask you again..." (-1:22), I feel I've addressed those initial concerns.

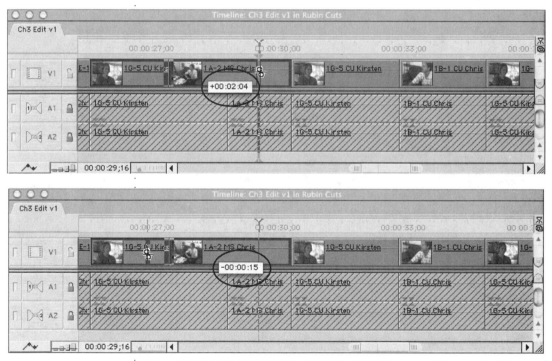

The edit is highlighted with a dark line (thick, representing a selection of both the Out and In point at the edit). The top image is rolled to the right; the bottom Timeline is rolled to the left. Keep an eye on the tooltip. It tells you the number of frames and the direction.

You may also notice as you drag left and right that the edit point you are holding in your hands (click-hold-drag) is snapping between points: from the location of the original sound transition to the playhead, and so on. Because snapping is *on*, you can precisely roll to likely spots for the trim, or even return an overlap to a straight cut. If you want to roll to a position other than a marked (and snapping-friendly) spot, you may need to turn snapping *off* to execute the trim. We'll leave it on for now because snapping is a powerful force in the Macintosh editing world.

> *Final Cut Express has another way to perform this Roll edit quickly. It's called Extend edit. The name doesn't really merit memorizing as long as you understand what it does. I'm going to break from tradition and show you a keyboard shortcut. Select a cut. Stop playing the sequence at the spot where you want the edit to occur, and press E on the keyboard. Cool.*

Here's a review of the rolling shortcut method:

1. Shuttle around in the sequence to the precise spot where you want the transition to occur.

2. Get the Roll edit tool from the Tool palette.

3. Click and drag the edit point toward the playhead. It snaps to your parked location. Release the button, and presto—the edit point has rolled to this spot.

Roll edits are great. More than 90 percent of all my non-rippling trims are picture-only. As you'll come to see, you will almost never perform them in sound alone.

The Insert

In general, any time you add a clip to a sequence in Final Cut Express, you're *inserting* it. We did a fair number of inserts back in the last chapter. Inserts, like trims, can benefit from a non-rippling variation. A non-rippling insert is perhaps the crux of sophisticated-looking editing. In Final Cut Express, the non-rippling insert is called an *Overwrite edit*. The graphical elements representing the Overwrite edit are colored red because Final Cut Express knows there's a reasonable risk that you'll write over something you didn't intend to write over. But I don't consider them dangerous.

There are many reasons to execute an Overwrite in just video or just audio. In picture alone, you can use an Overwrite to insert a reaction shot of someone listening over a shot of someone speaking. In sound alone, it can be used to cover over a bit of audio you don't like (like an airplane flying overhead or the director speaking off-camera). When you're really skilled, audio-only inserts can be used to replace single words or parts of words marred by a bad performance.

Three- and Four-Point Editing

Ah, but first what may feel like a digression to help you prepare for Overwrite edits. Early in their education, students of editing face the often-confusing concept of three- and four-point editing. It's a little like explaining how to tie your shoes. It's hard to say in words, but it's fairly obvious once someone shows you. Hang on.

All shots in a sequence can be described using two key pieces of information: what portion of a source clip is being used, and precisely where it is placed in the sequence. It takes two specific pieces of data to describe each of those pieces of information: an In point and an Out point. Thus, every edit can be written down as four data points:

Source: In   Source: Out
(the beginning and end of the shot)

Master: In   Master: Out
(the shot's location in the Timeline)

To make any edit, you must know at least three of these four pieces of information. Another way of saying this is that if you have three of the above data points, you can always figure out the fourth.

These are the "points" referred to in the expression "three- and four-point editing."

Why haven't we talked about this before? We're in Chapter 3 and we've done a fair amount of editing without much "point" discussion. Because modern editing systems like Final Cut Express tend to hide all this point stuff except when you really need it. Hopefully, you recall that we marked an In and Out in the source material prior to inserting (or that Final Cut Express always sees at least two points in the clip, whether or not you place them). These are two of the points in three- and four-point editing. Final Cut Express always knows the first two points. You can move them, but they're always there.

But what about the third point? I did say you must have three to edit. The third point is always *where the playhead is parked*. When you make an insert, the playhead denotes the third point unless otherwise specified. That's why we've been able to edit making only two marks in the Viewer.

But there comes a time when those three points aren't the three you want to use.

Overwrite (Non-Rippling Insert) in Picture Only

Let's say someone is talking in a shot that has been cut into your sequence. It's a fairly long, boring shot of the person ranting on and on, and you want to show someone else (known in the biz as a *cutaway* or *reaction shot*). You want to specify a place in the sequence where the cutaway will begin and note where it should end. You do these by using the Mark In and Mark Out buttons—but in the *Canvas* (or Timeline), not in the Viewer.

Let's try it.

Assuming you've been following along, you're still looking at your copy of Rubin's Cut 1 in the Timeline and Canvas. If it's not up now, open it.

1. Play into the long rant by Kirsten. She is saying, "I found these next to the bed," and she's holding out something we can't see. (Around 18 seconds into the sequence.)

2. Lock the sound tracks, if they're not already locked.

   I want to see the bag Kirsten is holding, but I don't want to interrupt her speech.

   In truth, you could do this at any point before you actually execute the insert, but it's good to do it as soon as you think of it.

3. Play the sequence and mark an In and Out to show where you want a shot to go in Kirsten's rant.

During Kirsten's lecture, without interrupting her lines or natural pauses, I marked a spot (with an In and Out) where I want to drop a new bit of picture. The duration window in the Canvas indicates that this space is 02;03 seconds (while the reference is nice to have, I do hardly anything based on these precise numbers!).

Notice the In and Out marks in the ruler of the Timeline. This is the range where I want to place a shot. I already have a pretty good idea of what shot goes here; now, to find it.

4. Go to the Browser (of the Chocoluv Tutorial) and find the bag shot called 1J series CU Chocolate. Double-click it and watch it in the Viewer. There's lots of interesting material here. What you're looking for is an area of good material.

5. When you find it, stop on the first frame of that area and mark an In. I like this one:

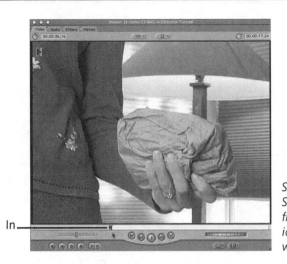

See the single In mark in the scrubber. Since we're looking at the head frame, you'll also see the Mark In icon in the top-left corner of the window.

I thought I'd want a shot of her shaking the bag or doing something else active, but it ended up being too much, and a segment of her just holding it relatively still was better.

If you pause and look around at the Viewer and the Canvas, you'll see three points: one on the source side and two on the sequence side. This is all that is required to make an edit.

6. Now you're going to do an Overwrite edit (a "non-rippling insert") in picture only. Drag the new shot in the Viewer onto the Canvas and drop it onto the red Overwrite box.

If you ever forget the difference between Insert and Overwrite, look at the graphic for a reminder. The Overwrite graphic tells you, "this drops on top of the sequence," as opposed to the Insert graphic, which says, "this goes into the sequence and pushes everything else down to happen later."

After you drop the shot into the Canvas, the Timeline reflects the cutaway.

The playhead ends up at the end of the overwrite when you're done, but I moved it so you could see the cutaway in picture only, clearly at a spot with no sound edits.

Three-point edits do not always have to be structured with an In on the source and an In and Out on the master. There are four permutations of the three-point edit:

- You know where the insert needs to be placed (master In and Out), and you know where the source material must start (source In); this is what we just did.

- You know what the insert (reaction or cutaway) shot is going to be (source In and Out), and you know where it must start in the sequence (master In).

- You know what the insert shot is going to be (source In and Out), and you know where it must end in the sequence (master Out); this is sometimes called *backtiming*.

- You know where the insert needs to be placed (master In and Out), and you know where the source material must end (source Out); this is another variation on backtiming.

Experiment with cutaways in the picture track for a while before moving on. You want to be comfortable with these functions before we do them in sound, where they are harder to visualize.

Overwrite in Picture in the Real World

If I could do only one thing really easily with an editing tool, it would be this. A simple concept with famous potential. So many kinds of projects demand this function—for instance:

Music videos. A music performance is both picture and sound. You can't, however, make edits in the sound track, but you want to see more than just a person playing a song. Picture-only cutaways are great to show people watching, details of the instrument, wide establishing shots, all without their own sound but without affecting the existing performance sound.

The first shot of musician Thomas Dolby Robertson is the performance with synchronous sound. The second is a cutaway that can be used to create some visual interest. It looks as if these were shot simultaneously with different cameras (and it's great if they were), but in truth the cutaway shots that I want to insert in picture are often "stolen" from other songs or even other perform-ances and do not sync to the music, so they need to be placed carefully and not be too long.

Interviews. Like a music video, an interview may have long stretches of someone talking on camera that need some spicing up with cutaways. Typical interview cutaways include shots of the interviewer (sometimes faked) or close-ups of the subject's hands or feet, or maybe items in the room that add to the content.

On the left, the interview shot; on the right, a wide shot (faked) to cut away and show some context. It's amazing how faked cutaway shots seem natural when the audio isn't interrupted!

Training videos: If you want to teach someone how to do something, you just need to shoot someone doing it. But this could result in one long, boring lecture and wide shot. Instead, insert some details of the items being discussed or wide shots of people listening. Tedious (but impor-tant) content needn't result in a tedious video—if you use picture-only overwrites to keep the images moving. More on these in Chapter 6.

Overwrite (Non-Rippling Insert) in Sound Only

In picture, Overwrite edits are easy; you can see what you are doing. In sound they are less obvious but still easy.

Let's replace sound in one of the shots, and do it with a sound-only overwrite, using your knowledge of three-point edits.

In the third shot of Ch3 Edit v1 (aka Rubin's Cut 1), you can hear me talking to Chris. I like his expression, but it's too bad I'm talking. In many cases you'd reject using this shot because the sound is wrong. But that would be a shame.

1. Before you forget, lock the picture track (V1) and unlock the sound (A1 and A2).

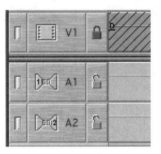

While we could replace the *entire* audio from 1C-1 ECU Chris (from the head to the tail of the shot), let's practice by just replacing the worst part.

2. Play through Chris's shot 1C-1 ECU Chris and stop before you hear the director (me) talking. Mark an In point.

Where does the bad audio start? Start by marking an In.

3. Play until the bad sound ends, and mark an Out.

With both In and Out marks in the Timeline, the bad audio region is defined.

Now that you have determined what material to remove, let's try a couple of different options for what to put in its place.

AMBIENCE

One way to fill that space is to use *ambience*—a production sound recorded during your shoot, when no one is talking or making any sounds. The ambient sound of the room, is also called *room tone*. Where do you find ambience to use? With experience you would know to record it while you were shooting your scene. If you hadn't learned that (or forgot to do it), the next best trick is to find a pause in a recorded take and hope it's long enough to fill the space you need. Since we need only a second or two, I'll bet we can find what we need.

If you give up, I found a bit here in 1C-1 ECU Chris:

For the best sound match, always start hunting for ambience in the take you are in. Look near the slate or at the end of the take. For personal projects, I often find good ambience in the worst shots—in places where I left the camera on by accident, for instance, or in long, boring shots I don't intend to use for anything. Remember, those long shots where nothing is happening are ripe with regions of silence. Use them!

1. In 1C-1 ECU Chris (or wherever you found some ambience), mark an In. I'm just estimating that I have enough pure ambience, without someone talking, starting from this point. We'll find out soon enough.

2. Now perform an Overwrite in the Canvas. The shot drops into the space you created with the marks and affects only the sound tracks. It should look something like this:

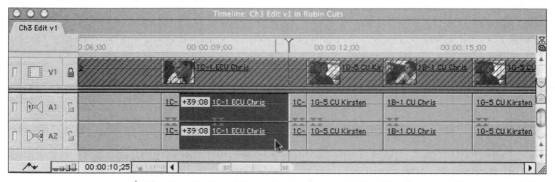

This insert of ambience looks strange in the Timeline, mostly because it is sound stolen from 1C-1—the same take we used in picture. Consequently, Final Cut Express is warning us that the sound is out of sync with the picture—which technically it is—39:08 seconds. Here, we did this on purpose, so we don't need to be concerned with the warning. If we had stolen the sound from another take, there would be no out of sync frame warning.

SLUG

Another way to remove material is to *slug* it; that is, to cut a bad shot out and replace it with a piece of black filler, called (of course) *slug*. In picture you see black; in sound, the filler is just silence. There are a few ways to do this, but in keeping with our experimentation in non-rippling inserts, you're first going to need to learn about a new kind of source material.

A small button at the bottom right of the Viewer brings up a pop-up menu that allows you to switch the source material from video (that you've collected in the Browser) to specialty video that Final Cut Express makes for you. Because Final Cut Express is *generating* this source material for you, it's called the Generator menu.

A modest button in the Viewer leads you to the Generator menu, which has options for adding new source material—not only text, but also color bars and an assortment of graphical elements.

1. Open the Generator menu.

As you can see, Final Cut Express can generate several kinds of specialized source material for you, including titles, color bars, solid-color backgrounds and shapes for special effects. The only one we're going to use now is Slug.

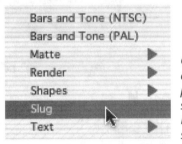

Check out your Generator options here. Text is the primary choice for anyone starting out (and we'll look at it in Chapter 4), but Slug is a solid second.

2. Select the Slug source from the Generator menu, and watch the Slug pop up in the Viewer.

There are some subtle differences between putting slug in your sequence and just having nothing there but a gap. Since it's the more conservative choice and is considered good form by most pros, we'll focus on slug.

Hmmm, not a lot to see here, but it's source material just the same.

You'll see the sprockets on the left side of the window, indicating that this is the beginning of the roll of slug. Final Cut Express gives you 2 minutes of slug here to work with. You'll need only a tiny bit.

3. Now that this source material is here, mark an In somewhere in the slug. You could just mark the first frame. I tend to click a little bit farther in (it's an old-but-good habit of not ever using the "first" frame of any shot).

While you could theoretically mark the first frame of the slug as the first frame to use, marking an In point somewhere within the clip will help you avoid unusual performance problems later on.

4. Back in the Timeline, we're starting with the ambience (from 1C-1 ECU Chris) we rolled in a few moments ago. Move to the head of this shot and mark an In point; move to the tail and mark an Out.

   In case you haven't been counting, this makes three points (one in the source, two in the sequence).

5. Drag the slug into the Canvas, and overwrite this sound.

How to Mark a Clip Existing in Your Sequence

You can mark a clip that is already cut into your Timeline using the following screen buttons:

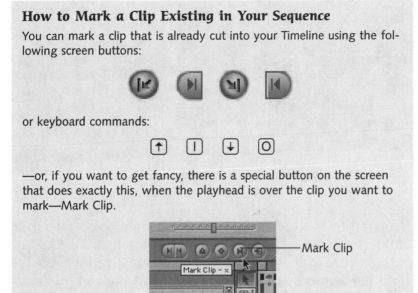

or keyboard commands:

—or, if you want to get fancy, there is a special button on the screen that does exactly this, when the playhead is over the clip you want to mark—Mark Clip.

However you get there, when you're done, your Timeline will look like this:

There are starting to be many details in the Timeline: the Mark In and Out icon is up in the ruler, and the clip we are marking is down in the audio tracks. Make sure this looks right before executing the insert.

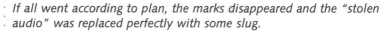

If all went according to plan, the marks disappeared and the "stolen audio" was replaced perfectly with some slug.

Using a slug is a fallback position when you don't have good ambience or don't have the time to go looking for it. But you will notice that the sound of silence is actually quite different from the ambience in the production, and the abrupt change can be as jarring as a bad edit.

Undo the slug and put the ambience back in. We'll work on the sound later.

Adjusting Your One-Track Shots

Once a video-only or sound-only insert is in place, there are lots of ways to adjust it. What you're going to find, however, is that as you move into more one-track modifications, your Timeline is going to start to get complicated. What was once a collection of simple, clear straight cuts (with all the sound neatly fitting under each picture shot) becomes a patchwork of picture and sound (overlaps, inserts of picture not linking to sound, sound inserts chopping up tracks). Any editor, no matter how seasoned, would start to get slightly queasy when it came time to make changes to a Timeline that looked like this:

This sequence is still made up of just one picture track and a stereo pair of sound tracks, but it has had many adjustments in picture-only or sound-only, so the edits don't line up neatly. It's actually a little hard to tell what picture goes with which sound.

But if you work to keep things in sync as you go, and move slowly when learning about these adjustments, the gradually growing complexity of the Timeline will be manageable.

Roll Edit, Part 2 (Trimming an Insert)

Any time you want to adjust a shot in either picture or sound only, it must be a non-rippling modification. This will guarantee that you never lose sync between picture and sound tracks. You used the Roll edit to create overlaps earlier in this chapter. It is just as simple to adjust an insert using the same Roll-edit process.

Since you're so familiar with Roll edit to do trims, I won't demonstrate how to do them here. But I encourage you to try one. If you find Roll edits are still a challenge, this is a good time to go back and practice them until they're second nature.

Lift (Non-Ripple Delete)

We used the Delete function (with and without rippling) in the last chapter to tighten shots and to get rid of unwanted material. We can do this in picture or sound alone as well, but we'll need to mind the sync.

Let's try an adjustment with Lift (a delete that doesn't ripple). The easy way to do this is simply to select the picture-only or sound-only shot you don't like, and press Delete.

1. Make sure the picture track is locked.

2. Select the ambient-sound shot you inserted a few moments ago.

3. Now press Delete.

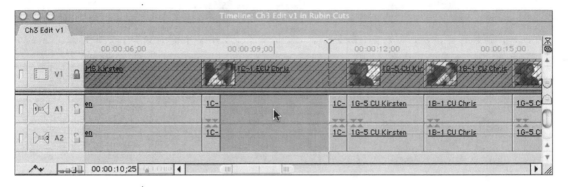

This certainly gets rid of the sound. Since you didn't ripple, the hole just sits there, and there is no sound while it plays. You'll notice that the gap you have left has many of the same properties as the slug you inserted earlier. It is considered bad form in basic editing to leave gaps in your sequence, but you can see how easy it is to remove material from your sequence and still keep the following shots in place, held in sync.

But there are some other tools for adjusting inserts as well. The inventors of computerized editing systems came up with some clever *macros* (single functions that perform what would otherwise be a series of actions together) to adjust shots in a sequence. These are no different from the basics you've been learning, but they combine a number of steps, with elegant results. Slip and Slide are simply variations on ripple trims, doing two ripple trims at the same time. And they are great for making small adjustments of cutaway shots—particularly picture-only cutaway shots.

Slide

What Apple calls the *Slide Item* tool (and I just call *Slide*) is an elegant and magical tool. Imagine that your insert shot is not glued into the Timeline but floating above it, like this:

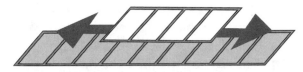

Imagine a shot floating above the Timeline—moving it doesn't create a hole and you can reposition the shot anywhere; the only change is that the material underneath it is obscured. This is the nature of Slide.

The Slide tool allows you to grab hold of the clip and move it (*slide* it) around in the Timeline to occur earlier or later in the sequence. Here's how it works in Final Cut Express.

You can find the Slide tool in the Tool palette. The icon representing Slide is a rectangular clip with simultaneous left and right Ripple edit icons on each side of the clip—which is exactly the type of edit you're doing.

1. We're going to do a Slide in the picture, so begin by locking the sound tracks and unlocking the picture.

2. In the sequence, find your insert shot of the bag in Kirsten's hand (1J-series CU Bag), and select it with the Selection tool.

   Actually, you don't need to select the shot to do the slide, but I want you to see what the shot looks like when it's selected, as compared with how it looks when you're about to Slide.

3. Go to the Tool palette and get the Slide tool. (If it's not immediately visible, it's under the Slip tool—click and hold to bring up other options for this position).

4. Once you've selected the Slide tool, use it to click this insert shot and select it.

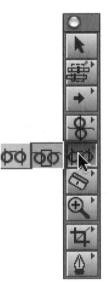

The screen shot on the left shows how the Selection tool looks if you click a shot; the screen shot on the right shows the Slide tool when you click the same shot. These little pointer changes are important.

5. Click and hold the insert shot. You'll see two now-familiar features pop up. First, the Canvas turns into the special two-up display. But rather than showing you the two frames at the edit point, as it does when you're trimming, it shows you the two frames of the tail and head *around* the insert shot. Since, presumably, you know what your insert looks like (it's a shot

of a bag), and you're not changing it, there's no need to show it to you. On the other hand, as you slide the clip around, this dual display will show you the frames to which the clip will now attach on either end.

The other familiar feature is the little tooltip, where the number of frames you've slid the shot are indicated (which I call the *shift-offset*).

6. Slide the shot to the left a little bit. According to my tooltip, I've moved –0:09; moving left is negative, so I just shifted the shot to the left nine frames, or just under a third of a second.

7. Let go and the Canvas returns to normal, and the insert shot is moved to its new location.

Technically, Slide does not change the In or Out of the insert shot, but it does move the In (and Out) of where the shot goes in the sequence. Most beginners will find the Slide function intuitive.

I exaggerated the amount of the slide here to help with visualization; the cutaway shot itself has not changed at all, but where it is dropped into the main shot (the one with sync picture and sound) has changed.

Slip

Unlike Slide, Slip takes a little more effort to understand.

This time, instead of visualizing the insert shot floating above the Timeline, imagine a hole in your sequence where the insert shot was, with the insert *underneath* the Timeline and moving around. *Slipping a shot* means moving the video you see in the hole, without changing or moving the hole itself.

It is as if you said to yourself, "This is where I want something to go, but this shot isn't exactly the bit of source material I want."

The Slip item tool is graphically depicted like Slide, except the Ripple edit icons are reversed left and right, indicating that the clip itself is being changed.

Now the clip is underneath the Timeline. You can move it around, but you can see only the part that is visible through the hole. Think of the hole as a solid window in the Timeline. Windows don't move, but sometimes things move around outside the window that may affect your view.

As with Slide, you can slip a shot by grabbing the Slip Item tool from the Tool palette and clicking and dragging a shot to the left or right. The graphical representation of the clip in the Timeline won't appear to move as you drag, but in the two-up display you'll see that the video underneath is adjusted.

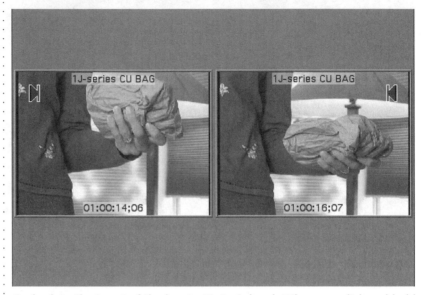

Go back to the insert of the bag in Kirsten's hand. When you click and hold this shot with the Slip Item tool, you'll see the Canvas change into the two-up display, showing you the head (left) and tail (right) of the insert.

Compare this with the earlier figures of Slide.

The counterintuitive thing about slipping is that as you drag the shot to the left, you are actually beginning the insert *later* (it feels as if moving to the left should start the insert earlier). As you drag to the right (as I did here), you'll see the shift-offset tooltip indicate that you are moving plus frames, and the shot shifts backward on the Canvas. Pause for a moment and just think about this. I'll wait here.

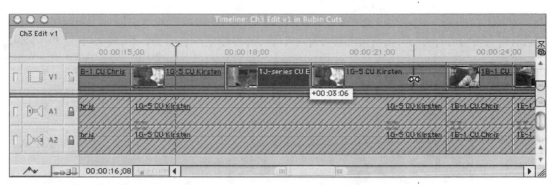

I'm dragging to the right (see the Slip tool). Don't get tricked by the position of the playhead.

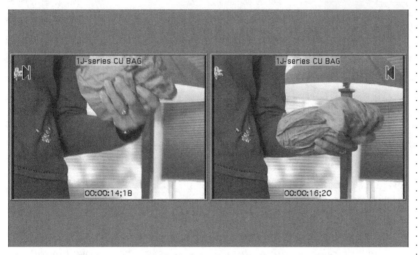

The two-up display provides helpful information; besides the images themselves, the timecodes in the lower part of the picture should help you navigate.

It's natural for Westerners to associate moving to the right with moving forward—we read left to right. But when you drag the insert to the right, you are moving the start frame of the shot earlier and earlier into the original clip. Watch the timecode numbers Final Cut Express shows you in the Canvas head and tail frames—they will always help you orient yourself as to which way you are moving the insert.

When you're done, let go. The Canvas returns to normal and the Timeline reflects the changed source material. Oddly enough, since the shot hasn't changed its Timeline location, the window will look pretty much the way it did when you started.

Before

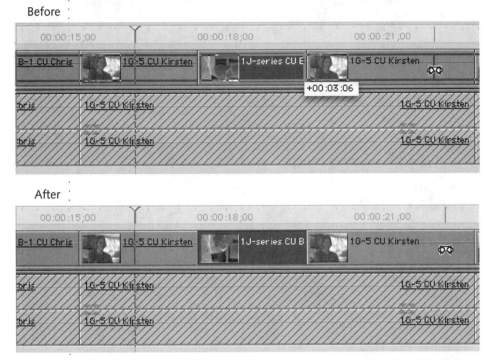

After

Unlike what happens with a slip, there's not much to see after the slide is done. Logically, of course, this is right—no shots have moved in this graphical representation. But this lack of visible change can make it tricky to know when you've done something.

Moving Shots Around

When digital editing systems were first being released just over a decade ago, they often were created by users who were frustrated with making demo tapes—a task that requires doing something quite difficult in videotape editing: moving shots around. Say you have three shots—1, 2, and 3. They are in a row, and you think, "Hey, I should put 3 right after 1." You would simply want to grab 3, drag it between 1 and 2, and let go. But as you may have seen from even these basic editing tutorials, editing isn't really much about shuffling shots around. As neat a feature as this is, when working with narrative material, you won't use it all that often.

Still, for many kinds of projects you'll want to move shots around, so it's important to understand how it works. This is technically known as *Timeline trimming.* It means that you're making edits and changes by looking at the graphical display and adjusting relationships there, as you would rearrange slides. You don't even need to watch the video itself to make these decisions.

An iMovie Moment

iMovie is particularly adept at this shot–moving thing; the clips in the Timeline can be worked with in the "eyeball" viewer that disregards shot length and focuses rather on shot order. Final Cut Express isn't nearly so simple as this, but you can still achieve these functions with it.

As you can probably guess, the essence of moving shots around involves these steps:

1. Select a shot.

2. Click and drag it to a new location.

3. Let go when it's in the right place.

These can be described more specifically in the terms we have been using in this chapter and the last: Ripple delete a shot from one place and then ripple insert it back into the sequence someplace else. Final Cut Express uses the terms *overwrite* and *swap* when you drag clips already in the Timeline around to new locations. Of course, Final Cut Express will want to know where to do the insert, and it will want to know if this is a ripple or non-ripple adjustment.

1. Go to the sequence you've been working on, and click and drag the shot of Chris fumbling with his ring. Right now, the sequence goes from Kirsten to Chris saying nothing, to a shot of Chris fumbling with his ring, and then back to Kirsten.

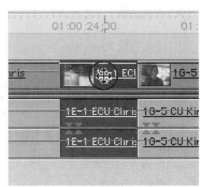

When you click a shot, the pointer changes to this generic "move it" pointer.

But if you start to drag the shot somewhere, the cursor changes to the (default) Overwrite pointer and a little window pops up to let you know how far you've moved the shot.

If you just drag the ring shot to a new location and let go, Final Cut Express will delete the shot from its original location without rippling—which will leave a gap—and insert this shot by overwriting wherever you let go. If you're trying to swap the ring shot and the shot of Chris saying nothing (going from A-B to B-A), this won't work.

2. Go ahead and play with this. As soon as you drag the clip even a few frames, notice the Overwrite pointer (the down arrow) appears, telling you that you're in Overwrite (non-rippling) mode. The down arrow is saying, in effect, "This shot is going right here, over this." The shadow of the clip you're dragging is solid and dark.

The odds are good this isn't what you wanted to happen. Maybe this simple drag and drop worked in iMovie, but not here. You've created a bit of a mess by simply dragging and dropping a shot—leaving a hole, going over a shot you liked, and still not accomplishing anything.

3. Just for the record, I've never needed to make this particular modification. Undo it. Everything should go back to normal.

Let's try this again. Grab 1E-1 and try to swap position with the shot before it, 1B-1.

4. Exactly as before, click and drag the ring shot to the edit point after Kirsten and before Chris, but don't let go. While you're dragging, hold down the Option key. The pointer changes from the Overwrite pointer into the Swap edit pointer, and the shadow of the shot you're dragging changes into an outline.

This is what you want to see when shuffling shots around. Click, Option-drag, let go.

5. Now, when you let go, the B-shot moves to the position before the A-shot, and the A-shot shoves down into the space left by the B-shot. There are no gaps, and the two shots have changed positions. In other words, the gap was ripple deleted and the B-shot was ripple inserted into its new location in one simple move.

Success! After swapping shots, 1B-1 and 1E-1 have changed places.

For the right kind of sequence, this is a fun activity—reorganizing shots like cards in a poker hand. As I said before, it doesn't come up all that often, but it does come up—particularly in non-narrative material (stuff without a script). I have one warning, and it's the reason I'd suggest avoiding swap edits: There are a number of odd occurrences you are liable to trigger when you're holding down Option while working in the Timeline. If you don't press it at just the right moment, you might get confused about what exactly happened. The Option key has many uses in Final Cut Express, and you'll probably make some mistakes while practicing Swap editing, but you'll end up learning a few handy new tricks in the process:

- To do a Swap edit easily, just remember not to press Option until you get the clip to its new location and are almost ready to let go.

- If you press Option before you click and drag the clip, you'll copy the shot you're moving. The original stays put and the copy goes to the new location.

- When you drop a clip in its new location (regardless of whether it's a copy or the original shot you're moving), you'll do either an Overwrite or an Insert, depending on when you let go of the Option key and the clip.

I recommend that you practice these Option-key moves in a duplicate sequence that you can delete when you're done, because getting your timing right can take a little practice. Have fun. But don't say I didn't warn you.

Life In and Out of Sync

Everything we have been doing in picture only or sound only was executed carefully, so as not to go out of sync: Roll edit of picture only, Overwrite edit of sound, Ripple delete of linked picture and sound. All prevent you from ever losing that precious relationship known as *sync*.

But in controlled situations, going out of sync is not all that bad. Sometimes losing sync is a necessary step in a multi-staged solution to some problem. Film editors are particularly good at moving in and out of sync effortlessly. It was only with the advent of videotape editing that editors became particularly stressed out about going out of sync. As an editor, you may want to start getting comfortable moving in and out of sync; it's an important stage in your development as an editor. Hang on.

Let's do a Ripple edit, a rippling trim, in picture only.

1. Lock the sound tracks.

This should be familiar, except that we've been careful in the past to do rippling trims only with sound and picture tracks unlocked. Already I get a little skittish seeing what's about to happen . . .

2. Double-click an edit point, and adjust the B-side alone just a few frames. (I'm going to shorten the B-side ten frames.) As you remove frames from one side of the cut and not the other, you can see what's coming.

Cut seems OK? It's not.

You're out of sync. Let's take a look at the Timeline.

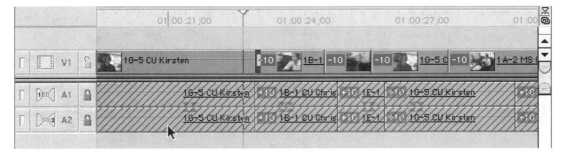

It's hard to say exactly what the problem is: Either the picture is ten frames earlier than the sound (–10) or the sound is ten frames later than the picture (+10). I guess it really doesn't matter. Something has to change in order to bring the tracks back together.

It's a little hard to see with the sound tracks still locked, but Final Cut Express puts a big red notice on any picture shot that is out of sync with its production sound. In this case, we took ten frames off the head of the picture, so from there through the end of the sequence, *all* pictures are ten frames out of sync—*the move rippled all the way to the end.*

If we look closer (and unlock sound tracks for clarity), you can see the telltale footprint of a shot out of sync. This is useful because when something is out of sync, you need to discern exactly where it *first* went out of sync in order to fix it.

A. Find that last shot that is still in sync. Here it is (10-5 CU Kirsten); it ends with a straight cut.

B. Here's the place where we did the trim. It's a little deceptive, as this shot also begins with a straight cut, but that's only because we did the trim, and all the shots after it rippled into the hole created by the ten-frame shortfall. The warning in the Timeline says the picture is –10 frames, or ten frames shorter than the sound. It also says the sound is +10 frames, or ten frames longer than the picture. Final Cut Express doesn't care how you fix it. Put ten frames back in picture, or take ten out of sound. Or some of each. It won't judge you.

C. Here's the first shot that actually looks out of sync in the Timeline. As in an earthquake, the picture track has slid, and you'll see the pattern created in straight cuts when all of them are rippled to the same extent.

If you're advanced, Final Cut Express also has more automated ways to restore sync, using contextual menus. You can investigate those once you've mastered this manual approach.

If you're like most editors, you'll simply perform an undo and execute your trim again, this time being careful to roll both sides evenly. But you could choose to be more selective about where the ten frames you need to adjust are going to come from. You could, for instance, do a series of small rippling trims, some in picture and some in sound, so that the net result is a resynchronization of picture and sound.

For instance, you could do the following:

1. Remove four frames of sound here using the Razor Blade tool and Ripple delete. Now we're only six frames out of sync.

2. Remove three frames of sound here where no one is talking, again using the Razor Blade tool and Ripple delete.

3. Lock the sound and turn on the picture, then perform a trim of the picture only, adding in three more frames.

As you perform the trims, you can actually *see* the frames being added to the Timeline and the out-of-sync–warning number getting smaller and smaller until the warning disappears.

Now your Timeline contains some unusual cuts. It's in sync for a while, then there are a couple of slightly out-of-sync areas, then it goes back into sync. While this isn't wonderful editing form, sometimes this kind of repair work is necessary as you try to solve various creative problems that only editing can solve. In this particular case, the two shots that are a few frames out of sync contain no talking in the sound track—they are basically picture-only shots with ambient sound. Consequently, there is no profound aesthetic problem.

I intentionally go out of sync and then get myself back only when I'm re-editing and I decide that a pause in the sound track is simply too long and I want to pull it out. In this case, I lock picture, and in the soundtracks only, I use the Razor Blade tool and Ripple delete to remove a second (or whatever is required) of unwanted silence.

The shot of the bag (1J) occurs at a place where there is a moment of silence in Kirsten's lecture. I want to lose the silence when it happens, but I'm not yet sure where to lose the equivalent amount of picture.

Here I've made Razor Blade cuts around the region of sound I want to get rid of . . .

MAKING MOVIES WITH FINAL CUT EXPRESS

. . . and Ripple delete. Bad sound is gone (great!), but the picture after this point is out of sync (hmmm). Now to decide how to make adjustments.

At this point I'm out of sync by the length of the sound I removed. To get back in sync, I need to remove picture from somewhere before anyone starts talking again. In this example, I pulled out sound beneath the insert of the bag. Now, I'll use a rippling trim to remove picture: a little from the bag insert, and a little more from the head of Kirsten's continuing dialogue shot.

A quick trim to take some frames off the bag insert . . . it was a little too long, anyway . . .

146

. . . and another little trim to take a beat off the head of Kirsten's dialogue shot. I know to take off exactly 24 more frames because the sync warnings indicate how far I have to go.

And now we're back in sync, but with a tighter track. All the red boxes with out-of-sync warnings are gone. Most people wouldn't notice the changes, but everything will move more smoothly and watching the video will be a little less dull when the audio track is tighter like this.

Putting It All Together

We've worked hard in this chapter to keep our separate picture and sound tracks in sync with each other. Without learning any new concepts, we applied some you already knew—trimming, inserting, and deleting (with both ripple and non-ripple varieties of each)—to picture only and sound only, and to both together. And we've learned that these few concepts embody virtually every function a professional editor would ever need. While there are shortcuts for most of these features, if you didn't feel like expending the extra energy (for instance, if you simply don't edit very often), you might never need to learn them.

Now that you have editing down (and I'm not exaggerating *too* much when I say that you know enough now to edit a feature film if you want to), let's take a look at some of the interesting results you can create simply by adding more tracks to the production. You won't learn any new tools or new functions, but you'll see that more tracks allow you to add richness to the basic production tracks you've been working on up until now.

Getting Fancy with More Tracks

Everything we've done up until now has been about editing *real* video shot with a camera: about cutting and choosing and moving things around in time and in order. You can also stack up pictures or sounds to great effect, to make *non-real* image tracks and sound tracks. One of the wonderful things about Final Cut Express is how easily it combines sound and picture together on multiple tracks to spiff up your project.

Adding more tracks to the basic video and audio tracks we've worked with in the previous chapters opens up opportunities for sophisticated use of special effects, for adding titles, and for laying down music and voice-over tracks. While none of these necessarily requires more tracks, each is best done in channels separate from the production picture and sound. This allows for titles that move independently over existing picture, or music that plays in the background as production sound volume is separately controlled. And while adding new tracks requires the same kind of principles you've already learned, it does complicate matters.

You manipulate picture in Final Cut Express pretty much the same way as you manipulate sound, but it's best (at least at first) to think of them separately. Mixing images together on multiple video tracks elevates simple editing to a level generically known as *special effects,* or more technically as *compositing.* This tends to tax your Mac hardware and dramatically slow down your workflow. Adding audio tracks, on the other hand, produces real-time results—in most cases, Final Cut can play up to eight channels of audio simultaneously, and with simple processing it can include as many as 99 tracks (compared with the paltry two you get in iMovie.) The creative opportunities of having multiple tracks can be dramatic.

In the previous chapter you learned techniques for treating picture and sound separately. In this chapter you'll build on that foundation by adding more picture and sound tracks to play at one time.

Adding More Tracks

There is really only one reason to use additional tracks in your projects: to make different sounds or images mix together and occur at the same time in the final sequence. For images, the main reason to add tracks is for executing special effects; mattes, keys, superimpositions, and some titles, for example, are all performed with multiple tracks. For sound, adding tracks allows a richer acoustic tapestry to accompany the picture: In addition to the production sound (that is, the sound that came in with the video images) and music, you might have effects. Sound effects are not just the explosions and gunshots you typically associate with movies. I routinely steal sounds from parts of the video I'm not using and move them into the tracks of parts I want to make richer—adding birds chirping, someone talking, a doorbell, a phone ringing.

The more tracks in a project, the more time-consuming and difficult it is to make changes to any part of the project. There are many more tracks to keep in sync. There are many more edits that might need adjusting if you make even a small change. Professional film and video editors lock *the picture cut before working on all the multiple-track stuff—music, effects, and so forth. It's a good rule. With Final Cut, a way to lock the picture cut is to duplicate that sequence and rename it, as you did with the final version in the last chapter, and then do your effects and new tracks in the duplicate sequence. That way, you can always go back to your locked picture cut in case of trouble or question.*

Sound

The easiest tracks to add are those for sound—they virtually never require much Mac horsepower to hear (as opposed to picture tracks, which may require time-consuming *rendering—* processing each frame to let you see changes).

And the easiest sound tracks to add are those for music, so let's start simple and build from there. Highlight the sequence Rubin Cut 2 in the Rubin Cuts project (again, without closing the Chocoluv Tutorial project). This is my quick pass at the scene from the last chapter, using only the tools and techniques we've been discussing. I suggest you make a copy (Edit > Duplicate) of Rubin Cut 2 to work in, which will allow you to have the original readily available for comparisons. In keeping with our naming system, I suggest you rename your copy Ch 4 Edit v1.

The options in the Sequence pull-down menu vary, depending on what you've highlighted in your Timeline or settings you've chosen. Don't be alarmed.

Adding Music Tracks

The first thing we'll do is add a couple of audio tracks. You add all tracks, regardless of whether they're for picture or for sound, in basically the same way, so what we do for sound is going to be similar for picture:

1. With the Timeline active, select Sequence > Insert Tracks.

    There are shortcuts, but it's fine to start with the mouse.

2. Enter 2 as the number of audio tracks you want to add. We'll use 2 to place the left and right stereo sound that is typical of music CDs.

Choosing Insert Tracks opens this dialog.

You could unselect the check box for Insert __ Video Tracks, but it doesn't matter, as long as the amount is 0.

But what about those other options—Before Base Track, After Last Target Track, and After Last Track? Before you do anything, back away from the Mac and let's talk.

There's more to adding tracks than creating new tracks; you also need to tell the software where to add them. "Where?" you might ask. "Why does it matter where the track goes, particularly if all the tracks play back at the same time?" *Very good question.* For sound, you'd be right: It really doesn't matter functionally whether music is stacked up on top of production sound or beneath it. But there are other rationales for track positioning, not the least of which are practical: to help you visualize these tracks and make working with them easier. For instance, at the very center of your Timeline should be the picture (on top), with the synchronous production sound tracks (left and right) on the bottom. If you add music, the music track probably shouldn't go between these tracks.

Here are the steps for inserting a single music track between the left and right production sound tracks. This is weird. Don't do this. Tracks that go together (such as left and right stereo pairs, and picture with its sync sound) should be physically proximal to each other. If you break this rule you'll probably make yourself crazy.

Visually, as well as organizationally, it's important to keep all that multi-track material that began as source together (like sync stuff or stereo tracks) in tracks close to each other. I'd add music low down in the stack. You can think of music as a "bed" that underlies everything else. Sound effects might be easier to think about (and therefore manage) as sandwiched between these other sets of tracks, although since I use sound effects rarely, I add that track to the very bottom (so I can ignore it most of the time).

In picture it's different. In picture, you look at these layers as if they were stacked up on a light table. An object in one layer will obscure objects in layers beneath. Consequently, layer position is very important in the video tracks. We'll look at this in detail later in this chapter.

Regardless of your personal logic for placing your tracks, it's still important to have control over where you put them. This track logic can be a little confusing, even for Final Cut experts. Here's a quick outline, in sound tracks, of Final Cut Express track-insert logic:

Before Insert After Insert

Base track —

Base tracks are closest to the line that separates video from audio.

Insert: Before base track.

Last Track —

Last tracks are farthest from the baseline, on the outside edges.

Insert: After last track.

Target Track —

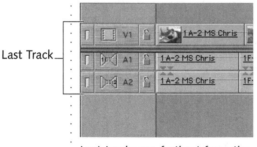 

Target tracks can be anywhere you select (set the yellow highlight in the track controls). In video there is only one target possible; in audio there are two, so Final Cut is concerned with the "last" target track.

Insert: After target track.

3. We want to add the new tracks *after* the last tracks we currently have, so we'll use the default setting (how convenient).

4. Click OK to confirm your choice and close the dialog.

Notice that you now have two new, empty audio tracks, A3 and A4, after (actually, *underneath*) tracks A1 and A2.

On the top, the Timeline before we inserted music tracks; on the bottom music tracks (A3 and A4, empty) beneath the production tracks (A1 and A2, which we had edited in the last chapter).

Let's undo (Command-Z) this track insert. I'd like to show this to you another way.

You don't have to go through that somewhat complicated process to add audio tracks. If you're dragging picture or sound directly to the Timeline, Final Cut knows enough to allow you to add tracks right then and there—no menus, no questions. Here, I'll show you how:

1. Double-click the clip david151 in your Browser to open it into the Viewer.

   This is a sound-only clip (in this case, *music*): a song called "David (151)" (written and performed by Suzanne Brewer). Notice the tabs in the Viewer; since this is a sound-only file, there are only two tabs present: Audio and Filters. There is no video or motion component to a sound file.

When you select a sound-only clip, you see an audio waveform in the Viewer. The louder the music gets, the taller the waveform—(the amplitude is increasing). The top and bottom tracks here are the left and right of the stereo pair. Notice that there are just two tabs in the Viewer (Audio and Filters). Don't panic. Sound-only clips are inherently less complex than picture-and-sound clips.

You can play a sound file as you would any clip in the Viewer. But you won't be able to drag it to the Canvas (or Timeline) by grabbing anywhere in the window the way you did with a video clip—a possible source of frustration. To drag sound files around, go to that icon of the hand holding a speaker located near the top right of the Viewer window. When you click that icon, your pointer becomes a hand (called the *drag hand*), and you can treat the sound the way you would any draggable clip.

Look for the hand-and-speaker. When your pointer moves over this icon in the Viewer, it becomes a hand, too— appropriate for grabbing sound and dragging it around.

2. Use the hand to drag the sound clip directly down to the Timeline, in the space below track A2.

Watch what happens when you get there—technically speaking, you're making an audio-only non-rippling insert in tracks A3 and A4.

Before: *As you drag the sound directly into the Timeline, the ghostly shadow of the new tracks appears in the space beneath the lowest audio tracks. Also, the pointer indicates that it will insert the sound as an Overwrite—which only means that no shots will ripple when this material is inserted, even shots in other tracks.*

After: *And here the sound has dropped in; new tracks have been added for the music automatically, and no shots are rippled in any tracks. Exactly what you want when music lays down under a sequence you're editing. (By the way, don't become disoriented after you let go of the shot—Final Cut Express will cue you up to the end of the music, which is minutes past the end of the picture; just scroll back to the beginning of your sequence.)*

This should look fairly reminiscent of other Timeline editing procedures: You can overwrite your target sound tracks with this clip; you can insert and ripple the existing tracks. But if you drag beneath the existing tracks and drop, you will automatically add tracks for the clip you're moving. Tracks A3 and A4 were added for the stereo music clip.

Extra credit: Now that we have a sound track, play the sequence with the production sound tracks muted so that you don't hear them (turn the green Track Visibility lights off); it's a compelling version with just picture and music. If you like, try recutting your picture and production sound so that there is no dialogue, just a montage of looks and emotions, as in a music video. Maybe take out some of the shots where people are talking; maybe use more emotional cutaway shots. I have included a simple example of a music-video version, labeled Rubin Music Cut.

3. Go ahead and play the cut in the Timeline with the music added.

   Interesting. Some of the edits actually work nicely with the music—like you're some kind of genius. That's one of the neat properties of music: It often syncs up with the picture in ways you may never have anticipated or planned.

4. We're not going to mix this track yet, but since we already covered adjusting audio volume levels (in Chapter 2), take this opportunity to lower the music volume a little (I suggest somewhere between –4dB and –8dB, according to your taste), so it doesn't compete with the production tracks.

5. Now that music is here, let's ignore it. Until otherwise noted, lock your music tracks (so they don't get changed, moved, or adjusted in any way) and turn them off (so you don't hear them while you work).

   They'll still be there when you need them, but you won't need them for a while.

This is a perfectly good time to take a break from editing and examine some of the advanced aspects of sound tracks and their relative volumes—known as a sound *mix*.

The Sound Mix

Once you understand how three-point edits work in sound (which we did in Chapter 3), you have begun your experience as a *sound editor*. In Hollywood filmmaking, the sound editor is among a group of specialists whose jobs include putting all the tracks of a film together and making sure the volume of each is appropriate. Sound editors get their material from the *editor* who is responsible primarily for the picture cut and the associated production sound—the sync sound that is shot on location. An editor might use the occasional sound effect or some music to rough something together, but it's the specialists—sound editors, dialogue editors, music editors, and effects editors—who eventually complete these refinements. For instance, *sound mixers* put all the tracks together and make sure that the volume of each is appropriate for what is happening in the movie.

Final Cut Express is a post-production tool—not just an editing system. As a Final Cut Express user and a student of holistic video, you now understand that you can handle the picture cut, but you can also manage the audio editing, the mixing, the special effects and titles, and even some color correction, without getting up from your chair. While we are dedicated here to getting a good picture-cutting foundation, often the most important aspect of having "good picture" is good sound. I've said it before, but it's worth repeating: Bad picture (bad shooting, bad edits, bad content) plus good sound is remarkably acceptable; good picture plus bad sound (bad edits, poor mixing) is stunningly difficult to watch. The sound mix is one component of good video.

ADJUSTING AUDIO LEVELS, PART 2

The goal of an audio mix is to create a single, seamless sound track out of material produced from a wide range of audio-recording conditions. Adjusting audio levels like a sound mixer is a simple but important first step into the realm of making a good-looking sequence.

When video is recorded on location, the microphone on the camera records production sound. Every time you move the camera, the volume of the sound may change, as well as the degree of noise the microphone picks up from the surroundings.

If I'm recording you from far away, and I turn up the volume to hear you better, I am also increasing the volume of the background noise. If I'm recording you close up, I don't need to increase the volume much to get a nice, clear signal, so I have probably picked up very little background noise.

As we discussed in Chapter 2 (in the section "Adjusting Shot Volume Levels") you can adjust the level (the volume) of each shot individually or of an entire track. And as with everything in Final Cut Express, there's a keyboard way to do it and an onscreen method. The onscreen method is the basic raising and lowering of the red line from the Clip Overlays control.

In case you forgot, here's the Clip Overlays control, which you use to access the onscreen volume controls for shots. It doesn't take a change of many decibels (dB) to have a large effect on sound volume.

Go back to Chapter 2 if you have issues with changing gain. The basic method described there is good for the occasional clip sound adjustment but is tedious for adjusting entire sequences. If you want to raise or lower the volume of a number of shots, select the shots you want to adjust and go to the Modify menu.

There are two important choices in that menu: Modify > Audio and Modify > Levels.

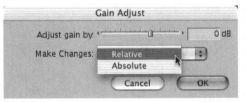

Modify > Audio (left) presents some good shortcuts for many panning and level adjustments. Modify > Levels (right) brings up a dialog where you can adjust the absolute or relative volume of selected shots.

The Modify > Levels options are a little more technical than the Modify > Audio choices. Modify > Levels brings up the Gain Adjust dialog, which has specific gain-adjustment tools.

Here's your chance to determine if your gain adjustment will be relative *("make it louder by a little bit") or* absolute *("set the volume to* this *level").*

"Absolute" sets all selected shots to precisely the same dB, no matter what their levels were when you started the modification. "Relative" moves all the selected shots up or down by a given dB amount from their starting positions.

Sometimes it's best for beginners with little time to work on video projects to skip messing with levels—it's time-consuming and demands a quiet room and good speakers or headphones.

Often more effective is simply adding audio cross fades at transitions where there is a discernable change in room ambience. You could spend as much (or more) time working on sound as on picture.

One surprising mistake that professionals make is working in an environment that is too *quiet. If you do your mixing in a totally silent room, you may not be considering how the project will ultimately be heard: in a noisy office, classroom, or kid-filled home. After finishing a mix, pros will sometimes revisit the absolute level with some ambient noise added to the room, to guarantee that even the quietest sounds can be heard in the place where the video will ultimately be experienced.*

AUDIO CROSS FADE

An *audio cross fade* turns down the volume on the first shot (the A-side) over a short period of time (the default is 1 second), while simultaneously turning up the volume on the B-side over the same period. One fades out as the other fades in. I like to think of these as a poor man's mix. Often, when two shots simply have different-sounding audio and I don't feel like spending a lot of time playing with the various advanced Final Cut features for tweaking audio (volume, pan, EQ, DeEssing, pass filtering, and so on), I just add an audio cross fade across the transition to soften any differences. About 75 percent of the time this works like a charm.

I don't add audio cross fades, by the way, until I am otherwise done working on my edit. All of these cross fades obscure the audio tracks and visually complicate re-editing. But they're easy enough to add or remove as required, so if you have a cross fade that's bothering you, just delete it until later.

A cross fade, whether in audio or video, is a *transition effect*. Final Cut executes transition effects by having you literally drag the effect (icon) from the Effects tab (in the Browser) and dropping it on the transition where you want it to occur. Keep this in mind as we do the audio cross fade here, and later when we do similar transition effects in video.

Let's go back to the sequence we've been working on one last time. Cue up to the beginning and start playing it.

Even between the first two shots, there is an appreciable level change from one to the next. If you want to deemphasize the audio edit, soften the change.

This second shot would benefit from a smoother audio transition.
Compare this "before" shot to what is about to happen.

Now we're going somewhere we've never been before: the Effects tab in the Browser. Select the tab and you'll see an assortment of folders. Open the one labeled Audio Transitions.

If you snoop around in the Effects bin you'll find the Audio Transitions hanging out; there really aren't that many prebuilt audio transitions (as compared with, say, the myriad options for video transitions). As far as I'm concerned, that's the way it should be. I don't want to be spending my afternoons messing around with these things.

1. Click and drag Cross Fade (+3dB) onto the audio transition between the first two shots of the sequence and let go.

2. Now play across the transition, listening carefully.

3. Undo the cross fade and play across the transition again, to note the difference.

4. Use the Redo command (Command-Y) to put the cross fade back in.

5. Play across the transition one more time, to train your ear to hear the subtle differences between an audio cross fade and a straight cut.

In the top Timeline you can see me dragging the cross fade from the Browser over to the place where I want to drop it. The silhouette of the transition snaps to the edit (which is good), and I can clearly see it straddling both sides of the transition. After I let go, you can see it in the bottom Timeline.

Note that there are two default cross fades offered: 0dB and +3dB. These are highly simplified names for some sophisticated audio manipulations. I generally use the +3dB option when going from take to take in similar-sounding shots, and I use the 0dB version when the shifts are larger, say from one scene to a completely different scene. The bottom line is that you should just try them. If one works, great; if it sounds odd, try the other.

That helps a little. (It helps even more if you raise the audio level a few dB in the first shot as well.) In some ways, adding a cross fade is like making a short overlap, moving the sound and picture edits away from each other.

We won't spend any more time here on audio cross fades. But they are your first step in transition effects and foreshadow our work in the next sections on fancier things, like picture effects.

Titles and Text

Remember when you added slug to the sound track back in Chapter 3? That was the first source material generated by Final Cut Express. Titles are essentially another kind of source material that Final Cut Express will generate for you. For the most part, you can manipulate these titles like any shot in your sequence, but because they're often superimposed over production picture, working with them is also a first step towards understanding compositing and effects.

Creating Title Text

A title begins with the source material Generator button in the Viewer. Let's go there now.

Generator

It's good you ignored this until now. Slowly, as we do more in Final Cut, we'll investigate the functions behind some of these buttons on the screen. iMovie has a far simpler and still powerful relationship to text and titles, but in essence the Final Cut Express method is more flexible and powerful.

1. Click the Generator button (below the jog wheel in the Viewer) and select Text > Text from the pop-up menu.

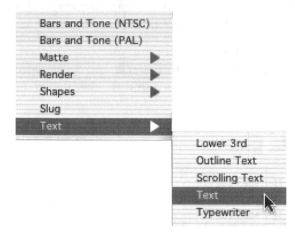

This presents the most basic text option. The Viewer displays a new internally generated source, a *text* source.

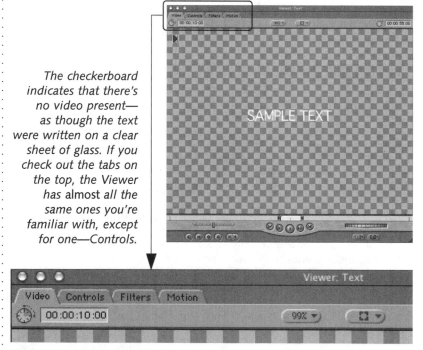

The checkerboard indicates that there's no video present— as though the text were written on a clear sheet of glass. If you check out the tabs on the top, the Viewer has almost all the same ones you're familiar with, except for one—Controls.

While it might seem that the Video tab is pretty important when you're working with titles, the Controls tab is your main landscape for setting up what your title says, and so on.

Because this source is picture-only, the Audio tab has been replaced by Controls. The Controls tab contains the primary information about your text clip.

What has been generated for you is a default clip of text ("SAMPLE TEXT") that is 2 minutes long. In the middle of that 2-minute clip, a 10-second shot has been marked for you (denoted by the In and Out marks). You are now parked at the In.

If you drag the playhead to the end of the scrubber bar, notice that the time in the Current Timecode field at the top right scrolls up to 1:59:29, which, if you start with frame 00, indicates 2 minutes.

But this default text isn't the text that you want to add. Select the Controls tab. An entirely new-looking window of controls fills the Viewer.

With not nearly the user-friendliness of the iMovie title tools, this still is a powerful title engine. That being said, it's the first significant departure between Final Cut Express and Final Cut Pro—your title capabilities here are modestly curtailed.

Titles in Final Cut Pro

Final Cut Pro has two columns at the right of the window that allow you to animate titles through a variety of parameters—for instance, rather than making a title 36 points tall, you could have the title start out at 0 points and slowly grow to 100 points over the course of a shot. Same with "position" and every other attribute. Keyframes (which we'll discuss a little bit later on) give you this functionality.

The Controls tab is where you can change what the title says, its font size, its color, tracking, and other basic font parameters. Click one of the categories (listed down the left side of the window) to modify it.

2. First, change the text to read "Chocoluv."

3. Then adjust the font to something sans serif (I used Impact, but any clean headline font will do) and in a significantly larger font size: The default is 36 points, which is pretty small on most television displays; try 100.

Here I've put in a new title and changed its size and font. The Text > Text options we selected originally are really designed for main *(big, one-line) titles, but you can have a few lines and press Return between them—they are still all treated as one object. There are other text choices for other kinds of titles (like MTV-style titles called lower thirds, scrolling type, and so on).*

4. Go back to the Video tab and see the results of your Controls changes.

The same title, as seen on the Video tab in the Viewer. Remember that the checkerboard indicates a title as if it were on glass. If you put it on a layer above a video clip, you'll see video through it.

The checkerboard background is a traditional way in graphics applications to indicate that there is *no* background; the title is floating as if on clear glass. If you place this over video, you'll see the video wherever you now see checkerboard. If you place it *under* video, of course, you won't see it at all. This is where the layer position really matters.

Click and drag on a tab to pull the window out from the stack and move it on the screen. When I'm doing titles, I always pull the Video tab in the Viewer over the Canvas. Now when I make adjustments in the Controls tab for this title, I can watch the effect on the Video tab without having to toggle back and forth.

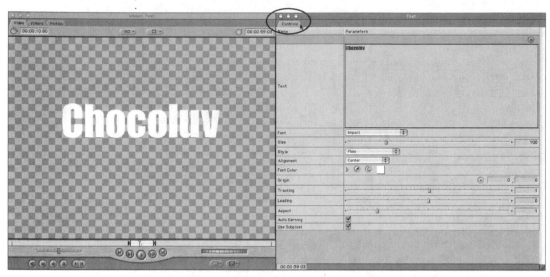

Pull the Controls tab over the Canvas while working on titles. If you want to put the tab back, just click the red close button on the Controls tab, and it will return to its original position.

Titles are not necessarily effects that require a new video track. Let's look at two ways to treat titles, first as just another shot added to the existing (V1) track of video and second as a new track.

Adding a Title to V1

Instead of adding the 10-second title that Final Cut Express defaulted to (the time between the In and Out points in the scrubber), let's add only a few seconds.

1. Go to the Mark In point of the title in the Viewer and click Play; slowly read the title to yourself, and stop when you think it's long enough.

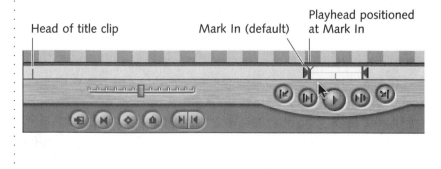

Head of title clip   Mark In (default)   Playhead positioned at Mark In

Why do we start in the middle of the title clip instead of at the head? It's an old habit left over from older technologies with their associated drawbacks. In general, it's so that you have more title both before and after your clip, in case you want to lengthen it in one direction or the other.

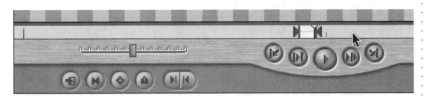

2. Mark a new Out when you feel the time is right.

I marked 2 seconds or so. Notice that the Timecode Duration field in the top left shows how long you've made the title.

Sometimes it's tricky to figure out if you're actually "playing" a title. One way you'll know is if the small triangle in the Play button is yellow, instead of black. Another way is to watch the timecode changing in the Current Timecode field in the top right of the Viewer.

You also could type a precise length in the Timecode Duration field and press Return. Titles, in particular, are good places to work with editing using timecode, although we won't discuss that in this book.

On the left is the clip duration in the Timecode Duration field when we marked it on the fly. On the right I've retyped a precise duration of 2 seconds for my title. Easier? Harder? Some people hate typing any numbers and prefer to work by "feel." Others find it fast and efficient to type numbers for various editorial functions.

3. Now, instead of adding a track in V2 (as we did before), target V1 (the Target Track control in the Timeline should be yellow, and likely already is) and insert the title before the first shot, as if it were any other clip in the Viewer.

When you click anywhere in the Viewer (Video tab), you can drag the title around—either to the Timeline directly or to the Canvas to insert into the sequence like any new material.

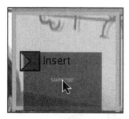

Remember Insert? To insert the title, position the playhead at the beginning of your sequence (where you want the title to go) and drag the title from the Viewer to the Insert button in the Canvas.

Now the title is placed in your sequence in pretty much the same way that any video clip would be. If you see the red bar and need to force Final Cut Express to render, select Sequence > Render All.

4. When it's done, play the sequence.

5. Now play the sequence with the music back on so that you can hear it. Music serves many purposes, but sometimes you may want to use the rhythm and pace of the song to help identify timing in other tracks.

Real-Time vs. Rendered Effects

When you add an effect or title to your Timeline that requires some extra processing by your Mac, the thin render indicator bar at the top of the Timeline turns a different color. If the color is green or yellow, you can play the effect in real time, without rendering. If the color is red, you can still see a single frame at a time, previewed in the Canvas when you aren't playing, but you'll need to render this area of the Timeline in order to see the effect actually play.

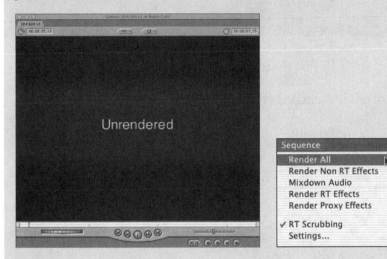

There are two primary ways to get a shot rendered. You can select the shots and then choose Sequence > Render Selection. Or you can simply render everything in your sequence by selecting Render All.

Some basic effects in Final Cut Express can be seen in real time without rendering. The more GHz in your CPU (1.4 GHz is better than 800 MHz, for instance), or the more CPUs you have (dual processors beat out a single processor), the more likely it is that your Mac can show you an effect without rendering—which is, of course, the best situation. As I've said, more CPU power plays little role in editing but a significant one in working with effects.

Unlike iMovie, Final Cut Express doesn't render anything unless you specifically ask it to. This may sound like a drawback, but as is often the case, building effects is a many-staged process, and you wouldn't want to waste time rendering your effect while you're building it and every time you tweak it—at least not until you think you're done.

6. It feels to me like the title is too short. I don't know how long it should be. But I do know that as I hear the music, I *feel* the point where I think the title should end and the picture should start. After I see the title play with the music, it feels more like it needs to be about 5 seconds into the music or so. Play to where you feel the title should end, and stop there.

7. Now that you have parked the playhead where you want something to happen (in this case, where the title should end), get the Ripple Edit tool from the Tool palette, select the edit-point end of the title, and drag it to the right, to the playhead.

When snapping is on, you'll be able to pop it right to the playhead where you want the shot to end. All the other shots (in picture and sound together) ripple down to make room.

Here are the three steps (which should be familiar by now) for trimming a shot: (1) Select a transition with the Ripple Edit tool; (2) click and drag to lengthen—it will snap to the playhead; (3) let go when you're there.

If you don't have real-time (RT) effects active (probably because your external video is on), you'll see something interesting in the render bar at the top of the Timeline: The part of this title that was rendered before is still rendered, but the new length is not—the red bar is only over the added part of the title.

Re-rendering may not be required for entire shots, but sometimes only for parts of shots in the Timeline. Here about half of this shot needs to be re-rendered, as indicated by the red bar above the ruler.

As you can see, a title is pretty much like any other clip, even when edited into a sequence. The difference is that, like many effects, a title must be rendered to appear. But a title over black is one of the simplest of all effects to render, so on any Mac it will probably be a short wait.

Adding Titles Using New Picture Tracks

Often, when you add titles, you will want them to overlap (superimpose) with pictures, and to do that you will need to add new picture tracks.

Adding tracks directly to the Timeline for titles is comparable to the way we dragged music to the Timeline without using the Add New Tracks function. Let's create a superimposed title card. This one is going to be a sort of MTV-style label, in the lower third of the frame, on the left:

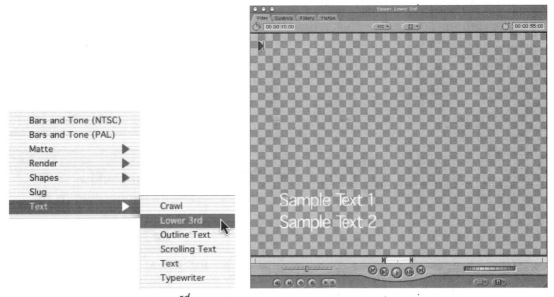

After you select Text > Lower 3rd from the Generator pop-up menu, the Viewer shows the default title. Of course, this is sort of useless, and your next move is to switch the view from the Video tab to the Controls tab.

When generating text, the Controls tab in the Viewer is often more important than the Video tab. Select it to adjust the material in the two text boxes. Let's enter something in each:

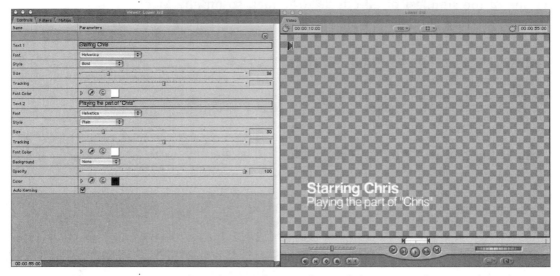

I can adjust the text, font, and size of the two text boxes in this title variation. To help me see what I'm doing while I do it, I've again pulled apart the Video and Controls tabs.

I made the top text bold (36 points, the default size) and the bottom text regular (30 points, a little smaller), but they're both in the same Helvetica font.

1. Using the Mark Out button on the Viewer, shorten the title to just under 3 seconds. (Or you could type the exact duration in the Timecode Duration field in the top-left corner of the Viewer.)

2. In the Timeline, play and stop at what feels to you like a good spot for the lower-third title to start.

But wait! When you play the sequence, you don't see it. Oh, right, the Canvas is underneath the Video tab from the Viewer. It's there; it's just hidden. Close the Video tab (click the red button at the top of the window) and you'll reveal the Canvas again.

3. With the playhead exactly where you want the title to begin, drag the title down to the Timeline until it snaps to the playhead. Let go.

A new track will be added for you. Just keep an eye on the inserting pointer (make sure it's doing an Overwrite and not an Insert).

Playhead   Overwrite pointer   Shadow of new clip (title)

The snapping feature is great for an activity like placing a title. Just park the playhead where you want something to happen (and this is perfectly logical because you have to watch your sequence to find that spot, anyway), then drag the title to the Timeline.

4. Drop the title *above* the V1 track. Notice that a new video track (V2) is added, and the title is in it.

That was easy, but of course we're not done. Don't bother rendering it yet—the title is too hard to read like this.

If you want to spot-check how this title looks without rendering, click in the time scale above the shot to move the playhead into the title. If you click Play, it will tell you the shot is "unrendered," but if you just click and step frame by frame with the arrow buttons, you should get an idea of how it would look if rendered.

Creative note: It can be jarring to start a title exactly at the start of the shot it is superimposed on. Give the viewer a moment to "read" the background shot, and then bring in the title.

It looked fine in the Viewer; it appears fine in the Timeline; but now that I see it in the Canvas, with the background material, the title in small white letters is hard to read over the video. You're not stuck—you could make the font bolder or the type larger, but I have another suggestion. You'll need to go to a different tab to fix it.

Adding a Drop Shadow

Here's our first fairly significant departure from the "way things tend to work." I said in Chapter 1 that the only way to get something in the Viewer is to select it in the Browser. The edits appear only in the Canvas. But there's an exception to these general rules: You can double-click a clip in the Timeline to load it into the Viewer. When you do this, you are effectively taking a shot from the finished sequence and putting it up in a work space where you can adjust it—in the Viewer.

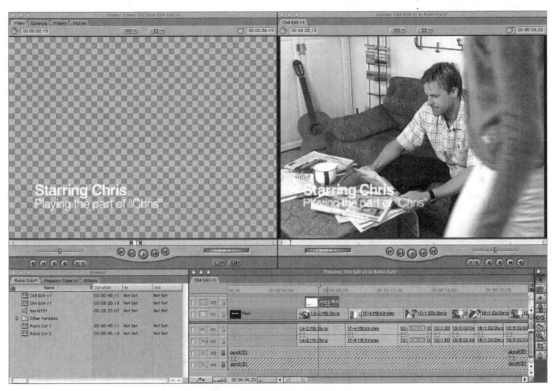

In the Timeline I moved the playhead to a point in the first shot where the title is superimposed. You can see the combination of title and shot in the Canvas above it. I also double-clicked the title itself (the clip is highlighted in the Timeline), which put a working copy of just the title back in the Viewer (top left). Because it is technically still in the Timeline, changes made to it in the Viewer are made in the Timeline.

Those little dots in the scrubber indicate that the shot in the Viewer is actually an adjustable bit of the Timeline. When you see those, it's a dead giveaway that something is up.

A shot brought to the Viewer from the Timeline is not much different from clips taken from the Browser, except that changes made here are incorporated into the sequence in the Timeline right away. It's as if you were adjusting shots in the Timeline itself, even though you're working on them in the Viewer space. The big advantage is that when you're done working on them, you don't have to save the adjustments or put them back in the Timeline; they just *are*.

Let's double-click the title effect we just created in V2. It's selected in the Timeline, and it appears in the Viewer.

While this title looks very similar to the raw title before it was cut into the sequence, it isn't the same. It's now composited over picture, so it looks different. Not so good. Click the Controls tab and you'll see the area we entered in the text itself, the font and font size, and so on. We're not changing any of this.

Now click the Motion tab.

A number of physical attributes of the frames you're looking at can be modified here: the frame's size, rotation, crop, distortion, opacity, and motion blur. The odd one here, for me, is Drop Shadow, which doesn't seem like a frame attribute so much as a text attribute. Still, if you're going to do text or titles of any kind, it's critical to know where Drop Shadow is and how to use it. I believe that all titles in video need a drop shadow. It can be subtle, but it increases the legibility of text onscreen, in particular when there is competing visual information in the form of a moving video background.

If you click the check box by Drop Shadow, you'll see the default setting for this effect appear on the Canvas. (You want to see it in the Canvas and not on the Video tab of the effect, because to make these kinds of judgments about an effect, you're likely to want to see it in the context of the other video in the sequence.)

If you don't like the default (and I don't), open up the Drop Shadow feature by clicking the disclosure triangle to reveal a small window of the Drop Shadow parameters.

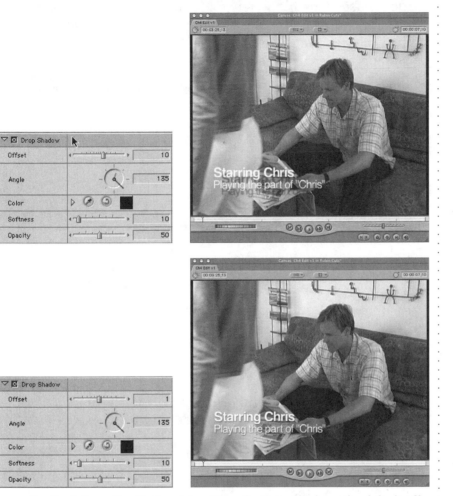

On the left are the Motion tab settings for Drop Shadow. The default off-set of 10 pixels is too great (above)—the shadow doesn't do much to help separate the title from the background. By making a smaller offset of 1 pixel (below), the drop shadow works a little better.

The one we're going for is Offset; its default is 10, but let's change it to 1. Depending on how busy the background image is and the size of the title (among other factors), a subtle drop-shadow offset runs in the range of 1 to 4. Set higher than 4, the shadow loses the ability to help the main text stand out from the background. Once you've set your new offset, go ahead and render the title (Sequence > Render All).

A drop shadow, while a potent solution, won't solve every title readability problem. White titles over a light or mottled color video frame with moving shadows—which we have in Chocoluv—are always going to be hard to read. Still, a drop shadow is a good start.

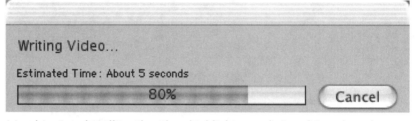

I tend to "render all" rather than highlight one shot and "render selection." But it really depends on what you're doing: If you have lots of effects in your sequence and you want to take the time to see only one of them, of course "render all" is not what you want. You'll end up waiting around for effects to render that you're not interested in.

You might try a different drop-shadow offset. If you change any parameter of the effect after rendering, you'll notice that the red bar is now back in the Timeline. Because you changed something about an already-rendered effect, you need to render the effect again—that's what the red bar is telling you. After you review the effect, if the title feels too long or too short, you can easily trim its length with a trim or the Razor Blade tool. Note, by the way, that shortening an effect doesn't require Final Cut to rerender the remaining part—as long as the frames in that part haven't changed.

Variations on Title Placement

Moving the location of a title on the screen can dramatically affect how a title feels to a viewer. Main titles are created in the center of the display by default; this makes some sense but defies the aesthetic rule of thirds, which aids in good screen design. To move the text you have two options:

On the Controls tab, you can click the plus button next to Origin. This resets the location where Final Cut places a title with respect to the video frame. The default origin is in the center of the text box (0, 0 in *x, y* coordinates). When you click the plus button, you will see the origin in the window, and if you click elsewhere in the frame, the origin (and thus the title) will move accordingly. This is the most appropriate method of moving a title around.

Video	Controls	Filters	Motion
Style	Plain		
Alignment	Center		
Font Color	▷ ✎ ©		
Origin		0 ,	0
Tracking			1

Style	Plain		
Alignment	Center		
Font Color	▷ ✎ ©		
Origin		0 ,	110.22
Tracking			1

The alternative doesn't move the title, per se, but moves the entire frame. On the Motion tab you can scale and move the frame—which of course moves and scales the title. Center on the Motion tab works the same way as Origin on the Controls tab. The results may look the same, but the method is profoundly different.

Video	Controls	Filters	Motion
Name	Parameters		
▽ Basic Motion			⊗
Scale			100
Rotation			0
Center	⊕	−60 ,	70.11
Anchor Point		0 ,	0

Basic Transition Effects

A transition effect is a modification to the way one shot ends and the next begins. Examples of transition effects that might be familiar include dissolves, fades, and wipes; all modify the way a shot begins or ends (and consequently, how it joins with the adjacent shots).

I call the junction between two shots a transition *even though Final Cut thinks of these as* splice *or* edit *points and reserves the term* transition *for the special effect itself. I often refer to an edit point as a transition (which is correct) and call the effect you might apply to a transition a* transition effect. *A sequence without transition effects is often described as* cuts-only.

There are variations on how transition effects are oriented as they are placed on a splice point (Start On, Center On, and End On Edit), and ample customizations are possible, but we're going to focus exclusively on the Final Cut Express defaults for transition effects.

Transition effects are stored in a folder on the Effects tab of the Browser (left). Inside the Video Transitions folder are transition-effect variations, including 3D Simulations, Dissolves, and Wipes. Dissolves are some of the most commonly used transition effects. On the right you can see the pre-built types of dissolves you might want to use.

The most commonly used special effect is the transition effect, and the most common kind of transition effect is the dissolve. Let's open the Dissolve folder in Transition Effects and look at the two most important variations. Understand these, and you might not need any other special effects for most of your video editing.

Fade In, Fade Out Dissolve

Fades are a sophisticated (yet surprisingly simple) way to ease into and out of titles and opening and closing shots of video. Fade outs create a feeling of *closure*. Fade Ins are a wonderful *reveal*, like a curtain opening. Most commercials sport a ten-frame (fast!) fade at the head and tail. Many television shows start and end each act with a fade.

A fade-*out* will gradually darken a shot to black, usually over the course of a few seconds or less. A fade-*in* does the reverse.

Here's an interesting view of a fade-out, called a filmstrip view (and not really practical for anything but book illustrations); you can see the shot growing dimmer with each successive frame until it's gone.

In Final Cut Express, two fades are prebuilt back-to-back as a sort of convenient option if you are using fades in the middle of a program. This Fade In Fade Out dissolve, like many special effects in FCE, is represented as an icon you can drag and drop. You drag the dissolve from the Effects menu in the Browser and drop it over a splice in the Timeline.

> ⬚ Fade In Fade Out Dissolve

The icon in the Effects bin (in the Browser). I'm not sure this effect is properly named: I think it should be Fade Out Fade In, *since that more accurately describes what it provides.*

For shots that are the first or last in a sequence, that don't seem to be attached to anything, place the transition at the beginning or end (respectively) of the shot.

1. Drag the Fade In Fade Out icon to the first shot in the sequence, the Chocoluv title. Watching the snapping and shadows, place the icon over the head of the title and let go. Final Cut uses a 1-second default duration for the effect, which is often about right.

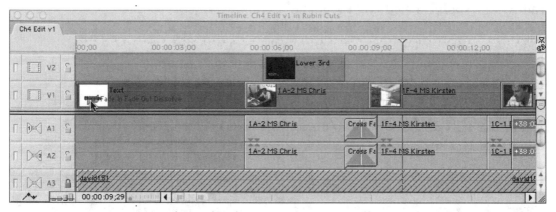

Visualizing the placement of transition effects can be difficult, but with a little practice it's pretty effortless to get the effect to the right transition. Here I've placed it at the head of the first shot.

That wasn't too hard. There may be a red bar over the effect, indicating that it needs to be rendered. You can render it if you wish.

2. Let's add three more of these transition effects. We'll add the first dissolve to the end of the title and beginning of the first video shot. At this location we will fade out the title and then fade in the next shot, so we want to drop the effect directly over the edit point; it should look evenly distributed over the transition:

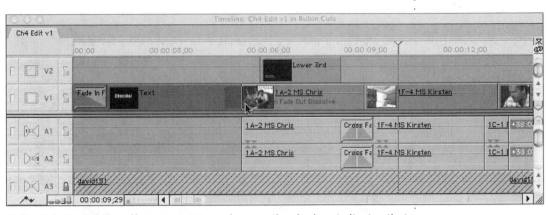

Before I let go of the effect, I want to make sure the shadow indicates that I'm centered on the transition and not skewed to one side or the other. It snaps into place, so getting it there is really easy. After I let go, the effect shows up in the Timeline (and looks a lot like the cross fade we put in the audio track earlier).

Now the simple title card fades in and out, and the first shot of the program fades in. But wait: *Something interesting is happening here.* When you place a fade-in at the beginning of the first shot in a sequence, the entire duration of the effect (in this case, 1 second) is spent fading in the first shot. *(Duh!)* But when we add the same effect to a transition between two shots, as we did at the end of the title card, half of the 1-second duration is spent fading out the first shot (.5 seconds, or 15 frames) and the other half is spent fading in the second shot. In general this is pretty smart of Final Cut, but the fade title card is now a little off balance (it fades in slowly but fades out more quickly).

3. There are a number of hip ways to change the duration of an effect—in this case, the fade-in. It can be done in the Timeline by clicking and dragging; it can be done a few different ways in the Viewer. Let's do a quick one: Double-click the effect in the Timeline (which, as you recall, moves a working copy to the Viewer) and modify the number in the Timecode Duration field in the top left.

I don't like typing numbers, particularly timecodes (with all those colons and semicolons!), but on occasion it can be fast. Here I changed the default fade duration from 1 second to half a second (00;15)—the good news is, I only had to type the semi-colon and the last two digits to do it.

If you examine the icons that Final Cut placed in the Timeline for the two (theoretically identical) fades, you'll see that the first one shows a little right triangle, depicting *black* starting *full* and disappearing (to the right) as we go along. The second fade-in/fade-out has two of these icons back-to-back, going from the shot, to black, and back to the shot. This is a somewhat traditional way to indicate effects across transitions.

A fade-in (left) looks a little different from a fade-in/fade-out—which is occurring on the right. The same transition effect, placed in two different kinds of locations, produces two different kinds of results. Notice how the fade-in/fade-out on the right is the same as the cross fade in sound.

In truth, Fade In Fade Out icons shouldn't look the same as dissolves that create overlapping material (like the cross fade in audio or the cross dissolve we'll try in a bit. These are traditionally shown with an X centered on the edit.

Remember, all titles improve when they begin and end with fades, even really fast ones. I'm going to add ten-frame fades to the beginning and end of the lower-third title to make this a little nicer. This time I won't center the fade on the edit point, but begin it there.

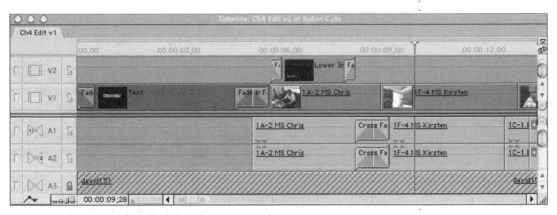

Now the lower-third fades are in. These are in close proximity to transitions in the V1 track, and if they're too close (or particularly if they overlap), they may look clunky, like a mistake, when you play the video. It's generally good to keep transition effects away from other transitions; if the material doesn't allow that to happen, just be sure to watch the results carefully.

> *Fades effectively shorten a shot, so an almost-too-short shot will feel shorter if you've applied a fade-in/fade-out to it. Plan the length of titles accordingly.*

Cross Dissolve

The next most basic transition effect is popularly called a *dissolve* but is technically referred to as a *cross dissolve*—an effect pretty familiar to most people: The A-side fades out at the same time as the B-side fades in. A *center-point dissolve* is one in which, at the location of the edit—the midpoint of the transition—you see an image that's 50 percent shot A and 50 percent shot B.

Here's that filmstrip view again, this time demonstrating a dissolve. If you want to see brilliant and complex use of these dissolves, watch the opening sequence in the movie Apocalypse Now. *The visual montage of overlapping images in multiple layers is a paragon of the art form.*

Unlike a fade, in which there is no overlapping of images in the A and B sides, a dissolve replaces one picture with another. Where a fade provides some sense of closure, a dissolve moves you forward. But most important, because the two shots in a dissolve can be seen onscreen at the same time, the content of those frames needs to be considered—how they look superimposed.

Even though I often use fades, I hardly ever use dissolves— I'm particularly cautious in mentioning them, because they tend to be overused or misused by beginners. Dissolves have many fine uses (including the depiction of time passing gently between scenes), but these uses hardly ever include transitions within a scene, particularly one in which a conversation is taking place. Still, dissolves are handy and merit some examination.

Something to think about: The longer a dissolve is, the more attention it draws to itself. While sometimes this is your goal, generally you don't want your transition effects to demand attention, and so you want dissolves to be relatively short (a second or so) rather than luxuriously long (3 or more seconds), *Apocalypse Now* notwithstanding.

How to Add a Transition

A cross dissolve (or cross fade in sound) adds frames of material that are not present in the Timeline in the cuts-only version of a sequence. For instance, when you add a cross dissolve, Final Cut must extend the video of both shots being shown so that the scene can slowly switch (that is, *dissolve*) from one to the other.

Below is an illustration of two shots cut together as a simple splice—sort of how they appear in the Timeline.

To create the centered dissolve, both shots must be extended by the same amount. A 1-second dissolve adds 15 frames to the tail of the A-side and 15 frames to the head of the B-side. Thus, inside Final Cut, a cross dissolve looks like this:

Additional material needed
to make the dissolve

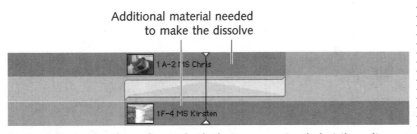

Notice how in the above figure, both shots were extended at the splice point when the dissolve was added.

Now here's a tricky concept that frustrates many beginners. There are times when you want to make a dissolve and Final Cut prevents it because it sees that there isn't enough material in your underlying source clip to execute the effect. If, for instance, the B-shot's In point started only 10 frames into a clip, then it would be impossible to add 15 frames to the head—there's not enough material. That's why FCE (mysteriously, sometimes) won't let you add a transition effect that extends the shot.

Another tricky thing about adding any transition effect (including dissolves): Even if Final Cut doesn't warn you, there may be an aesthetic problem. The 15 frames added (automatically) will be material you haven't previewed yet. It's possible that the new material will look bad when it becomes part of the dissolve and is mixed with the other shot. Maybe it's a slate, maybe it's another character or scene. (These are sometimes called *flash frames,* because they often produce a little flash or "bump" in the transition.) Whatever the reason, when you perform a dissolve, you always want to review the result closely to see how it looks.

Let's add one dissolve to this sequence, between the shot of Kirsten standing watching Chris and the one of Chris looking up. It's about the only reasonable spot for a dissolve, as it might give the feeling that she's been standing there a bit. (On the other hand, it might not work.)

1. Drag the Cross Dissolve icon from the Effects tab of the Browser and drop it when it's centered on the transition.

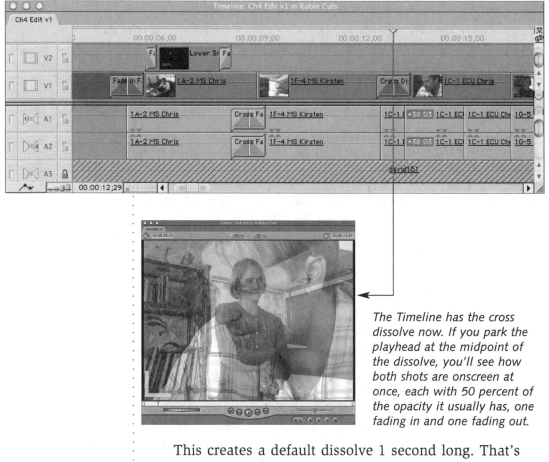

The Timeline has the cross dissolve now. If you park the playhead at the midpoint of the dissolve, you'll see how both shots are onscreen at once, each with 50 percent of the opacity it usually has, one fading in and one fading out.

This creates a default dissolve 1 second long. That's not unusual for a dissolve, but you might want it to last longer.

2. Double-click the dissolve icon in the Timeline to open it in the Viewer.

This should start to be a familiar activity. Rough something in, and then refine it. You can adjust many of the subtle features of this dissolve in the Viewer.

3. Enter a new duration in the Timecode Duration field at the top left. It now says 01;00, or 1 second; change this to 02;00.

By now, entering timecode might not have the paralyzing effect it once did. Still, I type as little as possible—in this case I selected the Timecode Duration field and simply typed 2 to indicate 2 seconds.

When you lengthen the effect, the icon of the dissolve in the Timeline also changes, to accurately represent the time covered by the transition.

It's all right, I guess. You can keep it or delete it, as you like. To delete it, just select the dissolve in the Timeline and press Delete. The transition will be restored to a cut.

Other Transitions

There are other transition effects you can test out, too. A *wipe* transitions from an A-shot to a B-shot using some kind of geometric pattern. While they are in separate folders, transitions like Iris, Page Peel, and Slide are really just variations of wipes. Have fun with these. There are a myriad of possibilities in the custom wipe and wipe-parameter-variation department. At some point in your spare time, I suggest experimenting with the transition effects included in Final Cut Express.

From left to right, a Clock Wipe, a Checker Wipe, and a Jaws Wipe. There are so many wipe options, it's dizzying. They're all kinda hokey and generally do the one thing you don't want an effect to do: draw attention to itself. Still, they're fun, and in the right video, if not overdone, they're useful between scenes. Watch the original Star Wars *if you want to see a typical (but properly campy) use of wipes.*

- An **Additive Dissolve** is like a cross dissolve, but the brightness of the images is added together instead of averaged out. It can look like a fade-in/fade-out to white instead of black.

- A **Dip to Color** is like a fade-out/fade-in, but rather than fading to black, you can select the color you'd like to dissolve in and out of (the color you see full on at the midpoint of the transition).

- A **Dither Dissolve** is an interesting transition that breaks an image into a noise pattern and then back to an image. It's fancy and trendier, and therefore easily overused.

- A **Non-Additive Dissolve** is like an Additive Dissolve, but the images do not add, and thus result in a dissolve through black but with a slightly different visual effect.

- A **Ripple Dissolve** is the most like traditional wipes. This transition looks like a pond ripple (made by dipping your finger in a pool of water) and is slower to render because it takes a bit more processing than most other transitions. (Don't confuse this effect's "ripple" with the editing concept rippling. They have nothing to do with each other.)

Video Favorites

Any effect that you use frequently can be dragged from the Effects folder (or from a sequence) into the Favorites folder. A copy is created there, so you can conveniently store your frequently used (or custom-modified) effects.

I keep six basic effects here. I find that this small number of favorites handles many of my editing-effects needs, but of course you may add your own favorites as you work. You can also rename them if you want to better describe the effect.

- Fade In Fade Out Dissolve
- Video Cross Dissolve
- Audio Cross Fade (+3dB)
- Audio Cross Fade (0dB)
- Image Control (the whole folder, but particularly Tint)
- Color Corrector (for emergency adjustments of white-balance problems)

Keyframes and Compositing

Video plays at 30 frames per second. If you wanted to draw 30 pictures and play them one after another, you could create a 1-second animation. Think about how long it takes to draw 30 pictures. Now think about how long it would take to draw a full-length movie.

One of the ideas that came out of early advances in animation was that when you're animating something or someone, you don't really need to draw all 30 frames. Not initially. What's most important are key moments in the character's motion. For instance, a moving hand starts in one spot, and after a few seconds you want it to be in another.

Eventually all the frames between these two moments must be drawn, but when you're working out the animation in the first place, you need only begin with the most important, *key*, frames.

Thus, the art of animating—whether you're using a computer-generated character, a flying logo, or a hand-drawn animal—begins with establishing the key frames, or *keyframes*. Then, later, you go back and do the laborious drawings between them—called *inbetweening*.

Why am I telling you this? Because if you want any professional control of titles and motion effects, you must fully comprehend this idea of setting keyframes and then letting the computer do the inbetweening. In a very real way, you are animating titles and many effects when you use them in video.

The management of keyframes is one of the critical differences between Final Cut Express and Final Cut Pro. Your ability to set and visualize keyframes is limited in Final Cut Express—limited in your control to set them and limited in the scope of functions to which they can be applied.

Investigating keyframes is therefore beyond our basic introduction here, but as your editing skills grow, your interest in special effects (in general) and setting keyframes (in particular) may increase, and at that time you will want to explore Final Cut Pro.

All I will say at this point is that Final Cut Express does have a button that inserts keyframes into your Timeline. It looks like this:

The Add Keyframe button can be found at the bottom of the Canvas, nestled among other comparably obscure little buttons that mark things in your sequences (from the left: Mark In, Mark Out, Add Marker, Add Keyframe, Mark Clip, and Match Frame).

If you place keyframes at the start and end of a shot or title, you can often adjust the parameters of the video (for instance, the size or position) at each keyframe, and Final Cut will animate the effect for you. It's sort of crude, but it's an introduction to a complex and fascinating set of tools.

Compositing: What It Is and Why We Aren't Doing It Here

This is not a book on compositing. But I do think it's important to understand some of the basic ideas of compositing and how Final Cut Express addresses them.

Compositing is the art of stacking up layers of video and making them look good in the process. When you stack up video layers, you have to imagine that they are piled up on a light table and you are watching them from the top down.

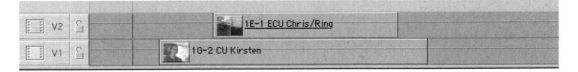

If a layer is opaque (opacity = 100 percent), then you're not going to be able to see anything underneath it. If a layer is translucent (opacity = 0 percent), then it will be a clear window, and you won't see any of images in the layer itself. This layer opacity concept is an important first step in understanding compositing.

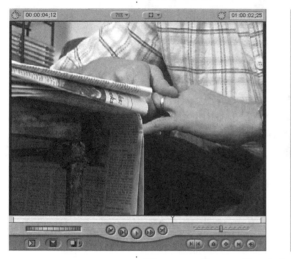

These are the results of stacking shots, layer one over layer two, as we did in the above Timeline. Not much to see on the left, where layer one is 100 percent opaque. On the right its opacity is 30 percent, and you can see layer two underneath.

But video in a layer doesn't always need to be full screen. The video can be shrunk to fill only a portion of the screen. Doing this results in a kind of "window-in-a-window" (or picture-in-picture) feature, where you can watch two independent moving pictures (sometimes called *video streams*) at the same time. The ability to resize video and move the little box on the screen is the next basic step in compositing.

Now both layers have 100 percent opacity, but layer one (the top layer) has been reduced to 30 percent of its former size. On the left, the topmost image is in the default position, centered; on the right I have moved it (choose Center on the Motion tab) to the lower-right corner.

But if that were all that compositing could do, it wouldn't be all that interesting. You've been working with video images that are full screen in a quadrilateral format that has a rectangular kind of geometric shape (technically speaking, an *aspect ratio* of 4:3). But there are tools that will allow you to cut out *parts* of an image. Cutting out bits and pieces of images and compositing them together into a new whole image is what's interesting, and it produces most of the impressive power of image compositing. I would suggest that the special ability to cut out pieces of an image (using *keys* and *mattes*) is the third, and most important (and complicated) aspect to compositing.

Here the topmost image has been filtered with a color key, so you can see through only the parts of it that have the chosen range of color. This, by the way, is how TV news programs put an anchorperson in front of a map or other background—by having a big screen behind them that's solid green (or blue), and then replacing the green (or blue) with another video stream. This specific color (or chroma) key is widely used.

By cutting out video, repositioning and resizing the bits over other video, you begin to sense the nature of video compositing. There is much more to it, but hopefully this short introduction will allow you to see how these often-complex effects integrate into Final Cut. And while they can be executed in this simple software package, fine keyframe control makes it considerably more functional and manageable, something that is lacking in Final Cut Express. When your video interests are sufficiently developed, your hardware sufficiently powerful (compositing is where you'll truly feel the effect of having more CPU power), and your free time sufficiently lengthy, Final Cut Pro may prove the optimal product to push compositing to the next level.

Filter Effects

A *filter* effect "processes" a selected shot, changing the way the image on the screen looks by changing (à la Photoshop) the pixels in each frame of video. Filters can blur and sharpen shots, adjust color and noise, and even give the video a film look. Filters are also used in conjunction with compositing, to facilitate the creation of mattes and keys.

Examples of a few wacky filter effects (from left): Pond Ripple (in the Distort bin), Diffuse (in the Stylize bin), View Finder (in the Video bin). Some of these are, of course, really fun. You could spend all day messing with filter effects.

Filter effects, like speed effects (coming up in the next section), generally take more processing power and time than basic transition effects and titles. To make matters worse, filters can be added to shots that already have filters, and as they stack up, the rendering time can expand dishearteningly. Some of this problem can be mediated by setting up Final Cut to render with lower quality video, but that is beyond the scope of this book.

I'd like to present a very plain filter effect just so that you can see one in action. It's one I use often: Tint.

Basically, Tint converts a color image into black-and-white (technically called *grayscale,* because it has many shades of gray) and then adds a single-color tint on top of the gray. (And believe me, there are a handful of ways to create this result using different filters or color-correction tools.)

Sometimes poor video production value is due to bad lighting, bad color temperatures (yielding odd colors), or mismatched colors between shots. Also, it is the color part of a video signal (called chrominance) *that reveals poorer quality camera technology and image compression. The black-and-white part of the video signal (called* luminance) *will be of higher quality than the chrominance. Thus, in many cases, you can lose the color and increase the* apparent *image quality.*

1. Drag the tint effect from the Effects tab in the Browser and onto a shot in your Timeline, and poof!—the shot looks like one from a black-and-white movie, because the default tint color in this effect is no color.

2. Double-click that shot, and it appears in the Viewer. Go to the Filters tab and you'll see where the Tint filter has landed. If you want to see what the default parameters of this filter are, you can check them here. If you want to change those settings, you also do that here. Tint is nice and simple, with only two parameters (color and amount).

Not too much complexity here on the Filters tab. Tint has only two parameters. Some filters have dozens and dozens of adjustments you can make to customize them. Did I say not to waste too much time with these things? They're so much fun, you can lose an afternoon messing with the controls.

3. You've dropped this filter on the first shot in the sequence. About a 4-second shot. Select Render All.

Tint works in the same way that all filter effects work: It is applied to a shot, and it has parameters associated with it that can be accessed in the Filters tab and, in some cases, animated with keyframes, if you're ready for that work. Of course, we don't need to filter any of these shots, and so once you've checked out what it does, go ahead and undo it. Unless you are in love with the effect and feel like doing it to all the shots in the sequence—and feel like waiting for a big render. On second thought, don't do it.

Again, if you're going to start getting into keyframes and animating effects, I recommend moving to Final Cut Pro. It's not that they can't be done at all in Final Cut Express; it's that they have been made so limited and secondary that it's a struggle to master them in this software. They're far easier in Final Cut Pro.

Filter Effects in Audio

I said earlier that you might have some advanced audio work you'd like to do to a clip: changing its EQ, notching out an unwanted frequency, adding reverberation, and so on. These work in the same way as video filters, and if you have particularly advanced tendencies toward your sound post-production, of course feel free to experiment with them.

Basic Speed Effects

Speed effects are rendered effects you can use to modify the playing direction and speed of a shot. Speed effects are useful when, due to some problem in production (too short shots because the camera-operator was impatient, for instance), you need to fix a shot to make it useful in your sequence.

My favorite uses of motion and speed effects, in order of my tendency to use them, are the following:

- Make too-short shots long enough to use by slowing them down. If you have only 25 good frames of a shot that you think should run about 1.5 seconds, slowing down the good frames can make an acceptable shot out of what would otherwise be garbage.

- Make bouncy, jarring moving-camera shots—which I shouldn't have tried to do without a tripod—more usable by slowing them down. Slower shots with camera movement will minimize the nausea factor.

- Reverse the direction of a shot when I pan or tilt, and letting it move from, say, left to right instead of right to left.

- Create a comic effect by speeding up a shot (by far the rarest of my uses)—what I call the Keystone Cops effect. Making, long boring shots "better" by speeding them up is no replacement for simply editing them, but that's a creative decision for you.

You can apply speed effects to shots already in the Timeline or still in the Viewer. Because speed effects must be rendered before you can see how they look, I don't recommend changing the speed of a clip in the Viewer. But once a clip is just a few seconds long, as cut into the sequence, it's fair game for necessary adjustments.

Let's say we want to make Chris's stunned reaction a little longer, but there just isn't enough material on the source side to lengthen the shot in traditional ways by trimming.

1. In the Timeline, select the shot you think is too fast (or, of course, too slow). Make sure that when you select the shot to modify, you are selecting only the picture part; if you select picture and sound, the sound will get modified, too, and slow (or fast) sound is probably not going to be what you're shooting for. This is one of those times when you want to unlink the picture from the sound before selecting the picture and modifying it.

I unlinked the tracks (see the two separated halves of the Linking control in the top-right corner of the Timeline) before selecting the picture shot I want to modify.

2. Choose Modify > Speed.

Modify > Speed (left) takes you to the Speed dialog (right).

This brings up the Speed dialog, where you can select the amount of the modification and a few other interesting aspects of motion effects.

I focus on the Speed setting, which I would change to below 100 percent to slow something down, or above 100 percent to speed things up. I tend not to use the Duration setting, but you can always enter a precise duration here, and FCE will calculate what kind of speed-up or slow-down is required. The Reverse setting comes in handy once in a while; it changes direction rather than speed—letting the end of the shot be the beginning. Frame Blending is a software adjustment Final Cut can make that improves the look of the rendered shot. I keep it on all the time, but it's most useful at speeds of about 40 percent or less.

Changing the speed of a shot to 50 percent makes it slow down by half, doubling every frame, and therefore the shot takes twice as long to play. That's a significant speed change.

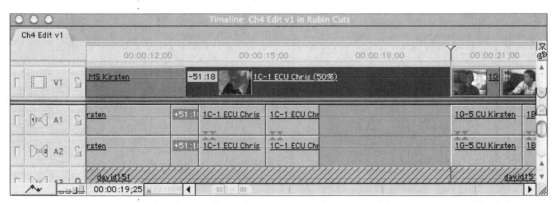

The slower shot of Chris is now longer, and because we modified the picture alone, Final Cut Express rippled the sequence to keep all the following shots in sync with their sound (which is good). The Timeline graphic now includes the amount of speed change (50%).

In our case, slowing down the shot by half makes it a little long, and you'll see when you render and play it that it looks different from the other shots. Only small changes in speed will go unnoticed by viewers (assuming that's what you want.)

3. Select Undo.

4. Choose Modify > Speed again, but this time change the Speed setting to 80 percent.

5. Render again.

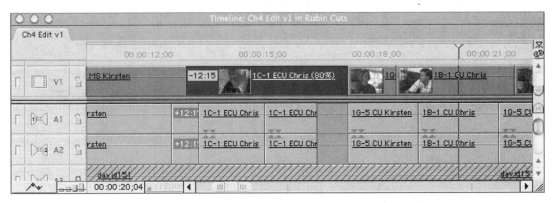

This is a far less noticeable adjustment, and sometimes it's your only option when you're working to wrest a particular feeling from the uncooperative source material.

By the way, if you had performed the speed effect on both picture *and* sound, the sound would have been augmented as well, often with undesirable results—but there would have been no gaps in the Timeline. The alternative we chose was to adjust picture alone. This, however, created a gap in the sound track. The gap is not really a problem, and you can fill it with slug if you want, but it's better to either do a non-rippling trim of the sound or insert some ambient sound, perhaps the same (quiet) sound in the tracks used just before the gap (sometimes called *stealing audio*).

Putting It All Together:
A Title Sequence

Creating a project's title is sometimes more complex than the editing of the project itself. It can be simple, yes, but if you want to try special effects and filters, creating a title sequence is a safe harbor, limited to a short format (5–15 seconds, probably). And while the titles can easily be incorporated into the edit of the main sequence (as we did earlier), it's often more efficient to separate them, since they are built in such different ways.

I do the following for a down-and-dirty, all-purpose opening when I have no time to mess around but I'd like something distinct:

1. Create a new sequence for the title; I call this something like Title Sequence v1.

2. Pick a shot (pretty much any shot).

3. Blur it, by going to the Effects tab and choosing Video Filters > Blur > Gaussian Blur and then select 20 pixels in the dialog. (When you start getting more advanced, try other modifications to this background image from the Video Filters selections.)

4. Make a title card with large, bold, white letters and a 3-pixel offset drop shadow.

5. Find a short riff of music, and drop it under the other tracks.

6. Stack the elements as follows: music (A1, A2), blurred background video (V1), title card (V2). The music should be longest, then the background, then the title.

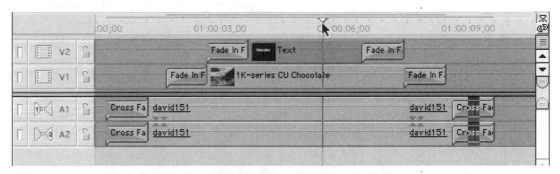

The Timeline nicely shows how the elements are stacked up and when they occur in time. There are so many variations possible, of course, that people make careers simply out of designing and building titles.

The elements should stack up like a little pyramid, so that the order of events is as follows:

- Fade in music.
- Music plays.
- Fade in background.
- A moment later, fade in title and hold it long enough to read twice, slowly.
- Then fade out title.
- Fade out background.
- A moment later, fade out music.

As your desire for complexity grows (and you could save this for your first Final Cut *Pro* project), you might try to animate the titles—for example, animate how they arrive on and exit the screen. You could use different effects on the background, maybe in combination and maybe with different levels of animation over the course of the video. And finally, experiment with the music; it could be an acoustical montage, with combinations of production sound and music fading in and out. You'll start to see why you might want to keep this project self-contained in its own sequence rather than building it on top of your edited sequence.

Adjusting the Final Cut Interface

Once you start building sequences with lots of layers, neither the default interface nor the Standard interface may be your preference. Before we end this chapter, let's look at the ways in which Final Cut Express allows you to modify your work space for the specific kinds of tasks you might be working on. When we started the tutorial we adjusted the interface arrangement so that each Final Cut Express window was in typical editing proportions.

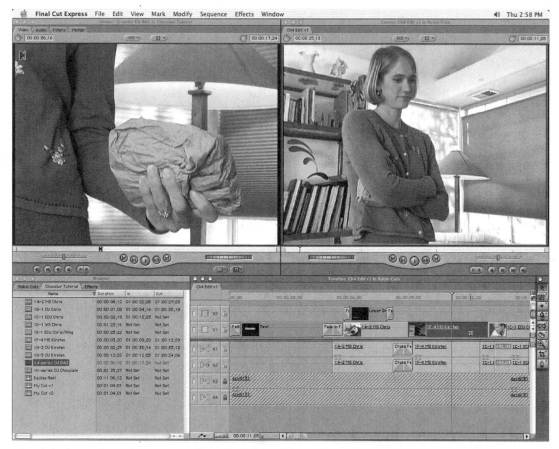

The default Final Cut Express interface has two video tracks and four audio tracks stacked up in the Timeline for starters. This is not ideal, since you really need only one video and two audio tracks most of the time; you can pretty easily ignore the additional tracks if you want. Now that you know all about tracks, the interface isn't nearly as daunting as it might have been before.

But each of the four primary windows can be resized and repositioned (they drag around easily and snap together neatly) according to the kind of work you do, the size of your display, and your aesthetic preferences. There are a handful of variations you might want to consider. Final Cut has a few preconfigured layouts prepared for your editing pleasure, nestled within the Window menu. You can start with those or experiment on your own. I'd like to show you a few of the different screen layouts and how they make different aspects of your work clearer and more efficient.

Formats for Editing

The Timeline is one of the most critical aspects of the editing display. Often, you'll want it to occupy the maximum horizontal space across the screen. Because most movie editors are principally concerned with one (or maybe two) picture tracks and two (or maybe four) sound tracks, their Timelines do not need to get much larger vertically: three to six tracks usually fit nicely in the default height.

If you want to see more than will fit without scrolling the Timeline window up and down, don't forget the Track Height control, embedded in the Timeline window frame, which you can use to enlarge or minimize the track height (the *thickness* of each track).

The Browser, however, can be much smaller. As you may have noticed in prior chapters, the Browser need only list the names of shots to be useful. So my first suggested reconfiguration of the interface resizes the Timeline and Browser:

Above, the standard Final Cut Express interface, showing the Browser and Timeline areas; below, the same areas adjusted a little (by dragging the bottom-right corner to resize each and moving them as necessary)— a pretty useful adjustment for many kinds of projects.

Because of the importance (and sheer quantity) of material the Browser holds on professional projects, Hollywood editors (often working with tens to sometimes hundreds of hours of source material) tend to run two Mac displays at a time, with one display dedicated *entirely* to the Browser. This allows the second display (usually on the right) to show only the Time-line, Viewer, and Canvas.

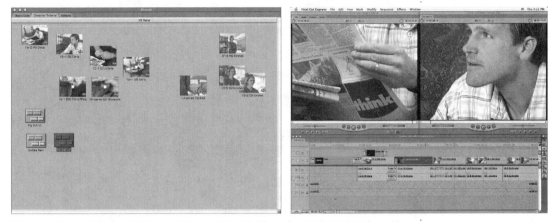

Here are two side-by-side monitors with our Chocoluv Tutorial. When the Browser is used full screen in this way, it becomes more feasible to view the clips as icons, (or sometimes picons—*short for "picture icons").*

Custom Formats

You might want to alter your default interface if you're working on something that specifically demands a different workflow. If you plan, for instance, to use many special effects, the length of the Timeline may be less important than its height, and space for the Effects window becomes more important, resulting in a configuration like this:

Predesigned for you in the Window > Arrange menu is the Wide option, which is pretty good for building composite heavy (lots of layers) effects. Most of the interface is dedicated to the Timeline, a fair amount to the Browser, and two small windows are provided for the video itself. Interesting set of priorities, no?

In the Window menu are options for different prebuilt screen formats, as well as the means for saving two of your own.

Investigate the Final Cut Express-provided layouts first, but on some afternoon when you have time, experiment with the layout you're most comfortable with. Final Cut Express has a convenient way for you to create two custom-configured layouts:

1. Arrange your windows in a way that you really like.

2. Hold down the Option key before you pull down the Windows menu.

3. Select Set Custom Layout 1.

Window		
Send Behind		
Arrange ▶	Set Custom Layout 1	⇧U
	Set Custom Layout 2	⌥U
Tools		
✓ Viewer ⌘1	Standard	^U
✓ Canvas ⌘2	Alternate	^⇧U
✓ Timeline ⌘3	Standard 16:9	⌥⌘U
Audio Meters ⌥4	Cinema	
	Wide	
✓ Browser ⌘4	Dual Screen – Editing	
Effects ⌘5	Dual Screen – 16:9	
Timeline: Ch4 Edit v1 in Rubin Cuts		
Viewer: 1E–1 ECU Chris/Ring in Chocoluv Tutorial		
Canvas: Ch4 Edit v1 in Rubin Cuts		
Browser		

Custom layouts become important when you start to find your own way of working and develop preferences for screen layout. I'm sometimes frustrated by having only two layouts that I can save, but it's not unreasonable; I make one for basic editing and one for either logging (organizing source material) or working on effects sequences.

As you see, you can save only two custom window layouts. I suggest that once you have developed some preferences, make a customer interface for basic editing; save the second one until you get into special effects.

Customizing your interface isn't a one-shot deal; you can continue to refine the way your screen looks as you learn more about editing and take on additional tasks in the post-production process. To change your custom setup, just rearrange the windows the way you want them and then reset your custom layout.

Although fundamental editing concepts and tools can be described in a chapter or two, this chapter barely touches on the kinds of fancy things you can do once you lock in your basic story structure. Remember, though, that effects tend to slow down every part of post-production, due to the increased complexity that comes of adding more tracks (keeping them in sync, knowing what's there, having more objects to keep an eye on at any given time), as well as rendering and rerendering composited materials, filters, and animated changes to shots. This chapter introduced you to the power that adding tracks can create. You now have the foundation for exploring the depth that Final Cut Express affords.

Congratulations! You made it to the end of the tutorial for Final Cut Express, and survived my canned, scripted material. I hope that through all the detail and vocabulary, you've realized that there are actually only a couple of basic editing concepts that you apply and reapply in different ways to perform the craft of editing. It doesn't take much to do a lot. Going through the tutorials methodically may have been hard work. But your reward will be in how you apply it all to your own projects.

Your personal video may not look anything like the tutorial video. No worries. The next part of this book will take you through more practical applications of your skills. It will show how to use Final Cut Express in real scenarios, and ultimately how to apply these theoretical concepts to projects you may find yourself working on.

Becoming Your Own Assistant

No question about it—editing is the fun part. And Final Cut Express makes it pretty enjoyable. But many aspects of post-production work are not quite as exciting: setting up equipment; dealing with technological problems; capturing and organizing materials; and out-putting videotape dubs or DVDs for distribution. Many of these tasks are repetitive, noncreative, and time-consuming. But don't get me wrong: they are also mission critical and important. Mastery of these basic supporting tasks can make your editing enjoyable and go more smoothly. If I had to generalize about these activities, I'd say they are primarily related to either getting video into your Mac or getting it out when you're done.

If you're like me, you probably don't have someone to help you do all the geeky technical and laborious work. But it has to get done. So you'll need to be your own *assistant editor*. There is a great tradition in Hollywood for how people learn about editing: You begin as an apprentice to a professional editor. You fetch the coffee and you get to see the editor work once in awhile. Then, after some time, you might become an assistant editor. Assistants do all the grunt work, including supervising much of the post-production. While the editor is the creative master of the project—the one who makes the aesthetic decisions and generally handles the editing system—the assistant is a critical part of the process. The editor and the assistant are a dynamic team.

Which brings us to you.

The past few chapters have been for editors, about *editing*. Now you'll need to take off your editing hat and learn a little about being your own best assistant.

As your own assistant, your job will be to do the following:

- Organize clips efficiently
- Capture video quickly
- Output your final (or intermediate) cut sequences to digital tape
- Prepare your final cuts for burning to DVD

Managing Video Projects

Your first job as an assistant is to manage the post-production process. What that involves depends largely on the project. The *amount* of material shot for a project is one factor to consider: More material probably means a greater need for pre-organization. The *style* of production is the other factor: It determines how you'll label and retrieve the shots.

It's best to make decisions about labeling and organization before you begin editing. This organizational phase of the project can take a great deal of time, and how much time you spend should be weighed against the total time allotted for post-production. For home projects, I want to spend as little time organizing as possible. For work projects, I don't want to waste time, and I am willing to be a little more methodical; a little labor spent organizing and labeling saves a lot of time if you're sharing materials with other people and while you're editing.

Decisions that you make early on, such as how to label videotapes and how much hard-disk space you need, have an impact down the line on how long it takes to complete your project. For example, although keeping timecode unbroken is work you do while shooting, the consequences of it are felt only in postproduction. You must also consider the trade-off between how long it takes to find video you're looking for (much easier with well-organized tapes) and how long it takes to label and describe all the shots.

Media organization is hardest to do when you're just starting out. I mean, why come up with a filing system or numbering paradigm when you've got only three digital cassettes and this is your first project? On the other hand, you can start with good habits early on, or later you may wish you had. Whether you want to get organized from the start or wait until you have too many unlabeled tapes to deal with and Capture Scratch folders in other Capture Scratch folders inside untitled folders all over your hard drives, here are some techniques you'll need to know.

Continuous Timecode on Videotapes

You saw in the first few chapters of this book how timecode plays a role in the measuring of video clips—lengths, durations, when things occur in the Timeline—but it has a critical role in your ability to use and manage your source videotapes. For videotape organization to work, and for Final Cut to effectively maintain the video process, you should have *continuous* timecode on your videotapes.

In iMovie you never have to worry about timecode; it ignores that number from your videotapes, so you can, too. If you want to, you can set up Final Cut Express to ignore timecode as well. (It's a preference setting.) *But this doesn't excuse you from your organizational responsibilities.* This timecode is for *you*, not just for the computer. In spite of its geeky appearance, it's your friend, and the lingua franca of the professional world.

When you shoot with a digital camcorder, it automatically records a timecode number on every frame, starting at the beginning of the tape (00:00:00;00). When you stop recording and then start recording again at a later time, even if you turned off the camera, the timecode continues on from where you left off. By the time you finish recording on the tape, the timecode has counted unerringly all the way to 60 minutes (or whatever). Now, every bit of video you've recorded on the tape has a unique timecode number.

Even when you stop recording and remove the tape from the camera, then put it back in, the timecode will wonderfully keep on counting from where you left off. There's only one way to mess up this system: rewinding and playing the tape. I'll bet you do this all the time, but it can lead to a problem.

If you watch your tape and play past the end of recorded material, you'll be looking at a frame that is blue and that has no timecode. There's nothing wrong with this (yet), but if you start recording again while you're parked on the blue frame, the timecode counter will start over at zero and you'll have a "break" in the timecode. A gap (even as short as a frame) between segments of recorded material sends the entire organizational process into some degree of havoc. Unless you start recording over a part of the tape that already has timecode, when you start shooting anew, the camera will restart counting.

A tape with broken timecode (if viewed in a hypothetical Timeline) might look like this. After the recording stops, there's a gap of blue—it could be short or long—and then the video starts again, with the timecode reset to 00:00:00;00. You end up with a bunch of shots on the tape starting at :00;00, which is like trying to find something from the index of a book when the page numbers randomly restart at 1.

There's nothing wrong with the video itself, and the timecode that is there will still tell you how long each segment of video runs. But now there are multiple places on the same tape with the same timecode number, and finding shots you want (for you or for the Mac) gets a lot harder. The timecode won't indicate if one shot comes before or after another. For that, you'll have to guess or make detailed notes to yourself. The result of broken timecode is often that you must tediously shuttle tapes back and forth, looking for one shot or another.

Tapes with broken timecode are not a total loss; they can be used, and they can be fixed. Once you understand more about working with your source tapes and capturing video, we'll look at how to use or fix tapes with broken timecode. But from here on out, work hard to keep the timecode on the tape in your camera unbroken.

My number one method for doing this is to remember to *bump* the record button (that is, to shoot some video) after I'm done shooting a project, and before I plan to rewind the tape and watch it. (As silly as it sounds, *bump* is actually the professional term for this.) I either shoot the floor or my hand or nothing (keeping the lens cap on). But whatever it is, it's just 5 seconds or so. That way, when I'm done previewing my tape, as soon as I roll into this garbage material, I can stop the camera and still be parked on a frame with timecode (as opposed to rolling into the blue). Then I can just record from there, without any fancy cuing up or tedious shuttling around.

If you haven't taken the tape out of your camcorder, you can take advantage of a feature that many camcorder models have called End Search. It automatically rewinds your tape and finds the last frame of video you shot, allowing you to restart recording from right there—and thus keep timecode continuous. It's a nifty feature, and tapes with IC Memory can achieve the effect (at a significant price) even if you do remove the tape from the camera. I tend to use the cheaper (non-IC Memory) tapes and opt for recording a little garbage right before I shift into VCR mode or before I remove a tape.

Labeling Videotape Cassettes

The most common problem for people working with video is probably managing the tapes. It may seem obvious to do so, but many people don't use that little label that comes with every videotape—or if they do, they don't write anything useful on it.

Every videotape must be labeled. If you haven't done it before, start doing it now. If you have tapes that are unlabeled, go back and put labels on them.

If you do nothing else organizationally, make sure that all your videotapes are *uniquely* labeled and numbered. But what to write on the label? This is subject to personal preference, obviously, but I have a suggestion that works for me. If this is a tape you shot in your digital camera, put an *S* on it. *S* stands for *source* (or, if you'd rather, *shooting*) tape. It contains the raw material you will put into your Mac for editing. If this is *master material* (the output videos of Final Cut), you could write an *M*. That's pretty much all you need. On the outside chance you also have old tapes you've dubbed into the digital format, label these separately, and use an *A* for *analog material*.

After the letter, add a number. Start with 1 and go from there. (I'm up to tape S113. The videotape I shot for the Chocoluv Tutorial was S070.) This number is technically known as a *reel number* (since cassette tapes are also called *reels*). Three-digit numbers will make for years of videotapes.

Source tapes. I have piles of them. For years I purchased raw videotape in 5-box cases, and used the empty cases to hold the reels. At some point years later I converted to true cassette racks, holding dozens of reels in slots.

There is a strong inclination to name tapes with text labels (Summer Vacation) or a date (9-2003). While Final Cut can handle a range of text reel names, it's difficult to know how to put away tapes with names or dates. And it won't be easy to tell if you're missing one. If you do use text or dates, it's wise to also use a basic reel number described above.

Once a tape has a reel name, you can use it in Final Cut, you can log it, and you can put it on a shelf to use later, at your convenience.

In a few years, cameras might not record on linear video-tapes but rather on nonlinear DVDs. While this will make watching unedited source material pretty easy and will let you store the media more conveniently, it won't change much about labeling the materials. So get in the habit now, regardless of how technology may evolve.

Creating Log Sheets

Once your tapes are labeled, it's a small step to write down on a sheet of paper important notes about what's on each one. I've enclosed a blank log sheet template on the DVD (in the ~Extras folder), but you can design your own based on your needs and experiences.

TAPE # S10

DV LOGSHEET

start time	end time	date	description
00:00		4/23/01	Jonah on floor
4:10			Jen paints toes
6:00			Jonah sleeping
7:00		4/25	Visit T+K
8:00			kids in garden
10:00			flowers
11:00		4/26	BATH!
14:00			Uncle Jeff arrives
15:30			Surf Trip to lighthouse
18:00			drummers @ beach
18:10			waves
20:00			Jeff surfs
25:00		5/10	Plant Garden
29:00		5/14	Plaster hands/feet for Grandma

My log sheets are simple but useful: The reel number is on top. The body consists of a timecode reference point (primarily just the minutes part—round off the seconds and skip the frames), the date shot, and a quick little note about what the material is. No need to put a lot of work into describing individual shots, just regions of material.

Writing notes on the tape label itself is problematic; the label is small, and you have to pull the tape off the shelf to review what's on it. In contrast, when making notes on a simple sheet of paper, one page per tape, you have ample room for whatever information you want to write down, and pages are easily managed together in folders or binders.

When you hit a critical mass of log sheets, you could move them from a folder to a binder with divider tab pages.

I flip through the pages of log sheets looking for a particular piece of video and then quickly fast-forward to that spot on the tape, and play it for myself or friends. With no log sheet, you might never find bits of video recorded in the past, except by accident some time when you least expect to.

Shot Names in Scripted and Unscripted Projects

All video projects fall into one of two categories: *scripted* and *unscripted*. Each type of project will direct you toward one or another method for naming and organizing the material you shoot.

Unscripted projects are shot in a news or documentary style. They have little or no planning (no scripts, no storyboards), little or no production tools (no tripods, boom microphone operators, or light kits), and probably no actors. There are no slates and no scene names, and there is no obvious way to label and organize the project. In these cases, shots themselves can be organized by the date you shoot them (for example, "04-15-02 morning") or simply by serialized numbers (such as "shot 01"), which represent entire tapes or large parts of tapes.

Scripted projects, whether a video for work or school or even the Chocoluv scene we've been working on, must be highly organized before the shoot. They involve some degree of pre-production, shot planning (maybe storyboarding), and on- and off-camera talent. For these projects, the editor's connection to the shoot is often through the script, lined with notes from production. We looked at a lined script on the Chocoluv Tutorial in Chapter 2. Scripted material means unique scene names and discrete planned shots, and it will likely be logged and broken down into individual takes (again, as was done for the Chocoluv Tutorial). In the end, you label shots in Final Cut so that you can easily find and access each one as needed, based on scene and take numbers.

Two typical slates: on the left, one of our Chocoluv markers; on the right, a slate from a feature film. While you may not use slates for syncing picture and sound, the data on them is important for keeping material organized and will be used to tag this video through the entire process.

The tradition for scripted projects is to use some kind of visual slate during the shooting so that you can quickly find where each shot starts on the tape. You'll also have some data on the slate so that once the shot is separated from the tape, you'll always know what it is and where it came from. The shot-naming system must be standardized and consistent throughout the shoot. When you're creating log sheets, you may use these names there, too (although I tend to use a more general scheme for the paper log sheets and leave the detail work for the computer). A classic scene-naming method is to use the scene number followed by the take number, separated by a hyphen (or occasionally a period or underscore). Thus, Scene 1, Take 5 is "1-5" or sometimes "Sc 01-5," although the *Sc* is somewhat superfluous.

Name	Goo	Description	Reel	Length	Au
5-1/1		CU COOK reveal CHARLIE	007	00:00:41:17	48
5-1/2		CU COOK reveal CHARLIE	007	00:00:14:27	48
5-1/3		CU COOK reveal CHARLIE	007	00:00:19:02	48
5-1/4		CU COOK reveal CHARLIE	007	00:00:26:00	48
5-1/5	✓	CU COOK reveal CHARLIE	007	00:00:19:16	48
5-1/6		CU COOK reveal CHARLIE	007	00:00:21:12	48
5-1/7	✓	CU COOK reveal CHARLIE	007	00:00:24:20	48
5-1/8		CU COOK reveal CHARLIE	007	00:00:13:26	48
5-1/9		CU COOK reveal CHARLIE	007	00:00:16:11	48
5-1/10	✓	CU COOK reveal CHARLIE	007	00:00:35:08	48
5-1/11		CU COOK reveal CHARLIE	007	00:00:21:10	48
5-1/12	✓	CU COOK reveal CHARLIE	007	00:00:21:29	48
5-1/13		CU COOK reveal CHARLIE	007	00:00:20:22	48
5-1/14		CU COOK reveal CHARLIE	007	00:00:17:15	48
5-1/15		CU COOK reveal CHARLIE	007	00:00:20:28	48
5-1/16		CU COOK reveal CHARLIE	007	00:00:11:18	48
5-1/17	✓	CU COOK reveal CHARLIE	007	00:00:20:16	48
5-2/1		WS COOK looks around	007	00:01:17:05	48
5-2/2		WS COOK looks around	007	00:00:51:16	48
5-2/3	✓	WS COOK looks around	007	00:00:52:24	48
5-3/1		CU CHOP onions	007	00:00:29:12	48
5-4/1		CU Onions pan to WS CHARLIE	007	00:01:07:08	48
5-4/2		CU Onions pan to WS CHARLIE	007	00:00:33:11	48

Here's a Browser bin for Scene 5 in my feature film; notice that the setups in Scene 5 are labeled 5-1, 5-2, and so on, with the take number after the slash. Scene 5-1 has 17 takes! It's a good thing you're seeing this in list view—17 icons of the same scene would look pretty much the same and would be basically useless for figuring out which one I want to use.

Managing Disk Space

When organizing the move from videotapes (and someday DVDs) onto your Macintosh, the first thing you may want to consider is the total amount of source material compared with the hard-drive space available. To have a "proper" editing experience, you want to have enough room on your computer to fit all the source material.

If all the video can't fit, you have two options: Either do a pre-edit and *selectively* capture material (a sort of linear edit before the nonlinear edit) or add external FireWire hard drives to increase your storage capacity. Hard drives continue to drop in price, with current hardware running about $2–$3 per GB (which translates into maybe $25 of disk space for every 1-hour DV cassette you use). This would be my recommendation; if you want a project to be simple, make sure you have the hard-drive space to hold all the source material for your video.

As my feature film project expanded during a long production schedule, I added new external hard drives to meet the demand. By the end of the shoot there were five 120 GB drives strung into the Mac.

There is a third option: Use Final Cut Pro instead of Express. Final Cut Pro offers a lower (offline) resolution feature, which lets you trade high-quality DV resolution (at 4.5 minutes per GB) for sub–VHS-quality Photo JPEG resolution (at 45 minutes per GB). However, this adds more steps, more work, and more chances for mistakes, and is rarely the ideal solution. You're better off sticking to DV resolution in Final Cut Express and keeping your projects controlled to fit in the hard-drive space you have available—in most cases it will be plenty.

Media Files vs. Data Files

Digital video makes for large computer files—as you've seen, 1 GB of hard-disk space holds less than 5 minutes of video. When digital video (and digital audio, for that matter) is stored on a computer, the file is known as a *media file.* But media files alone are not functional units for editing. In fact, you can't edit with media files. You need something else—a bit of information in your project—that understands and can find your media files. Having a fuller grasp of these kinds of files and how Final Cut deals with them lets you move projects between Macs, revisit old projects, or fix problems in current projects with comfort.

When Final Cut Express creates a new project, the project is a repository of all kinds of data (sometimes called *metadata*) about media files. *But a project is not a media file.* Neither is a clip or a sequence. A clip (the object in Final Cut that most resembles a media file) is a tiny data file that is *linked* to a media file.

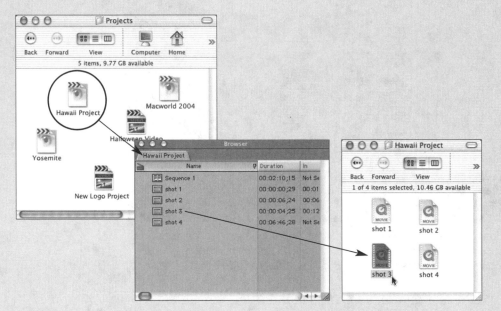

It's important to recognize media files, project files and clips, and how they are related. On the left are some project files (some from Final Cut Pro and some from Final Cut Express) on my hard disk. One is from my trip to Hawaii. In the middle is the Browser in that Hawaii Project, filled with clips. These clips are connected to large media files. On the right is a folder on my Mac holding the media files (notice that the icons denote the QuickTime format) associated with the clips in the Hawaii Project Browser.

Collections of Final Cut data files, which we know as *projects,* are relatively small. All the data (the Final Cut project file) for my recent 15-minute annual retrospective video amounted to only 350 KB, though the associated media files nearly filled a 40 GB hard drive. The full-length feature film I cut in Final Cut Pro had 40-plus hours of video on 600 GB of hard-drive space; after I labeled everything and put together a number of versions of the entire film, the project file was still only around 10 MB.

continues on next page

Media Files vs. Data Files *(continued)*

Here's a big idea: *A clip can exist without a media file connected.* (Say this out loud a few times and think about what it means.) When a media file and a clip lose their link, the clip will remain in the Browser with a red line through it—it's then called an *offline clip.*

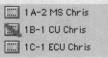

A clip icon with a red line through it is offline—as in not connected to a network. This state should not to be confused with offline editing and offline resolution, which are completely different.

A clip could be disconnected from its media file because you've renamed the media file, because the file has been moved, or because it has been deleted from the computer. If it has simply been moved or renamed, it can be relinked to its clip by selecting File > Reconnect Media (then you'll have to go find it!). If it's completely gone, you can recapture the clip by dragging it into the Capture window.

When a clip is unlinked from its media file after editing, the Timeline denotes the missing shot by "whitening" it. It also puts a red bar above the Timeline indicating that something needs rendering (which I think is kind of a dumb waste of rendering energy).

If you go ahead and play a sequence with missing media files, this unmistakable warning shows in the Canvas. Reconnecting the clip to the media file fixes everything. But you have to connect not only the clip in the Browser but also all the disconnected shots used in the Timeline.

As long as you have the Final Cut project file, you can always re-create all your work from source tapes or move the project from Final Cut Express transparently into Final Cut Pro. (This is a departure from the way iMovie works—with iMovie, you can't revisit old projects after their media files have been deleted.) It is critical to keep project files safe and backed up. Lucky for us, this is easy because they are so small. Media files do not need this kind of special care. As important as they are, they are de facto already archived on the source videotape they were captured from. When you are done with media files, you can delete them from your hard drive with reckless abandon.

Creating New Projects

When you create a new project, two actions kick into motion: the creation of a project file (which has to be saved somewhere on your hard disk) and the creation of a handful of folders for the media and render files that Final Cut expects to arrive shortly. These all must be strategically placed if you expect to find them again easily. If you don't name and place them, Final Cut will assign them default names and locations—which is fine if you're just starting out, but it could be an organizational problem in the long run.

You can use a number of organizational strategies with Final Cut Express, each dictated by the particulars of the project. This is my own quick-and-dirty method of basic organization for personal projects.

1. Select File > New Project.

    This opens a new, untitled, and unsaved project.

2. Select File > Save Project As.

    In the dialog, navigate to the hard drive where you will keep your projects. (Note: The default location of these files is the Documents/Final Cut Express Documents folder, but if you change the default, it's easy to lose them.) I keep project files and media files separate, on separate drives. My projects reside on my main drive, and media is generally on a large external drive. For the moment, we're saving only the project.

3. Now name your project and click Save. The project file will be stored where you indicated.

But you're not done yet. Now you need to establish a pathway from your camera onto your media drives. If you don't adjust the pathway, the default directs video to your system drive—the drive with the OS. This may be OK if you're just starting out or messing around, but for a variety of technical reasons, your system drive isn't a great place to maintain the *mega-*superenormous media files (each of these files is usually 1 or more GB, and probably the biggest file your Mac has ever seen).

1. Select Final Cut Express > Preferences.

Final Cut Express	
About Final Cut Express	
Preferences...	⌥Q
Easy Setup...	^Q
Services	▶
Hide Final Cut Express	⌘H
Hide Others	⌥⌘H
Show All	
Quit Final Cut Express	⌘Q

2. Select the Scratch Disks tab.

The Scratch Disks tab is important and not intuitively obvious in how to work. Final Cut insists that there always be at least one drive on your Mac selected as the destination for your media files—and if you don't pick one, it does. But you can Clear the default selection, and Set a new one. And you can have more than one. It will fill up the first it comes to, and then move on to the next—so you also might change the order of drives in the list. When you pick a drive, Final Cut Express will automatically create three folders there for media. They are:

- Capture Scratch—For source video and audio media you've pulled from tapes
- Render Files—For video render files the program creates invisibly when you are executing special effects, for instance
- Audio Render Files—For audio files created for you when Final Cut Express deems it necessary

Preferences

General / Timeline Options / External Editors / Scratch Disks \

Video Capture	Audio Capture	Video Render	Audio Render			
☑	☑	☑	☑	Clear	Set...	71.4 GB on Drive75
☐	☐	☐	☐	Clear	Set...	<None Set>
☐	☐	☐	☐	Clear	Set...	<None Set>
☐	☐	☐	☐	Clear	Set...	<None Set>

Waveform Cache: (Set...) 33.8 GB on Alpha-X/Users/mr/Documents/Final Cut Express Documents

Thumbnail Cache: (Set...) 33.8 GB on Alpha-X/Users/mr/Documents/Final Cut Express Documents

Autosave Vault: (Set...) 33.8 GB on Alpha-X/Users/mr/Documents/Final Cut Express Documents

Minimum Allowable Free Space On Scratch Disks: 10 MB

☐ Limit Capture/Export File Segment Size To: 2000 MB

☑ Limit Capture Now To: 30 Minutes

(Cancel) (OK)

Once you've set your scratch-disk path, you generally don't need to come back here. Your media files will be stored in the Capture Scratch folder on the drive you set here. The names of the automatically created folders, you may notice, will match up with the checkbox columns in this tab.

I've made this mistake: When you start your second project, it is not uncommon to mess things up by changing your scratch-disk path from (in this case) Drive75 to Drive75/Scratch Disk. You end up with scratch folders inside other scratch folders, ad infinitum. You pick the drive or the folder, and Final Cut will either find the proper scratch folders or create them.

Now that these preliminary items are set, you're ready to work. When you capture material from DV tape, it will automatically go into the Capture Scratch folder. The clips you work with in the Browser will be linked to the media files in this folder. When you're done with a project, the media files in these three folders can be purged (I just drag them to the Trash).

I say three folders, not four, because the default for Final Cut is to keep video and audio together on the same drives. You can tell it not to, but separating audio from video during capture is not recommended with DV, so keep them together and therefore use only three folders (video and audio both go into the Capture Scratch folder).

As you edit, Final Cut may need to render effects for you (all the dissolves, composited shots, titles, and the like that we created in Chapter 4). Final Cut Express will then automatically create, name (very cryptically), and place the effects in the Render Files folder. Ditto for special sound work that needs sound rendering, although the files are placed in the Audio Render Files folder.

● ● ●		jens.plates	

Name ▲	Date...ified	Size	Kind
Cut v2–FIN–00000016	3/14/03	3.4 MB	Final ...vie File
Cut v2–FIN–00000017	3/14/03	3.4 MB	Final ...vie File
Cut v2–FIN–00000018	3/14/03	3.4 MB	Final ...vie File
Cut v2–FIN–00000019	3/14/03	3.4 MB	Final ...vie File
Cut v2–FIN–00000020	3/14/03	19.6 MB	Final ...vie File
Cut v2–FIN–00000021	3/14/03	8.8 MB	Final ...vie File
Cut v2–FIN–00000022	3/14/03	8 MB	Final ...vie File
Cut v2–FIN–00000023	3/14/03	3.4 MB	Final ...vie File
Cut v2–FIN–00000025	3/14/03	3.4 MB	Final ...vie File
Sequence 1–FIN–0000000a	3/14/03	3.4 MB	Final ...vie File
Sequence 1–FIN–0000000b	3/14/03	3.4 MB	Final ...vie File
Sequence 1–FIN–0000000d	3/14/03	1.8 MB	Final ...vie File
Sequence 1–FIN–0000000e	3/14/03	472 KB	Final ...vie File
Sequence 1–FIN–0000000f	3/14/03	3.4 MB	Final ...vie File
Sequence 1–FIN–00000007	3/14/03	3.4 MB	Final ...vie File
Sequence 1–FIN–00000008	3/14/03	3.4 MB	Final ...vie File
Sequence 1–FIN–00000009	3/14/03	64.7 MB	Final ...vie File
Sequence 1–FIN–00000010	3/14/03	33.9 MB	Final ...vie File

(Window toolbar: Back Forward View Computer Home Applications Projects. 1 of 24 items selected, 10.52 GB available)

You will probably never need to go looking around in the Render Files folder—if you do, most of these filenames will make no sense. They are automatically named, and Final Cut Express knows when to use them even when you don't.

Caveat: This is a tidy way to organize everything you need, but as the volume of captured video grows and grows, the disk you have selected may get full. The Scratch Disks tab of Preferences has locations for other disks to be added (using the "Set" button in each row) so that when one is full, Final Cut automatically moves on to the next (assuming that you have more disks or available partitions). If I expect my video to exceed the space on one disk, I create a similar set of folders on the other drive and set the pathway (as we did in the second part of the above assignment).

The Scratch Disks tab in the Preferences is important to understand. It directs where media files are stored on your Mac. I tend to put my largest drives first and try to avoid using space on my system drive when possible.

Finally, when my project is done, I move it to a special folder containing all my finished-and-now-offline projects. I always keep these small but important project files safely backed up to protect my work.

Input: Capturing Video

It used to be that getting video into your computer involved *digitizing* analog video from tape. The process of digitizing is almost identical to what you do today in Final Cut when you capture: The video still must be moved in real time from a linear medium (the tape) into a nonlinear medium (the computer's hard disk).

In many ways, capturing video is a little like editing video. You mark In and Out spots on a length of "source" videotape where there is material you want to keep (in this case, video that you want to have available for editing). If you want to change the In point, you will probably roll the tape to a better spot and mark the new location. This can take a long time—rolling around, shuttling here and there, finding places to mark In and Out points, and then moving on. (It's not quite as bad as the old linear videotape-editing systems, but it's close, and it certainly gives you a sense of what editing used to be like.)

The Capture Window

You capture video using a special tool in Final Cut Express: the Capture window, which you access from the File menu.

There are a couple of key features to this window:

On the left is the big window where your videotape will play; beneath it are tools for controlling the digital video camera that is connected to your Mac. They look like the usual video transport controls, but they aren't simply moving digital files around—this time they're physically controlling the FireWire-connected digital camcorder. Before you can do much in the capturing department, you must make sure your camera is connected and communicating with Final Cut Express.

Tape Preview area   Available space and time   Videotape's "source" timecode   Data about the clip being captured

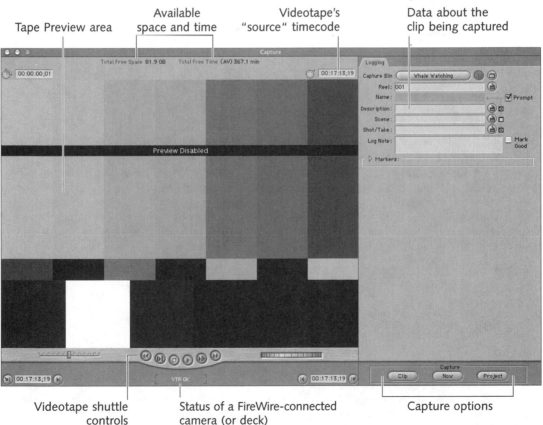

Videotape shuttle controls   Status of a FireWire-connected camera (or deck)   Capture options

iMovie rolls this screenful of info and controls into the main display, which is clever—but in Final Cut you have more options for how to label, organize, capture, and play your video, so you might need a little more space.

The Mac-Camcorder Connection

If you tell Final Cut Express to go to the Capture window and you don't have a camcorder hooked up and ready to go, Final Cut Express will balk—it understands (as should you) that precious little capturing is going to happen if your camera isn't ready. If it's not, the first warning you get will look like this:

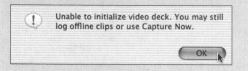

If you are OK with this and press further, you'll get another warning:

Pushing through these is fine if you're just snooping around, but you are going to want to connect your camcorder, turn it on, set it to playback mode (or VCR mode, or the like), and probably put a tape in it (although this isn't required for Final Cut Express to open the Capture window). While you're at it, it's a good idea to have your camera connected to a power source (that is, plug it in) so that it doesn't run out of juice in the middle of a big capture.

Even if, for some reason, Final Cut Express were communicating properly with your camera when you selected Capture, the cable could still could get disconnected (on purpose or by accident) at some point prior to capturing. (For example, I've mindlessly turned off my camera to save the battery, or on other occasions, the camera has simply run out of battery power while I've been working.) If for any reason the Mac-camcorder system is not hooked up and working property, you'll see this message:

"No Communication" is just one of the little messages that keep you informed on the status of your tape deck (which in most cases is your camcorder). "No Communication" is the one I least like to see (it means there is a technical problem, as opposed to a more benign message like "tape threading").

continues on next page

The Mac-Camcorder Connection *(continued)*

This is a problem and the cause could be one of many. Remember, your camera must be connected via FireWire, and the camera must be turned on and set to VCR mode. If you plug in your camera (or turn it on) *after* launching Final Cut, and the Capture window says that the camera is not communicating properly, begin troubleshooting by closing the Capture window and then returning to it. Every time you launch the Capture process, Final Cut Express rechecks for the camera (the message "Initializing Capture" will appear).

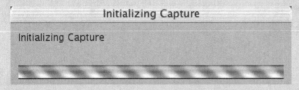

This "Initializing Capture" moment is giving your Mac an opportunity to look around, see what's connected, and make sure everything is OK.

If you close the window and then reopen it, and it still isn't giving you control, you could relaunch Final Cut Express—but that probably isn't the problem. It could be hardware related (your camera; the cable) or software related (a problem with Final Cut Express control protocol for this make or model of camera; external video is off or missing; a Final Cut Express glitch). Try disconnecting and reconnecting your camera. If you have one, try a different camera or cable. As a last resort, restart your Mac (still with your camera turned on and connected to the Mac with a FireWire cable). If that doesn't work, seek help from tech support from Apple and/or your camcorder's manufacturer.

Before you begin capturing, what you want to see is this:

When it says "VTR OK," you should be able to play, pause, and rewind the cassette in the camera using the Final Cut controls, and the color bars in the preview window will be replaced by video images. You won't be able to see the camera's built-in timecode (or *data code*—the time, date, and other camera information the videotape invisibly records) displays over the picture in Final Cut Express, even if you see them on the LCD of the camera. But the timecode should be visible in the Current Timecode field at the top right above the image.

Even if the timecode is visible in your camera (left), you won't see it during capture in Final Cut Express (right). But it's being read and can always be found in the Current Timecode field (on the upper right). Notice how the timecode on the camera matches the (circled) display in Final Cut Express.

Below the video frame is the familiar array of transport controls for play, stop, and so on—the keyboard shortcuts work for controlling the camera as well. There are a couple of other buttons at the bottom left of the window, but we are going to ignore those for now.

At the right side of the window is a tab for your logging information (the metadata we referred to earlier). It contains reel number, description, notes, and so forth. This data is what Final Cut knows about a media file. When you organize, search through, or sort clips, you're using the information entered here.

When clips go into the Browser, they're going into the Capture Bin—a *conceptual* folder (you can't see it) that we have simply been referring to as "the Browser." If you do nothing to change it, clips you put in the Browser are kept at this most basic *(root)* level. But you can create folders in the Browser to help organize material. These folders are also Capture Bins, and you can have bins in bins, if that's the way you want to set things up. On small projects it's unnecessary to use any Capture Bin but the root. What you'll see in the data side of the Capture window is that the Capture Bin is listed—the default being the root level (which it auto-enters as the name of the project).

All this bin-root-log-capture stuff may feel complicated, but don't sweat it. Final Cut has default settings for everything, and if you never learn about it, the world will not end, your shots will be placed in the Browser just fine, and you'll never be the wiser.

Loading a Tape and Entering Information

Capturing is about getting the material from the digital tape into the computer. Since Final Cut Express can read the time-code on the tape, you're spared the tedious job of typing time-code numbers as part of this capturing process. But there is one piece of data Final Cut Express *does* need you to enter: the reel identification. Everything else is superfluous for the novice (unless you have the time and inclination).

I harp a lot on this reel-number thing. It's so simple and so important, but because Final Cut inserts a default number in this field, it's easy to skip. Entering a reel number is the only way to let your computer know what tape you're using. With a reel number and a timecode number, editing software can *understand* every shot you use, even if you manipulate it, move it around in the computer, or delete it (and if you delete it, a reel number enables you to get it back pretty easily!).

On the left are the default settings for a new project. Compare them with the simple capturing setup on the right: Only the Reel field is filled in, and it remains unchanged for the entire tape. That's not too much work, is it?

When you eject a tape from your camera, Final Cut Express is watching. And when you put a tape back into your camera, Final Cut Express sees that, too—and prompts you to enter the all-important reel number it suspects has changed.

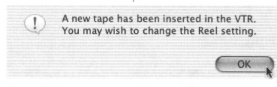

A new tape has been inserted in the VTR. You may wish to change the Reel setting.

OK

Final Cut Express knows that you've changed the tape and is urging you to enter a new reel number.

Whether the project is personal or professional, I do not enter scene or take numbers or any description of the clips I capture. For personal video projects (such as sequences of your aunt's wedding or a colleague's retirement party), with no scripts or slates, I am capturing every bit of video I shot for a given scene. In the time it would take me to organize this material, make notes, and break it down into small clips, I could have spent an hour actually editing. For scripted projects, or work videos, I sometimes enter scene and take information as the shot name. Then, if I enter basic description info, I only do it later, while editing or as part of the process of screening of material before editing. That's when you really familiarize yourself with your source material, and it's a good time to jot down descriptions or notes if you feel you need them.

Capturing Options

With all the necessary information entered (and that means "not much"), you can turn your attention to the buttons on the bottom right. Final Cut Express has three options for capturing your video: Clip, Now, and Project. We're going to mostly ignore Project and focus on the two you're likely to use often.

Clip is what you use to log and then capture in two short steps. Using the Capture window, you shuttle your videotape around, find where you want a shot to begin (mark an In), roll through it until you see where you want it to end (mark an Out), and then click Clip, which—after you give the clip a name—instructs Final Cut to rewind the tape, grab this media, and stop when it's done.

Clip is best when the quantity of material you want to use from a tape is significantly smaller than the tape as a whole. Say you're shuttling through your tape and you want one shot from right here. Or there are a few 15-second shots on the tape you need to get, but they are separated by large

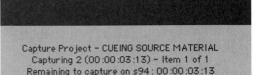

Capture Project – CUEING SOURCE MATERIAL
Capturing 2 (00:00:03:13) – Item 1 of 1
Remaining to capture on s94: 00:00:03:13

spans of time. Or there's really bad timecode on the tape, and you must be careful when you capture to miss those broken spots. But even then, I hardly ever use Clip—it puts a lot of wear and tear on my camcorder and tape, and takes significantly longer than other methods.

The Project Option

Final Cut Pro doesn't have *Project* but instead has an option called *Batch*, which is in many respects the same thing. You use Project when a tape has been logged and then all the media files associated with that tape have been removed from media drives; clicking the Project button regenerates all the media files and reconnects them to the clips. You use Batch when youre coming into the capturing process with a Browser full of clips with red lines through them, indicating they're not connected to anything—yet. Project automates the process of capturing all these shots again.

In my book (and this is my book), the capture option of choice for Final Cut Express is *Now*.

When a tape is rolling along, clicking Now starts capturing within a second or three, with no In or Out point selected— and no prerolling or cueing up or anything else. Just real-time, live grabbing of video. And it doesn't stop until you stop it, by pressing the Escape key (Esc).

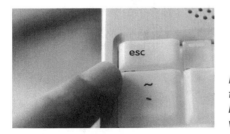

Press Esc to drop out of your capture. You might think the space bar, or return, or some other key would work, but you'd be wrong.

Even with only a vague idea of what is on a tape, and with unbroken timecode, it's easy to get your video captured into Final Cut Express and ready for work. Using the Now option you can suck a 30-minute tape into the computer in about 30 minutes (as compared with 40–60 minutes using other methods).

Then you can divide the long clip or clips into *subclips* for easier access, if you like. I treat my video in the computer much as if it were video on the physical (linear) tape—but with instantaneous (nonlinear) random access. For documentary-style projects, I don't know what I need or how I'm going to organize it at the get-go. By capturing long clips, I have that speed and flexibility. It's not right for everybody or every project, but often it's ideal.

Warning: When you capture using Now, there are two possible problems to be aware of. First, there's often a delay between the instant you click Now and the time Final Cut actually kicks into capture mode (usually related to your hard disk's being in an idle, resting mode and needing to warm up). Since your video is playing before you hit the Now button, there can be a difference of many frames between the time you want to start and the moment when capturing actually begins; the difference can even be many seconds long! Capture via Now is a crude method that assumes you can afford sloppiness. That's one reason I don't start and stop capturing frequently, preferring instead to grab the videotape in large chunks. For more precise capturing, you really have to use the other capture options.

Second, Final Cut Express works best with unbroken timecode. If you expect to be rolling into zones on your tape that have no timecode (a break, a discontinuity, a blue gap), you can set up Final Cut Express not to abort the capture when it occurs (but even then, when you stop the capture, it will warn you that the timecode is bad and you should recapture).

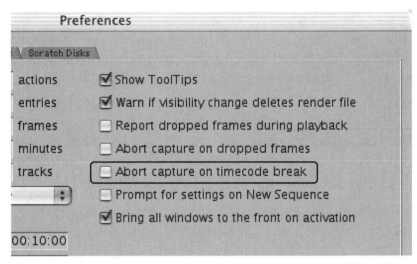

If you want to capture from a tape with broken timecode, you'll need to go to Preferences > General and tell Final Cut Express not to stop capturing if it sees a break in code. If your tapes are full of gaps, just uncheck this and forget about it.

If you edit with the clip anyway, the software will work, the source timecode will be problematic, and you will have problems if you need to recapture this clip for any reason (which may or may not concern you, but it is important to consider). I have also sporadically seen glitches in my captured video following a break in timecode, including picture and sound running out of sync from each other and the video itself disintegrating into noise and garbage. Unless you're prepared, don't use Capture Now if your timecode is spotty or sporadic on the source tape—but frankly, you shouldn't be using tapes recorded in this way.

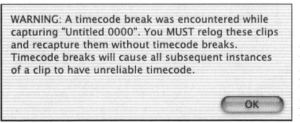

If you go ahead and capture a clip with bad timecode, Final Cut Express will grab it, but you'll get this ominous warning. In spite of what it says, you can probably use it for your purposes, but as I've pointed out, there could be problems down the road.

USING TAPE WITH BROKEN TIMECODE

Using Final Cut's clip-capture functions, you can surgically extract bits of video off a tape containing broken timecode. You'll miss a few seconds here and there, but it's not a total loss.

The problem is that if Final Cut Express doesn't see timecode on the tape while it's looking for something, it will get lost. You can manually control the camera to stop Final Cut from scanning in the wrong direction for the frame it's looking for, but you still need to mark In frames and Out frames to capture material in regions of the tape where it will not bump into a frame without timecode. This means marking points far enough from the timecode gaps that prerolls (when the camera backs up ahead of an In point to get a running start before capturing) will not hit them. And even then, you should keep your eye on the camera and capture before something unusual starts to happen.

FIXING A TAPE WITH BROKEN TIMECODE

If being this careful during the capture process strikes you as more laborious than you'd like, your best alternative is to dub your old source tapes to new tapes and in the process fix the timecode. Since few of us have two digital cameras sitting around to do a dub (and a special 4-pin–to–4-pin FireWire cable to connect them), I'll tell you how to manage it with one camera and Final Cut.

1. Make sure your General Preferences are set to allow you to capture video with broken timecode.

2. Rewind your tape to the head.

3. Start capturing (Now) at the head of the tape (well, near it anyway—you have no choice but to miss some of the video at the very head), and grab the entire tape as one big file, timecode warts and all.

   A 60-minute tape requires less than 15 GB of available hard-disk space, which is a lot but usually less than an editing system's minimum configuration.

4. After you capture the video, record it all out onto a new tape (File > Print to Video; or check out the upcoming section on Master Tapes).

During the recording the camera generates new time-code, and it will ignore the timecode problems sprinkled throughout the source.

Naming and Saving Clips

Rolling through your video and capturing on the fly using Now will place your media into the Capture Scratch folder, and it will also place this unnamed clip in your Browser. (This is, by the way, unique to Final Cut Express—a definite improvement over Final Cut Pro v3.) You still should take a moment to name it.

I like the way Final Cut Express drops clips in your Browser as soon as you've finished capturing them. They'll go in Untitled, but take a moment to give even a short, simple title to each. The clips will reshuffle to sort alphabetically by name as a default, but you can click the head of any column to make that the field the Browser will sort by.

My clip naming is crude at best. For personal projects—more documentary in style—I try to create as few clips as possible. Consequently, the clip names are simply sequential numbers, like "part 1" and "part 2" or "1 clip" and "2 clip" (this sometimes makes it easier for the Browser, which sorts alphanumerically, to place the clips in the order in which they appear on the tape).

While I might be tempted to use names like "good stuff" and "sunrise," these names will sort in ways that may make them harder to find. And since the source clips are long, trying to summarize the contents of each is usually futile.

Final Cut Express has many sophisticated tools for searching for material, but they are all predicated on entering key information in the metadata fields—on *logging* the video in the computer. To find all the shots with a sunset in them, for example, you would first have to have separated all the sunset shots (or marked points within shots) and entered the word *sunset* into the associated description field. While this is good for complex documentaries, it is overkill for short projects.

On projects with actual slates, or even those without slates but with discrete scenes or takes that I want to maintain separately, I still capture as described above (using Now)—in large chunks (sometimes as long as entire tapes)—with little regard for the divisions in the content on the tape. Once the tape is in the computer as a big clip, I break the clip into smaller units for working. Because these clip subsets are called *subclips,* I call this *subclipping*. It's a fine method of continued clip naming and organization beyond the work of capturing.

SUBCLIPS AND BINS

Once you've got a clip in the Browser, you can always select a portion of it to be a subclip—effectively a new clip, but one that has an identity related to the master clip from which it was spawned. Creating subclips is easy—about as easy as marking a shot.

Modify	
Make Subclip	⌘U
Remove Subclip Limits	
Make Freeze Frame	⇧N
Link	⌘L
Stereo Pair	⌥L
Mark in Sync	
Duration...	^D
Speed...	⌘J
Levels...	⌥⌘L
Audio	▸
Composite Mode	▸
Alpha Type	▸
Reverse Alpha	

1. **1.** Mark In and Out points in a clip that denote the material you'd like to be a subclip.

2. **2.** Go to the pull-down menu Modify > Make Subclip. If you do this enough—as you might if you had many tapes to subclip for a giant project—I'd recommend using the keyboard shortcut Cmd-U.

3. **3.** While the original clip is unaffected by this process, you'll see a new clip in the Browser, with a slightly different icon representing it.

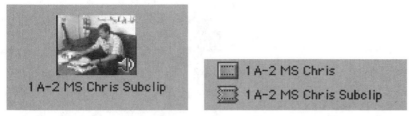

Subclips in icon view (left) don't look any different from the master clip from which they were created (although "Subclip" is appended to the name). In list view (right), however, they have fun little jaggy edges. Yet another advantage of the apparently-boring-yet-useful list view.

Once you have your subclips, you can rename them and leave them shuffled into the Browser, or you might choose to create special folders for the kinds of material you are managing in your project. These Browser folders are called *bins*. You can have as many bins as you'd like in the Browser, and you can have bins within bins, if that works for you.

File		
New Project	⌘E	
New	▶	Sequence ⌘N
Open...	⌘O	Bin ⌘B
Close Window	⌘W	
Close Tab	^W	
Close Project		
Save Project	⌘S	
Save Project As...	⇧⌘S	
Save All	⌥⌘S	
Revert Project		
Restore Project...		
Import	▶	
Export	▶	

To create a bin, select File > New > Bin. The option is only available when the Browser is active.

Now you can drag clips, subclips, or any items you want into a special space to facilitate your personal organizational strategy.

On a feature film I recently worked on, I had a bin called Raw Tapes (for entire tapes captured as clips), and I had bins for each scene. After I subclipped a tape, I moved the tape clip into the Raw Tapes bin, and moved the appropriate subclips into their respective scene bins. In the end, I had bins for every scene in the film, and inside those I had all the subclips I needed to edit the scene—without regard for what tape the shot came from. I also had bins for my sequences.

Here's a Browser full of folders (called bins*) for each scene, and within each bin are all the shots I needed to edit that scene. While this is for a feature film with upwards of 40 hours of source material, the organizational method is the same as for smaller (or larger) projects.*

Importing Music from CDs

For reasons I don't fully understand, getting music from a CD into your Final Cut Express project is harder than in either iMovie or Final Cut Pro. It's a two-stage process that I will outline here. Hopefully, this will change in future versions.

Importing is not really like capturing; it's how you get still images and graphics files into your project, as well as how you pull in music files. We imported the tutorial files in Chapter 1. Now we'll go through the steps for getting music from a CD in your Mac's disc drive. In the title of this section, I'm using the term *importing* loosely; before you can import the file, you have to do some work.

1. Insert the CD into your Mac's disk drive. It will launch iTunes automatically, which is good. If for some reason it doesn't, go ahead and launch iTunes.

	▲	Song Name	Time	Artist	Album
	1	☑ Seventeen Again	4:55	Eurythmics	Peace
	2	☑ I Saved The World Today	4:53	Eurythmics	Peace
	3	☑ Power To The Meek	3:18	Eurythmics	Peace
	4	☑ Beautiful Child	3:27	Eurythmics	Peace
	5	☑ Anything But Strong	5:04	Eurythmics	Peace
	6	☑ Peace Is Just A Word	5:51	Eurythmics	Peace
	7	☑ I've Tried Everything	4:17	Eurythmics	Peace
	8	☑ I Want It All	3:31	Eurythmics	Peace
	9	☑ My True Love	4:45	Eurythmics	Peace
	10	☑ Forever	4:08	Eurythmics	Peace
	11	☑ Lifted	4:49	Eurythmics	Peace

If you're connected to the Internet, iTunes will automatically check a big online database for the names of your songs and other data about this album. I've inserted the Eurythmics' Peace album. If the database didn't identify the CD, tracks would be listed as "Track 1," "Track 2," and so on.

2. Make sure that iTunes is set up to import AIFF files, 16-bit, 48 KHz. If not, go to the Preferences and adjust the import settings.

Fix your settings in the Importing dialog (left), which you open from iTunes' Preferences. Don't forget to customize the AIFF settings for 16-bit sound at 48 KHz sampling: Choose AIFF Encoder from the Import Using pop-up menu to open the AIFF Encoder dialog (right). Sampling at 44.1KHz is common for CDs, but 48KHz is the default for DV and Final Cut.

3. Select the song you want to get from your CD.

4. Choose Advanced > Convert Selection to AIFF.

Advanced	
Open Stream...	⌘U
Convert Selection to AIFF	
Consolidate Library...	
Get CD Track Names	
Submit CD Track Names	
Join CD Tracks	
Remove Audible Account...	
Convert ID3 Tags...	

iTunes
Importing "Forever"

		Song Name	Time	Arti
1	☑	Seventeen Again	4:55	Eury
2	☑	I Saved The World Today	4:53	Eury
3	☑	Power To The Meek	3:18	Eury
4	☑	Beautiful Child	3:27	Eury
5	☑	Anything But Strong	5:04	Eury
6	☑	Peace Is Just A Word	5:51	Eury
7	☑	I've Tried Everything	4:17	Eury
8	☑	I Want It All	3:31	Eury
9	☑	My True Love	4:45	Eury
10	☑	Forever	4:08	Eury
11	☑	Lifted	4:49	Eury

Once you've established your preferences, the "Convert Selection to . . ." option in the Advanced menu will be completed with "AIFF" as opposed to, say, "MP3." Immediately after you choose this option, the selected song will begin to import. When it's done, the check box next to its title will have a green check in it.

All of this is just part one: how to get a song off a CD and into your Mac. Unless you've jiggered with the path settings in iTunes, this AIFF file is placed in your iTunes music folder ([system drive] > Users > [your log-in] > Music > iTunes > iTunes Music). That's where we will go to get the song and import it into Final Cut Express. You're done with iTunes at this point.

In Final Cut Pro you can import directly from a CD into Final Cut without the iTunes step. However, there are some potential problems with such directness—regarding sampling rates as well as media file linking. In order to eradicate the common mistakes, Apple just wiped out the functionality entirely from Final Cut Express.

1. Select File > Import > Files.

File	
New Project	⌘E
New	▶
Open...	⌘O
Close Window	⌘W
Close Tab	^W
Close Project	
Save Project	⌘S
Save Project As...	⇧⌘S
Save All	⌥⌘S
Revert Project	
Restore Project...	
Import ▶	Files... ⌘I
Export ▶	Folder...
Capture...	⌘8
Reconnect Media...	
Voice Over	
Capture Project...	^C
Print to Video...	^M

2. Now navigate to the iTunes folder where the file was placed, and select the song.

Remember that if iTunes didn't identify the CD, the artist and album names will be "Untitled," and the song will be called "Track 1" (or something similar).

Choose a File

From: 📁 Peace

Compilations ▶	Peace ▶	🎵 10 Forever.aif
Eurythmics ▶		
FreePlay Music ▶		
Unknown Artist ▶		

Show: Standard Files

Go to:

(Add to Favorites)   (Cancel) (Choose)

AIFF

Kind: Document
Size: 45.5 MB

If the CD and songs are titled, this search is very easy. When you reach the song itself, you'll see this friendly AIFF file icon (right). A magnitude of 44 MB is typical for a song in AIFF format. MP3 compresses files more and creates songs that are closer to 4 MB in size.

Once you select the song, a clip appears in your Browser *representing* the media file it has located. Remember, Final Cut isn't moving the sound file—it's still in your iTunes folder—but now some data about it (the clip) is part of this project. If you move the song, the connection might be disrupted, as with any media file. Don't move these around.

As you can see, importing sound files from a CD is really no different from importing any media files (JPEGs, MP3s, TIFFs) into Final Cut Express.

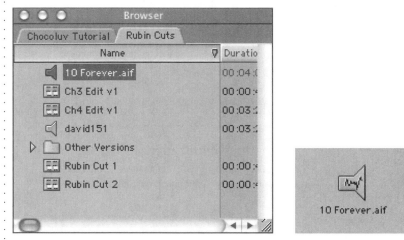

Success! The song has completed its journey from the CD to your Browser. Here's the icon in list view (left) and in icon view (right).

Output: Finishing Up

As the assistant, you captured quickly, on the fly, with only a reel number in the data fields. Next you slipped on your editor's hat and cut the material as you saw fit, refining it and making a few versions. Then you added music and titles and some basic effects. Now you're done. Here it is, still in the computer, but done. It's time to call in the assistant again to back up your work, master the final sequence to digital tape, and get everything ready for burning a DVD for your friends.

The Master Tape

A project isn't done until the final video is recorded in its high-quality DV format back to a master videotape. As I mentioned, I use different tapes for source material (which I shoot) and master material (which represents different cuts of the project). Now it's time to get an M tape, label it, and put it in your camera.

1. Label a master tape ("M1," for instance) and insert it into your camcorder, which should be connected to your Mac running Final Cut Express.

Nice and neat—a bunch of my master tapes in a box. Notice how all of them are locked, for their protection. Hey, where's my M1 tape?

2. On the tape cassette itself, make sure the REC lock slider is at REC so you can record on the tape. Whenever I pull a master tape from a camera, I always immediately switch the lock to SAVE.

The REC lock slider in recording (left) and save (right) positions.

By this point, you should be beyond all the warnings about your camera connection (which we went through on the front end of the process) while capturing; output to tape is kind of like capturing, but just in the other direction. Communication still must be established for these things to work.

3. Select File > Print to Video.

Print to Video is a crude-but-effective method for getting video out of Final Cut Express. In short, it formalizes the crude process of pressing Record on your camera and Play on your Mac. Final Cut Pro lets you place the recording at a precise timecode location on the tape, but Final Cut Express assumes that this degree of precision is not required for the amateur. Missing some functionality here is not a big deal, but in this case Final Cut Express is feels sort of primitive.

When you select Print to Video, the dialog by the same name appears; it allows you to set up certain add-ons to your sequence without really adding them to your sequence (if you follow me). When Final Cut Express plays your cut for recording purposes, it can add a countdown, color bars, tone, black slugs at the beginning and/or end, a generic title card, and so on, none of which show up in the sequence (or Timeline).

I keep the Print to Video settings very simple: a 15-second black leader at the head and tail. This ensures that if I ever want to get the video back off the tape and into Final Cut, I'll have handles from where I can easily start and stop capturing. The black also gives a solid space between this sequence and the next one on the master tape. By the way, in Final Cut Pro, this dialog is called Mastering Settings.

If your video is going to be dubbed to lots of other tapes, VHS tapes in particular, adding color bars and tone is a good idea. If you're going to send the video to anyone, a little title slate is also a reasonable addition. The traditional information for a title card is (a) the title of the video, (b) your name, and (c) the date.

I've changed the Print to Video settings to include a title slate (left). It's not an amazing titler, but it will do to label a video. On the right you can see the title as it appears in the output—it's pretty small in the center of the display.

You can play around with these settings for your own amusement. Many people, for fun, enjoy seeing a countdown before their project begins, or want to have a few seconds of color bars, but neither of these is necessary. I do insist on two basic settings: 15 seconds of leader (Black) before your video begins, and 15 seconds of leader after it ends. (Can you use 20 before and 20 after? Of course. Anything less than 10 seconds is probably too little; anything more than 30 is probably too much. When I'm in a funkadelic mood, I use 15 seconds at the head and 30 at the end (the *trailer*). This guarantees that your project is always neatly sandwiched between some useful chunks of black for easy access in the future.

Of course, by recording with ample black around sequences, it is easy to keep timecode continuous even on master tapes. By starting the next recording during the black leader at the tail of the sequence, the overlap guarantees a nice continuity of code.

4. Before you start recording, make sure you are viewing the right sequence (open it in your Canvas and double-check that it's active). Note that it isn't mandatory to output the entire sequence. If you want only a part of it, mark an In and Out within the sequence, and set the recording media in the Print to Video dialog to In to Out. If you don't have any marks in your sequence, the default In and Out points are the beginning and end of the sequence, and thus Final Cut will record the entire thing. If you are not sure whether you have marks there (and don't want to mess with this), just set the media to Entire Media and you'll get it all no matter what.

If you're making a tape for a loop—as for a presentation in a retail store or trade show—that you don't want to have to rewind every 5 minutes, set that up in the Print to Video dialog as well. Set how many times you want it to repeat and the amount of time between loops.

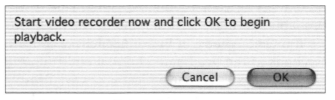

5. With all these settings established, you're ready to click OK. You'll be prompted to start the recording from your camcorder (or VCR—whatever is attached). When you are confident that the tape is playing and the camera is recording, click OK.

> Start video recorder now and click OK to begin playback.
>
> ⟨ Cancel ⟩   ⟨ OK ⟩

Final Cut Express will start playing your sequence the way you've indicated in the settings. I tend to watch the process (as opposed to leaving for awhile) just to make sure that nothing sticks or obviously messes up. The Esc (Escape) key stops this recording just as it does with Capture.

Recording your master to tape is the last step in the editing process. With a master version on tape, you can always choose to capture just the cut and make any adjustments to it you want (shorten it, change titles, compress to some as-yet-unreleased format). When you put a sequence on tape, you'll lose the separation between shots. It's now just one big clip as opposed to an edited sequence with discrete shots that can be trimmed. This is bad if you really want to re-edit, but it's great if you want to handle your video as a single element, for compression or for inclusion in some other project.

What to Record

In most cases all you really need is the final cut of your project, mastered to this master tape. But coming from a professional background, I have a hard time leaving it at this. I generally record at least one other variation of the project at this time. Because I sometimes revisit projects and want to make some adjustments, I save a version without titles, music, or effects—a *titleless master*—on the master tape as well. The edits are the same, but if I want to make small adjustments (tightening only), or change music or titles, this is the video I'll start from. It can be easier than reconstituting the entire project from the source tapes and project files (although that is always an option in Final Cut).

Along with the final cut and the titleless master, I sometimes keep an older version of the cut—usually the first cut—a version that is not so much edited as culled. This also provides a better starting point, should I want to revisit the project, without having to go all the way back to raw footage.

Finally, I sometimes place a final cut on a master tape that's separate from the one I have been recording on, so that I have two copies on separate reels, just in case there is ever a technical problem with one of the tapes. I do this only for very important projects, but it provides some peace of mind.

Of course, when I'm really in a rush, and the project is just for fun, I make only the one final recording and leave it at that. You'll have your own sense of risk and importance of the work you do.

File

New Project	⌘E
New	▶
Open...	⌘O
Close Window	⌘W
Close Tab	^W
Close Project	
Save Project	⌘S
Save Project As...	⇧⌘S
Save All	⌥⌘S
Revert Project	
Restore Project...	
Import	▶
Export	▶
Capture...	⌘8
Reconnect Media...	
Voice Over	
Capture Project...	^C
Print to Video...	^M
1 Chocoluv Tutorial	
2 Rubin Cuts	

Final Cut Movie...
QuickTime...

Exporting

Once the video is on the master tape, and before you start deleting media files, you might have a use for a few of Final Cut Express's convenient export options. All the export tools let you make some kind of digital file on your hard disk that is built from the work you have done.

There are two export options—Final Cut Movies and QuickTime—and each has a number of permutations. I will outline the three exports I use most.

QUICKTIME MOVIE (FOR WEB OR CD-ROM)

Save

Save As: Ch4 Edit v1.mov

Where: ▦ Desktop

Format: QuickTime Movie ▸   Options...

Use: Default Settings

Cancel   Save

If you choose Export > Quicktime, you'll get this Save dialog. The default format is for a QuickTime movie (.mov format), but this isn't always the format I'm shooting for. There are lots of possible QuickTime formats.

Ultimately, if you want to stream your video on the Internet, email it to a friend, or put it on a CD-ROM, you need to have a compressed version of your cut. The bandwidth required to play a DV-quality movie is high and the files are large. Compression will decrease the image quality (either a little or a lot, depending on the compression scheme and parameters you decide on), but it prepares the video for easy distribution.

If you do want to make a QuickTime movie, you'll still need to adjust the settings for your particular use. From the File > Export command, choose QuickTime. The default is a Quick-Time movie. Click Options to open the Movie Settings dialog.

Movie Settings

☑ Video

(Settings...) Compression: Video
(Filter...)   Quality: Medium
(Size...)   Key frame rate: 24

☐ Allow Transcoding

☑ Sound

(Settings...) Format: Uncompressed
                 Sample rate: 44.1 kHz
                 Sample size: 16
                 Channels: 2

☑ Prepare for Internet Streaming

[Fast Start ▾] (Settings...)

(Cancel) (OK)

Getting the Movie Settings correct for what you want to export is not a minor issue. Both Video and Audio (sound) need to be individually adjusted, and each has numerous variables. I find doing compression far more challenging than any of the editing work it took to get here.

Video compression is reasonably complicated. There are a host of methods for compressing video: you can make the image smaller (your digital video has 720 by 480 pixels in an image); you can decrease the number of frames presented each second (DV uses 30 frames per second); and there are many mathematical algorithms, called *codecs* (for compressor/decompressor)—such as MPEG-4 and Sorenson—that can work on the problem, each with different pros and cons.

Compressing video is its own expertise, and as with production issues like lighting and sound, it goes beyond the purview of this book. But I will scratch the surface here to get you into the process.

First of all, know that it isn't enough to call video "Web" video—how much you'll want to compress a project depends on how it needs to be received. Delivery over a 56K modem requires far more drastic minimization than is required for broadband connections like DSL and cable modems.

CD-ROM on the other hand, offers a far greater delivery advantage—bandwidth is not limited as it is for the Internet, and videos needn't be burdened with the added pain of downloading.

Not all video compresses the same! If you are making a video that you know must be delivered in a compressed format, either over the Internet or on CD-ROM, then there are a number of practical matters you can do in production and post-production to improve the quality of the video specifically related to how well it can be compressed. For instance, solid color backgrounds and non-moving subjects compress better than mottled backgrounds and moving subjects. (This also applies to moving cameras. So use a tripod and no pans). Titles should be larger. And keep the transition effects (wipes, fades) to a minimum—they don't compress as well.

In all cases, however, QuickTime videos must be played in QuickTime players on the computer of the recipient, and your codec and compression strategy must take into consideration the version of the player. QuickTime 6, for instance will play an MPEG-4 compressed movie, but earlier QuickTime versions do not; the Sorenson 3 codec sometimes doesn't produce as good-looking output as the MPEG-4 codec, but the videos it generates will play in older QuickTime v5 players. See?

To generalize this process and introduce you to some of the elements of compressing video, let's make a (somewhat typical) MPEG-4 video for a QuickTime 6 player.

1. Start with Video. Click on the Settings button (in the Movie Settings window) for video to bring up the Compression Settings dialog. Near the top of the window is a pulldown menu with a list of compression options. Select MPEG-4.

If you just want to make a DV file, identical in quality to the one you started with, you can select DV/DVCPRO-NTSC (or -PAL if you live overseas in a PAL nation) and you won't lose any resolution in your QuickTime movie. Don't compress the sound, and don't select Prepare for Internet Streaming.

The Compression Settings dialog for MPEG-4 Video.

Animation
BMP
Cinepak
Component Video
DV – PAL
DV/DVCPRO – NTSC
DVCPRO – PAL
Graphics
H.261
H.263
JPEG 2000
Motion JPEG A
Motion JPEG B
MPEG-4 Video
None
Photo – JPEG
Planar RGB
PNG
Sorenson Video
Sorenson Video 3
TGA
TIFF
✓ Video

Here are your video-compression options. Freak you out a little? It should. The best compression settings for a given bit of video is often deter-mined experimentally, and there are more precise tools than Final Cut Express for doing this, such as QuickTime Pro or Media Cleaner Pro.

2. In the Compression Settings dialog, set the quality you want. The slider in the Quality box is macro control, but the finer tools are down in the Motion box. Set the slider as high as you'd like, but then adjust the Motion settings. Here are reasonable values to enter:

> **For broadband Internet:**
> Frames per second: 15
> Key frame every 150 frames
> Limit data rate to 25 Kbytes/sec
>
> **For CD-ROM**
> Frames per second: 30
> Key frame every 300 frames
> Limit data rate to 100 Kbytes/sec
>
> For both Internet and CD-ROM you will likely want to make the video frame size smaller as well.

3. Click the Size button in the Movie Settings window.

4. Select Use Custom Size.

5. Enter new dimensions for your frame.

   320 by 240 (a quarter the screen size of DV) is common for compressed videos for CDs and Web, but you'd need to go smaller for those who have modems.

You make a video 1/4 its original size (and data rate) by shrinking the frame to 320 by 240.

6. As for audio, go to the Sound settings and select MPEG-4 Audio.

For broadband Internet:
22.05KHz
16-bit
Mono

For CD-ROM
32KHz
16-bit
Stereo

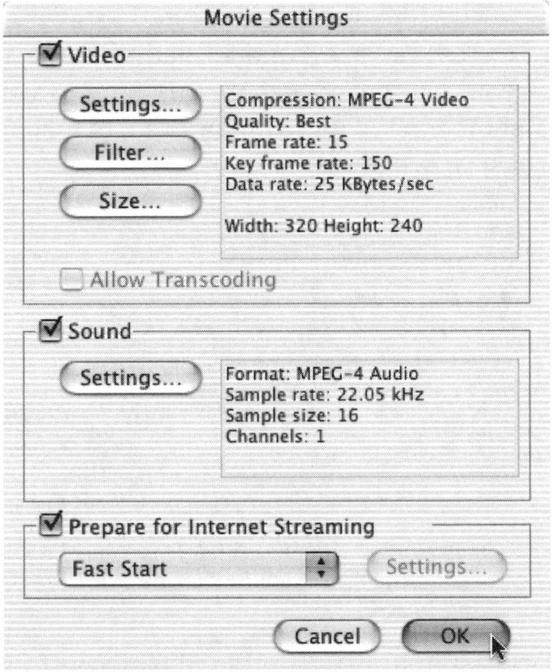

When you're done with all the settings, the Movie Settings window will summarize your choices. When I click OK it will generate a .mov file with these settings for the web.

A 45-second video in DV takes up about 165MB on a disk; compressed for a CD (with the above settings) the same video would take up less than 5MB and only 1.4MB for the Web. If you aren't sure if your recipient has QuickTime 6, you might opt for the Sorenson 3 codec, with comparable settings as described here.

Remember that these aren't your only options (far from it), and a key factor is the overall bandwidth your video needs to play as compared to the bandwidth of the viewing medium. Another factor is how large the resulting movie file is (some Web servers will balk if you deliver a file more than, say, 10MB). Experimentation is about the only way to get the right combination of codec, frame rates, frame sizes, and so on, to maximize the quality of your finished video.

EXPORTING STILL IMAGES

When you're parked on any frame—whether in the Viewer or the Canvas—you can always export this frame in the active window as a photograph, for use on the Web, to mail to friends, to put in books, or whatever.

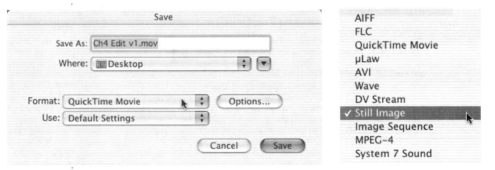

Another Export > QuickTime; the default setup is to export a QuickTime movie, which needs to be changed if you're making still images. Click Options and select Still Image.

The QuickTime > Still Image option allows you to select the image format (JPEG, TIFF, and so on) and give the frame a name. But before you jump into this, I offer three warnings.

First of all, be careful of the default formats. Final Cut Express v1 defaults to a PNG image file. If you want a JPEG, TIFF, or some other format, remember to adjust this.

Second, Final Cut Express never mentions that the resulting image will be a little distorted from the way it looked in video. If there's any movement in the frame, you'll see distracting scan lines. This is because what you think of as a *frame* of video is really two *fields* of video (effectively two half frames).

When there is very little movement in the frame, this may not pose a problem, but with considerable motion, the two fields may contain very different images, and the combined image will look odd. You can make a still image of the frame in Final Cut, apply the De-interlace filter (Video Filters > Video) to the still image in the Viewer, and then export the still image in the usual way. Or you can export first, and then use photo-manipulation software (like Adobe Photoshop) to de-interlace these scan lines. Neither method is elegant, but at the same time, neither is that difficult.

Before de-interlace (left) and after de-interlace (right).

The third problem is the shape of the video frame. I won't get too technical here, but the pixels in the video onscreen are not square; they're actually a little rectangular. So when you export an image file from DV videotape and look at it on a computer (where pixels are square), the 720-by-480–pixel image will get stretched. To compensate for this distortion, your image-manipulation software will need to squeeze the image into its original aspect ratio of 4:3, converting a 720-by-480 image into a 640-by-480 image.

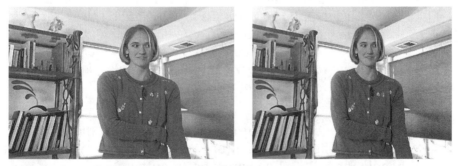

Before resizing (left) and after resizing (right).

After de-interlacing and resizing the exported file, it will look about the same as the original video frame.

MAKING DVDS

Video DVD is not an archiving format; it is a distribution format. The compression used to make DVDs (MPEG-2) may be remarkable, but it reduces the quality from where you started on DV. The quality decrease is often subtle, and even on a DVD you'll see a video that is comparable to (or better than) VHS tapes. It's just that after spending all that money on a digital camcorder (particularly if you bought a high-quality 3CCD camera), it seems a pity to reduce the quality of your product. In any case, you always want to keep the highest quality master you can (which is why you *finish* your project on DV tape).

With a Mac, there are principally two DVD-burning options: iDVD and DVD Studio Pro. DVD Studio Pro offers many professional DVD features, like interactive menus, unlimited numbers of clips within the disk size limit, and a wide range of design flexibility. For professional DVD creators, this is the way to go, but I find most of these features unnecessary for my business and personal DVDs—in particular when compared with how much time these features take to create. Consequently, I use iDVD for all my disc-making needs. It works very intuitively and is very drag and drop.

Don't confuse copying to a DVD and "making" a DVD. If you want to drag a video file to a DVD and save it there, you are just doing a big file copy—about a 20-minute process for 4.3 GB of data (the limit on common DVDs). But burning a video DVD involves a complex mathematical compression; 1 hour of video might take 2 or 3 hours to prepare and record.

All iDVD requires is that the video dragged to the DVD window be in the QuickTime (or Final Cut) format—then it will handle the MPEG-2 compression from there.

File

New Project	⌘E
New	▶
Open...	⌘O
Close Window	⌘W
Close Tab	^W
Close Project	
Save Project	⌘S
Save Project As...	⇧⌘S
Save All	⌥⌘S
Revert Project	
Restore Project...	
Import	▶
Export	▶	Final Cut Movie...
Capture...	⌘8	QuickTime...
Reconnect Media...	
Voice Over	
Capture Project...	^C
Print to Video...	^M

Save

Save As: Ch4 Edit v1

Where: ▦ Desktop

Include: Audio and Video

Markers: None

☑ Make Movie Self-Contained

Cancel   Save

If you want to make a DVD, the ideal option is Export > Final Cut Movie. If you choose this, you'll see the Save dialog on the right.

Export > Final Cut Movie is a convenient feature that outputs the discrete bits of video placed together in edited sequence as a single neat file. The resulting file is virtually indistinguishable from the original video in your sequence, because it's an exact bit-for-bit duplicate of the DV data that was on your tape and is in your source media files. If you select Make Movie Self-Contained, then you'll sit around for a while while Final Cut Express generates a new digital media file, at 4.5 minutes of video per GB. If you're making a DVD, this is not necessary. Unselect the Make Movie Self-Contained option, and Final Cut Express will make a tiny file that *points* to the media it used to make your sequence in the first place.

Save

Save As: Ch4 Edit v1

Where: ▦ Desktop

Include: Audio and Video

Markers: Chapter Markers

☐ Make Movie Self-Contained

Cancel   Save

I don't usually rename these movies, particularly when I'm going to iDVD, as I can rename them in iDVD as needed. With Make Movie Self-Contained unselected, the only real decision I have is about the markers. I use mine as Chapter stops.

Making a Final Cut Movie results in the creation of a small file, which is easy to drag into iDVD. (I start with these files on the Desktop.)

If Your Video Is Archived on DV Tape

If you've mastered a sequence to a DV tape and the media is no longer on your Mac, use the Capture function to bring in the video from your master tape as a single clip. Pay attention to where you save the clip on your hard disk—I make it easy for myself by saving it to the Desktop (or to a folder called DVD Sources) when I'm bringing in old material for disc burning. The media file (which is in the QuickTime format) for this clip can be dragged directly into iDVD if you want.

Sometimes when I bring in an old video, I see a few things I'd like to cut out before burning it as a disc. While I don't want to re-edit, I might want to tweak a title or fade here or there. Once you bring a video into Final Cut Express and revise it, you have to export it as a Final Cut Express movie as we did above.

If you simply want to take a video and make a DVD out of it, it's pretty easy. But in time you may have lots of videos, covering a range of years, perhaps, and you will want to put certain groups of videos together on specific DVDs. To manage this process, I also use Final Cut Express. As you have more and more finished projects, making DVDs can be as arduous an organizational process as editing. Here's what I do:

1. Make a Final Cut Express Project called DVD Mastering Project (or something like that). Keep it around for all your DVD-preparation needs. (Even when you delete media files, keep the project for your ongoing DVD mastering.)

2. As you build more and more master tapes, you will find that they become your *DVD source tapes*. Capture parts of these tapes into this project. I place all these raw clips into the Raw Tapes bin in the Browser.

3. Create a sequence for each video. This entails using the raw clip as the source; trim it down to just the part you want to burn to disc. It also allows you to precisely determine the total running time (TRT) of the video. I put the title of the video and TRT in the name of the sequence (see the figure).

4. Create bins for each DVD you are working on. I label DVDs the way I label tapes: MD1, MD2, and so on (MD stands for "Master Disc").

5. Drag sequences to the bins as you decide which videos you want on which discs.

6. Now you can export Final Cut movies for each sequence and place these in your DVD Sources folder on the Desktop. Keeping them there makes them easy to drag and drop to iDVD.

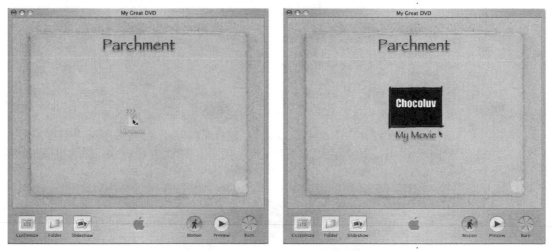

Just drag QuickTime movies or Final Cut Movies directly to the iDVD interface, rename them, find a poster frame (if you want), jigger with the template, and then burn the DVD. Note: If your media exceeds 60 minutes, iDVD automatically increases the compression, which *decreases* the quality of video on the DVD. As a general rule, therefore, I keep my DVDs at under 60 minutes of video.

Drag the finished movie file (QuickTime or Final Cut movie) directly into iDVD and let go. Not much easier than that.

The specifics of using iDVD and all its neat little features are beyond the purview of this book, but iDVD is so easy that you can probably work it out with little coaching.

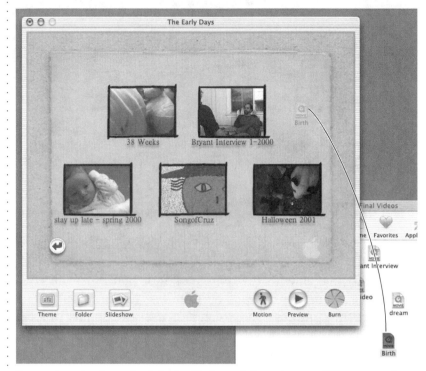

Drag a bunch of movies into iDVD, format them to your liking, even drag them around and rearrange them on the display. If you have more than six movies, you'll need to make a folder for the overflow.

Backing Up

When it's all over, I keep only my project files and throw out everything else. Project files are very small and unassuming files; they can be used to recapture all the video from source tapes, they can rerender all the needed render files, and they can be moved from computer to computer with ease. If you've used some still-image or music files, you may want to back those up in the same folder with your project file, since they can't be recaptured as easily. Another trick is to drag your Favorites folder from the Effects tab to the project tab before you save your last project version. Otherwise, Final Cut Express will lose track of them.

I not only keep a folder on my Mac that holds all my old projects, but I also periodically burn a backup of this folder on CD-R. I burn all my important personal files now—I used to use Zip disks, which are plenty big, but CD-Rs are convenient these days. However you choose to back up, I'll say only this: *Don't forget to do it*.

Putting It All Together

Apple has always specialized in keeping the geek factor to a minimum. Where geeks will want you to talk about your bandwidth, the compression choices you use, and the GHz in your CPU, editors—like most consumers—just want to make videos with as little hassle as possible. Now you know enough to handle both the editing and your own assisting.

I think that professionals, when teaching consumers, overemphasize all the assistant stuff. Organization is important, and if you have the time, it is something that really should get done. But aside from gaining some rudimentary knowledge and practicing some efficient behaviors, logging and organizing should be kept in check, and editing should get your maximum attention.

All the film school practice in the world is of questionable use when facing the daunting world of shooting a Little League game or your first training video for work. So as we leave behind the basics of editing and assisting, let's take one last chapter to see how this knowledge works in new ways when we apply it to the kind of videos we often encounter (or want to approach) in the "real world."

Your Video Projects

You know how to edit a movie now. *You really do.* Or a corporate training video or television commercial or, of course, your personal videos. There is a lot more to learn about Final Cut Express, but with the solid foundation you have developed in the earlier chapters, you can learn the software in more detail at your own pace. You'll learn lots of shortcuts and maybe a couple of interesting tools. But those are largely bells and whistles. As it is, you already know how to edit most kinds of video projects.

But what are your projects? Now that you know how to organize and edit video, what might you do with it? I'm going to depart from the tutorial and software instruction to address how you move from the controlled material of the tutorial to the vagaries of the real world. You probably already have a camcorder, and maybe piles of tapes sitting around waiting for you to finish this book. What can you do with those? We'll go into how to salvage problem footage that might seem unusable. Or you may have projects you've been hungry to attack once you understood editing; this chapter offers some tips on how to get good coverage and how to deal with the kinds of audio problems typical of personal projects. And finally, now that you are a video expert (of sorts), a world will open up to you as you see all the myriad ways you can apply your skills— we'll finish this chapter with a few ideas for the application of video skills for fun, work, and school.

What's in Your Camera Now?

I don't want to scare you, but it's going to be challenging to edit material you shot before you learned about editing. Sometimes it's best to put this old material on the shelf and start fresh, maybe not revisiting the old tapes until you have more experience and confidence in your editing abilities. There's little worse than the discouragement that comes of attempting a project too big and too complicated when you're just starting out.

I would suggest approaching your old material with three points in mind: (1) Your tapes may be unlabeled and scattered around your house; (2) the timecode on those tapes may have gaps (*breaks*) in them; (3) the coverage you shot may not be appropriate for editing in the way we practiced in the tutorial.

Is this what your tapes look like? Before you decide this is a lost cause, take an afternoon to start applying your organizational skills here, and see how far you get.

First, put labels on all your old tapes and give them each a unique reel number. Then log them on individual log sheets (as we did in Chapter 5). This is good right up until you start running into breaks in the timecode.

Remember that if there are gaps in the timecode, logging the tape and finding material on it (also covered in Chapter 5) will be challenging. But if you overcome these obstacles, you can get the video into Final Cut and try to make something concise and enjoyable from it.

Not having good coverage—just lots of random shots (and not very good ones at that)—is a bigger obstacle. Editing can vastly help to make the video more watchable, but there is only so much you can do. The most dramatic, and easiest, thing to do would be to *cull* the videotape down to a smaller pile of video. After that, you might combine bits of this tape with others and then make a moving slide show from it. Let's look at each of these options in a little more detail.

Culling It

As you learned in Chapter 2, with only the Razor Blade tool and Ripple Delete, you can roll through your video material and delete the really bad, hard-to-watch parts. Culling is sometimes your best option with old tapes—tapes recorded with incomplete coverage. If you drop the weird camera moves, lens-cap footage, shots of your feet as you walk, and moments when you didn't realize the camera was recording, will make more enjoyable videos.

The top image shows how I chopped up a big hunk of video with the Razor Blade tool. Below, I used the Ripple Delete function to throw away the bits of garbage. Actually, I kind of faked this picture—when I'm really culling, I chop and throw out as I go.

I sometimes use iMovie instead of Final Cut Express to do my culling. While iMovie doesn't have a razor blade tool per se, you can always drop an entire tape into the Timeline and use the Split Video Clip at Playhead tool (Command -T) to chop up the video. Then it's easy to switch from the timeline viewer to the clip viewer. From here I throw out garbage and rearrange the remaining bits into something tidier. What I end up with is more like a series of disconnected snapshots than a real story, but it's perfectly acceptable compared with the unwatchable alternative. You can then bring the culled video back into Final Cut Express for editing.

Compilation Videos: A Moving Slide Show

No matter how good an editor you become, having random scenes of video shot here and there without solid coverage makes it all but impossible to edit in the traditional way. What you can do, however, is find the good moments from a tape or a series of tapes, bring them into the Browser, and assemble them in interesting ways. This is a *compilation video*.

A compilation video is made up of lots of disparate shots tied together by a shared theme, such as time, location, or subject. For example, I've seen compilations with titles like "A Retrospective of Aaron's Life" and "Claudette's Wedding."

In a compilation, the goal is not so much to hide the edits between shots or make the camera invisible (as we did in Chocoluv) but simply to connect discrete elements that follow one another. In other words, it creates a *slide show*—but a slide show with moving video instead of static slides and without pauses between slides.

In many ways, a compilation video is pretty much what you can make in iMovie, and your home videos, regardless of your editing software, may often use the same approach: stringing together assorted good video shots in roughly chronological order.

Here is a brief outline of a way to use Final Cut Express to approach these projects:

1. Capture all your video for the compilation so that it's in the Browser as one or maybe a small number of clips.

On projects compiled from many tapes, there will of course be more (and shorter) clips in the Browser, but a Browser that looks like this is typical. Notice the long durations and the nominal clip names. They simply aren't important, and your time is better spent editing.

2. In the order in which the material was shot, scroll through each clip in the Viewer in real time, and grab the short bits that you like (they will probably be around 2 to 8 seconds each), keeping picture and sound together.

   Even though you have inserted shots containing both picture and sound, I respectfully suggest that you forget about the sound for the moment. Make edit decisions based only on picture. We'll leave the sound connected to the picture but reserve the right to drop it later.

3. Add new shots to the end of the sequence. Try at first to keep the shots in chronological order.

   Once in a while there will be a shot you strongly feel should go earlier than where it was in the shooting order—for example, an establishing shot of something. Of course, feel free to insert it where you think it should go.

   If you come across a shot you think makes a particularly interesting beginning or end, move it to the head or tail of the sequence. The easiest way to do this is to grab shots in the Timeline and drag them to where they should go, using the Swap Edit feature.

4. Once you've gone through all your source material, play the sequence with the *sound on*.

You're not listening for a cohesive narrative; you're listening for jarring edits. If you're going to try to use this sound track, all those one-track techniques you learned in Chapter 3 will come in very handy. Go through each sound edit one by one and either (1) do a rolling trim on it a little one way or another, (2) add a cross-dissolve in audio, or (3) delete the sound entirely or replace weird audio with ambience. The more disjointed the various shots are, the more likely it is that you'll want to drop the production track.

Now, whether you've fixed up the production track or not, it's time to decide if you want to add another pair of audio tracks, and if so, for what—music? A voiceover? The easiest to deal with is a music track.

A nice touch: End the music a few moments after the production. Normally I'd fade out the music track (as I did with the production sound), but professionally created music from CDs tends to include an ideal ending already (whether it fades or just ends cold). You can see in the decreasing amplitudes of the music waveform how the song fades out on its own.

You can easily add a voice-over using the Voice Over tool in Final Cut Express (File > Voice Over). To record it, either use the microphone on your camera in Camera mode or plug a better-sounding handheld microphone into the Mic jack.

As you edit personal videos more often, you'll probably find that you shoot more usable material, which of course positively will affect subsequent videos. Once you've experimented with compilation videos, you'll be better prepared to adjust your shooting to match your editing. As you gain experience editing, you'll think of shots that would have made that video better, such as establishing shots and reverse shots.

New Projects

Video projects can run the gamut from absolutely simple to extraordinarily complex. While post-production can also be simple or complicated, its range varies much less than the production. When you edit video you use generally the same kind of process whether you're working on a home video, a business training video, or a feature film. You can even use just one editing program (such as Final Cut Express). Production, on the other hand, can be as spontaneous as pulling your camera out for fun, or as ambitious as mobilizing for a small military action. I shoot candid, unscripted personal videos, but you may find that doing a little organizing (writing a script, having assigned actors, taking care in production by using tripods and lights, and so on) will better showcase your editing talents and produce remarkably useful videos that are worth the extra effort.

As I've pointed out, there are fundamentally two kinds of video projects: scripted and unscripted. Whether you're a professional or an amateur, you might approach your work from either of these directions at various times. Each provides different opportunities and challenges. Each creates different results.

No matter what kind of videos you make, when you're done, it's easy to distribute them. It's a cinch to burn them to disc, DVD-ROM or DVD-Video. DVDs also make videos easy to share, quick to watch and view again. DVDs are versatile, too, since they can be played on either television or computer.

In this section you'll learn about some of the issues of each type of video project. Unscripted projects, for instance, are fast to shoot (if you don't go crazy recording everything you point a camera at), but offer some editorial challenges—in particular, the handling of uncontrolled sound and improvising with imperfect scene coverage. Scripted projects require far more preparation and production effort but usually edit together rather easily. I'll offer some examples of each and highlight key post-production topics where applicable.

Your Unscripted Projects

The easiest projects to shoot, and perhaps the hardest to edit, are unscripted. They're easy to shoot because they require no preparation. They're hard to edit because, well, anything goes. You can approach them from many different directions, and the unstructured nature of the shoot produces material that's often challenging (with poor lighting and sound and possibly incomplete coverage to work around). Script or no script, the first step is always to shoot the best material you can. The next step is to work with what you've got. In my approach called "sketching" in video, I'll give you some guidelines on getting complete Hollywood-style coverage even though you aren't going to do any preparation for your shoot and you have only one chance to record. Then, since sound is so important to the professionalism of a finished project, I'll take an extra moment in this section to address how you might handle marginal audio quality in your post-production.

VIDEO SKETCHES

Shooting unscripted projects is similar to using a still camera: You take it out to shoot when the mood strikes. You may shoot sporting events, parties, your kids, friends, and even interviews. But what the projects all have in common is that it's hard to predict what's going to happen while you're shooting and what coverage you'll get—you don't really know if you're going to shoot something editable. You may have no alternative but to produce a compilation video from this material, but what you could aim for is a result I call a *video sketch*.

A video sketch is a short project, about 2 to 5 minutes long, created through about 1 to 2 hours of editing. Sketches are casual, candid, and a little rough around the edges. But the most important thing about sketches is that unlike most home video, they are shot using basic coverage techniques, giving them a sort of "Hollywood" flavor.

Sketches occupy a new place in the media spectrum: somewhere between the nonprofessional, unwatchable clichés of home video and the professionally produced and edited materials of videographers. Sketches are personal, idiosyncratic home-video, music-video, or documentary projects, but because they are post-produced, they're far more sophisticated than the video that regular folks ever used to create.

Even the most apparently mundane topics can form the basis for invaluable family videos.

In *The Little Digital Video Book* (also from Peachpit Press) I describe in detail how to make sketches, but here are a couple of basic guidelines you can use right away without having to learn everything there is to know about creating this type of project.

First of all, shoot no more than 15–20 minutes of video to make a sketch; that's a length you can thoroughly edit in just a couple of hours. If you shoot more than that, you'll only make the job of editing harder; it'll take longer to capture and review the material, and you might not finish.

Even more important than the amount of video you shoot is the coverage you create for yourself. It will make the difference between creating a good sketch and a typical home video. Making a video is not just shooting—it's hunting for (or maybe collecting) certain kinds of video that easily go together. And even though you don't have the opportunity to shoot multiple takes and ask actors to repeat performances as you move the camera from one setup to another, the natural repetitiveness of most events (walking, talking, eating, playing) makes it possible to get "real" coverage (the kind planned out in scripted productions). As you're shooting your next project, keep in mind that you need to get these types of shots (which should be fairly familiar after your Chocoluv experience):

- The same event in close shots and from farther away (use the zoom feature of a camera for this—don't move yourself).

- At least 10 seconds of one very wide establishing shot.

- Some key moment in your video covered with a shot and then a reverse shot (move yourself about 180 degrees from where you started shooting and shoot from the other side of your subject).

- As many insert and cutaway shots as you can easily shoot from where you're standing. Look for details of objects in the frame—still-life images that can move but have no important production sound: hands, knick-knacks, other observers, room highlights, windows, reflections, and shadows. Funny things that catch your attention—but keep these shots short: none of them should be much longer than 5 seconds.

Another important reminder: Don't move the camera while recording. It doesn't have to be mounted on a tripod to be steady, but don't pan, tilt, dolly, track, or do any of the other cool moves you see in movies and on television. Those shots are created by people with equipment you don't have and with preparation that is antithetical to the spontaneous unscripted-video process. If you have a tripod, use it if you want. But for the most part, do all shooting with a static and unmoving (and unzooming) camera.

When you've shot your home video with this professional kind of coverage, you can apply the editing skills you might save for scripted projects (like Chocoluv) to any unscripted moment—resulting in a powerful video.

The Lockdown Shot

A great shooting technique for unscripted projects that works for dozens of different kinds of subjects is called the *lockdown shot*. Put a camera down on something solid, press the Record button (remotely, if possible), and you get source material that can be edited into an interesting effect. Start and stop the recording, let time pass, and do it again. Or just let the tape roll for an extended period of time, knowing that you will edit small bits from the expanse of tape. You're creating video that's a form of time-lapse photography but not quite as scientific. If something is happening on camera, and the camera is locked in its position and does not move *even a smidgen*, you can dissolve from shot to shot and only the stuff that changed between the shots disappears and reappears. This is very cool for shooting temporal projects—an artist creating a painting, for example, or a construction crew erecting a building. The effect you can create is wonderful for highlighting motion against a still backdrop.

Although it's ideal if you have a solid tripod, you can use an inexpensive one since it only has to hold the camera still. (Fluid heads—required for any kind of smooth camera motion—make tripods particularly expensive. Without that need, any old tripod will usually do, including old ones used only for still photography. For this kind of shot, I've used the same $50 tripod for 20 years.)

But you don't even need a tripod. You can improvise on any surface as long as it provides a fair view of some scene. I've set cameras down on kitchen counters, parked cars, and stone walls. More important is a camera *remote control*, so you don't risk bumping the camera when you start and stop recording.

In Final Cut Express, use small parts of these shots that you want to tell your story, and place long (1 to 3 seconds) cross dissolves over the transitions. Set the video to music. It's a powerful effect—and so simple to execute.

Here are a few frames from a creative project: The camera was locked down while some friends and I painted a wall. The real elapsed time was 5 hours. I shot about 20 minutes and ended up using dissolves between a dozen 5-second shots for a satisfying 1-minute video. To see an example of using a lockdown shot, look at VidClip5 (double-click it in the Chapter 6 folder to see it in QuickTime, or watch it in the Sketchwork project in Final Cut Express).

DEALING WITH SOUND

Good sound is hard to get when you're just shooting casually, with little preparation and a consumer-quality microphone built into the front of your camera. There may be lots of ambient noise. Conversations may be hard to hear. Disjointed bits of music might be playing in some shots. But because there's no script (and no rules), you have a little flexibility in working with the mediocre sound you recorded while shooting.

As you edit your project with production sound, you'll base some of your edit decisions on what you're seeing, but you'll also base many on what you're hearing, which can cause problems. The most common pitfall is that you'll often wait to make edits when people are not talking. *But people are always talking.* Your shots may run on and on until you find a good break or a punch line. There may be no breaks at all. Consequently your shots will just sit there onscreen and will be hard to tighten up. Result: long dull videos.

If you're attached to the production sound track, consider that a fair amount of work will be required to edit it carefully (remember the overlaps in Chapter 3—they're going to be important). Add cross fades in the audio to smooth out abrupt changes in volume or content, and consider leaving the production tracks but adding additional tracks to the mix (as we did in Chapter 4). But all this still won't help you if the shots are long because you're listening to everything people onscreen are saying. For that you need more drastic measures.

When I address sound, I keep in mind two guidelines. First, the fewer tracks you work with at a time, the faster post-production will be. So by extension, cutting picture alone, with no production sound (or ignoring it while working), is the fastest and easiest approach to a project. It's not right for all projects, but it is a worthy method when first attacking a video. Second, virtually all professionals agree that to make a video feel finished, sound is more important than picture. So what do you do with the audio?

Drop the production sound! If you're willing to lose (or ignore) the sync sound from the shoot, you lose many of the clichés of home video. Shots can be much shorter—shots of 1 to 2 seconds are typical—if you ignore the audio.

Not using the production sound doesn't mean your video has no sound. It means that you use either music (which is nice and easy) or ambience (which is more difficult, but not by a lot). We experimented in Chapter 3 with replacing bad bits of audio with ambience. You might try creating all new tracks of ambience and deleting (or turning off) the production tracks altogether.

The Chocoluv tutorial showed how to reinvigorate a dull, scripted scene simply by losing the production tracks entirely and replacing them with music. Music alone or in combination with tracks of ambience is a dynamic improvement to most unscripted videos for a couple of reasons. Music forces your project to have a finite duration: the length of a song (3 to 5 minutes for most tunes). Music lends a structure to the project: The song delivers the story and mood, a beginning and an end. And if you've borrowed music from a professionally produced CD, you can get a professional-sounding sound track. Probably nicer than the noise you recorded during the shoot. (Don't forget that copyrighted music can be used only in personal, non-commercial projects.)

On the other hand, the noise you recorded during the shoot is the real sound from the event. After you've finished cutting the picture, you could find long stretches of audio from the shoot, audio that is not synchronous with the picture but still appropriate to the sketch, and cut it into the sound track. This kind of audio creates a sort of narration track, but a natural one. I recommend starting with one or the other—music or ambient sound—before venturing into a real mix of the pair.

In addition to ambience and music, you might also use the Final Cut Express *voice-over* tool to create a narration. The audio from a voice-over can be recorded on camera (with picture, even if you don't intend to use the picture) or directly into Final Cut Express (as sound only), and can further improve typical videos.

An Unscripted Interview

In the Sketchwork project, you'll find VidClip4, a 1-minute sketch that is a casual interview with artist James Carl Aschbacher. In it, I used the sound track from one shot and then cut picture-only shots "above" it to be illustrative. At first I cut the picture above the "narration" and maintained their sync sound; later I removed sync sound entirely, leaving only the narration. The interview wasn't planned as such, but anytime someone is talking on camera about anything, it's easy to use the audio tracks alone to create a narration. Then you can add new video. For more on James Carl Aschbacher's mural, visit www.aschbacherart.com.

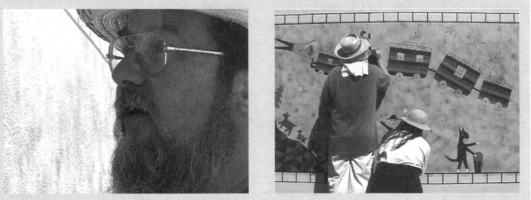

The close-up shot on the left is of the artist. I shot the entire interview at this angle, but I didn't use the video (for the most part). Instead I dropped video inserts over his picture, choosing to show moments during the painting of the mural in chronological order.

Your Scripted Projects

A different world of production opens up when you are willing to plan out a project in advance—writing a script, gathering up props, working on lighting and sound to get the best possible source material, and using actors (professional or just prepared) on camera.

Explaining the production issues associated with scripted projects is beyond the scope of this book. That being said, however, the process of editing scripted projects is virtually identical to that we used in Chocoluv—primarily because it, too, was scripted. You'll have multiple takes of each shot (you can keep shooting each line until you feel you've gotten it *right*); you'll have the same material covered from different angles, and much of what you'll do as the editor will be to decide what is the best performance and the best way to represent the topic with the material you have.

If you're new to video, you may have a few ideas for projects you'd like to try, but you may not have fully considered how many applications there are for your newfound skills. While video has been expensive and a bit of a specialty in the past, it has been used extensively for decades in commercial ventures. Here are some of the ways video has been applied, and some other ways it is beginning to be used more and more.

VIDEO FOR FUN

The first thing most people think of when they hear "video editing" is "movies." With little more preparation than I demonstrated in Chocoluv (but hopefully with a better script) anyone can gather friends and produce entertaining videos. As film industry folks in Hollywood will tell you, it's all about the idea—poor execution by amateurs is often forgivable when the concept of the video is solid.

Nevertheless, it's worth your time to read up on proper production techniques, such as how to light, use microphones, and operate a tripod or dolly. You can get away with crude production (like a shopping cart for a dolly), but I've found that the hardest part of production is writing a good script and orchestrating all the people required (both in front of and behind the camera). And once you go through all that work, it's only a little more work to do the production right.

- Pay attention to the sound. Have someone dedicated to the audio portion of the recording using headphones and possibly external microphones.

- Don't forget the lighting. It might take only one *key light* (although it's better to use a *fill light* and a *back light* as well), but you should have an assistant managing the light or lights, figuring out how to power and position them, and setting filters over them as might be required to achieve a specific effect. (By the way, a *gaffer* is a movie electrician; a *grip* moves props and lights around.)

- Find someone to manage script notes. One person should have nothing else to do but keep an eye on the script and make notes about what was shot on what tape reel, what the setups were, and which takes felt the best.

- Move the camera slowly and steadily if you're going to move it at all. This means you'll need a dolly (real or makeshift); you'll definitely need a tripod, and it probably should have a fluid head for smooth pans and tilts.

- Plan your coverage. A scripted project means you have the luxury of time to find the best locations to set up in order to cover a scene in an interesting way. Don't forget about getting all the bits you need to edit easily: close shots and wide, shots and reverses, cutaways, and some ambient sound before each scene.

Videos for fun are highly speculative ventures. Unlike videos for work (which may have a defined objective) or videos for school (which may be assignments), outside of your immediate circle of friends there is no specific target audience (or goal) for your project—or worse—everyone is your target audience. The vastness of the potential is both exciting and problematic. I would suggest keeping your initial projects inexpensive, simple, and manageable—and building from your success. The DV video format and Final Cut Express are perfect for this agenda.

When you've finished your fun videos, there are numerous venues for showing them, both on the Internet and in the physical world. Film and video festivals are always hungry for quality products. It's true that directors are sometimes discovered from their fun short projects, although it's probably better to look to these shorts as practice to refine your directing, writing, and editing skills.

As you gain experience with your "movies," you may wonder how to build on what you've learned. Of course, you can get more ambitious with longer stories, more complex staging and camera work, scripts with more locations and costumes, and perhaps special effects. You can also improve on image quality. The DV video you can produce with your consumer camera is of fabulous quality and, if it's shot well, comparable to that produced in many professional video formats (in fact, if you shoot it the right way it's even possible to transfer DV video to celluloid film for submitting to festivals). But you still may want to learn about better tools and media—such as 24P high-definition video and perhaps even film. The higher the quality of your product, the more opportunities you leave open for high-end distribution.

VIDEO FOR WORK

For the most part, big corporations have been using video for various purposes for years—not because big businesses needed video more than small businesses, but because the costs of the tools and expertise were such that only big companies could afford them.

As companies are often worried that business videos will be too boring to be watched, or that the material is inherently tedious (such as learning how to do something right or following a rule), business video relies heavily on production and post-production ingenuity. Funny or visually interesting content stands a far better chance of reaching the audience than a "talking head" sitting in an office. While this could mean all kinds of creativity in production (costumes, humorous scripts, fish-eye lenses), in post-production it tends to mean lots of special effects. Many effects require technical skill and serious processing power, and they probably exceed the comfort zone for Final Cut Express (or, for that matter, Final Cut Pro, although Final Cut Pro, particularly when combined with products like Adobe After Effects, can readily deliver such special effects). Others necessitate the use of specialized software, in particular when 3D models are employed to make objects that are eventually integrated with the video.

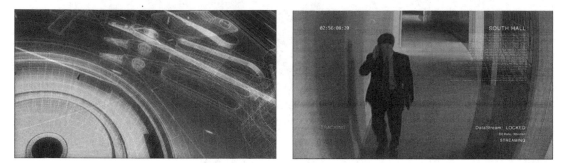

Sophisticated corporate videos often improve the impact of their message by employing 3D graphics (at left) or compositing effects (at right). These are fun but neither necessary nor feasible in every video.

That doesn't mean you can't create compelling business videos. Even though a video is important, it can be simple and effective. Think about the "Switch" campaign Apple used in its commercials—editorially speaking, they are very basic.

The most challenging part of making videos for business is the production: having a good idea and a clear objective, knowing your audience, writing a script, orchestrating the shoot (lights, sound, actors, sets), and using quality music. Ironically, you may find the post-production to be the most enjoyable and relaxed part of the process.

In general, business videos tend to be short, often only 3 to 6 minutes long, and fall into one of two categories: *internal* and *external*. Internal videos are for a company's private purposes; they're essentially for employees. These may be very conceptual—perhaps to articulate aspects of the company's brand—or practical—to train staff how to perform some task or communicate a new initiative. External videos are for a wider audience; they're usually still intended for employees, but they might also be shown to trade-show audiences, vendors, industry analysts, and, of course, customers.

The vast majority of business videos are for employees, and they are exceptionally pragmatic. It's important for every video to have a clear objective.

IDEAS FOR WORK VIDEO

There are as many video uses as there are businesses and people trying to communicate their messages. Here are some of the ways videos are put to use:

> **Training videos.** Training videos are a classic form of the medium. Employees or actors can act out specific scenarios—demonstrating problems that come up, or how to perform some task—with proper and improper outcomes. One common structure is to show an employee interaction and the unwanted result, and then show the proper interaction, followed by the ideal result. These can be used to heighten employees' sensitivity to issues such as sexual harassment, company drug policies, information confidentiality, and manager-staff relations.

The training video on the left (cropped into a movie-style wide-screen format to add a little sophistication) shows employees acting out a problem; the one on the right (in typical video proportions) demonstrates for employees how to perform a certain task.

> **Department videos.** Videos are a powerful way to put a face and personality on every aspect of a large organization. They can provide an avenue for one department to better understand others. Remote members of a sales staff can keep up with events from the home office or see how they are being supported by employees they don't frequently see. Upper management can use videos as potent messages to directly convey to staff when they can't literally be in everyone's offices discussing each issue of importance.

Winston George Whittaker
President and CEO

Executives can communicate their vision and message to large organizations in a far more personal and compelling manner by using video instead of printed memos.

Project videos. Any kind of future projection or visualization can be mocked up in video to illustrate what a job, product, or team might experience in the future. You can sometimes minimize apprehension about change by clearly demonstrating how that change will impact employees. In a big organization, a team might use a video to clearly demonstrate to management or other groups the details about a new project: its impact on the rest of the organization, how it fits into the company, and the potential results of the endeavor.

Field videos. Internal corporate videos are a fun means for teams of employees who travel for business to report back on their field experiences. Business trips to trade shows and conferences can yield short videos that let others better understand the trips' goals, vibes, and accomplishments. These videos can be silly and entertaining, or serious and educational. Videos from the field also allow customers to speak more directly to a company. The real customers can demonstrate to employees how products are being used in the field, and give testimonials about the success, quality, or effect a product has had.

Entertainment videos. Like the skits that staff members put on at annual meetings, holiday parties, and retreats, video provides a way to have some fun at work. Entertainment videos sometimes playfully poke fun at management (or customers!), provide parody and satire, and are excellent ways to break up more serious gatherings with levity and company personality. A good company compilation project is a *gag reel* of silly moments captured on camera throughout the year and assembled for the enjoyment of all.

Community videos. These don't deal with the intricacies of company policies and politics but are designed to help a community better understand what goes on at a large local employer. For such businesses, there is a natural curiosity about what goes on behind the gates—what does it look like in there, what are people doing, how are supplies received and shipped, and what is the long-standing relationship and commitment between the company and the community?

Recruiting. Videos are useful in recruiting—in giving prospective employees a strong emotional sense of the company's mission, its culture, its products, and its facilities. Recruits may have myriad choices in the job market, and as much as a company wants to select carefully, it also wants to attract a large pool of the best applicants. Videos can distinguish one company from another, particularly when the companies' goods or services are not quite as well known or distinct from others'. From corporate headhunters to employees staffing local job fairs, people charged with bringing in new talent will benefit from video materials.

Demonstrations. Retail stores employ video loops to entice pedestrians to enter the business; these videos demonstrate products, services, or just interesting images that communicate the company's distinct brand and identity. Inside stores, videos can show how products sitting idle on a shelf might be used and enjoyed. A clothing store can run video of a fashion show; an adventure-sports store can run short adventure documentaries that include products in action. Giving retail sales staff members great tools (of which video is one) augments their ability to reach customers.

Any complicated process is made simpler by clearly demonstrating it on video—in particular, when there are many steps or when the outcome of the effort is dramatic. Here, silver jewelry is being designed, but any project (from loading a parachute to baking a pie) makes for fun demonstration video loops for staff or customers.

Advertisements. Of course, the most common external video is the commercial, called a *spot* in broadcasting lingo. Traditional advertisements are 30-second and 60-second spots; the DV-quality video you make in Final Cut Express is sufficient for delivering ads in local and regional television broadcasts—assuming that production values (lighting and sound) are good. The DV format is excellent for running television commercials on a monitor during trade shows and at internal sales meetings (and board of directors meetings).

Quick Custom Commercials

If you want to create spots that are for one product or business but will play in different markets, try doing what some companies do: make a master spot—generic for all markets—and then copy that sequence and drop in one or two shots (often at the beginning or end) that customize the commercial for each particular audience. In this way, you can generate dozens of unique, customized commercials relatively quickly.

A variation on this is to provide a shot at the end of your commercial that is effectively blank, where the local television station or franchise (or whoever needs to deal with the customization) can add simple titles for its market. The traditional application of this is when a national chain—say, a car dealer—makes a spot and leaves this frame blank, and the local dealership adds its address and phone number to this blank "card" so that you know whom to call in your area. If you look at TV commercials carefully, you can identify these spots: They have high-quality production values throughout (they're often shot on film), and this one shot at the end with video-quality text (customarily added by the local TV studio).

VIDEO FOR SCHOOL

As more and more kids have access to computers and digital cameras, it's inevitable that they will be turning in their school reports on video. At first, the simplest architecture for a presentation would appear to be a slide show; using software like iPhoto, it's easy to have still images flow from one to another, with a voice-over track narrating events.

By moving to a video product like iMovie, the degree of complexity can increase—with moving pictures and a few layers of sound. But iMovie still doesn't open up video's full range of creative possibilities, and in many cases it can make the edit more difficult than necessary.

With Final Cut Express, students can explore how to manipulate sound and pictures to create compelling, informative, and entertaining shorts. Sound effects, voice-over narration tracks, moving graphics, and a sophisticated editorial style can be combined for great effect, educating students about both the content of their projects and the ways you can manipulate media to persuade an audience. There is perhaps no better education about the power of television than by allowing kids to see how media is constructed.

An interesting exercise is to give two groups of kids a common body of video material and then have one group cut a story from one point of view while the other group edits a story from an opposing point of view. Same content, different analysis and result.

SCHOOL VIDEO IDEAS

There is no end to the ways video can be used in educational settings. Here are some basic approaches:

Role-playing. Students can portray any notable person—famous or not. In literature classes, students can be writers and poets; in science classes they can be inventors or scientists. Anyone, from Neanderthal man and Genghis Khan to T.S. Eliot and Eleanor Roosevelt, can become a character in a short skit. Students learn how to research period costumes and products, develop sets and scenarios, and write scripts that highlight what this person's life was like—his or her influences, fears, great moments, and maybe tragic end. Videos can be made entertaining by adding characters, working on nationalities (as manifested in accents and language), and developing imaginary (but plausible) vignettes.

Parody. Students enjoy creating parody and satire from both current and historical events. By poking fun at news stories they gain an appreciation for issues, and they may add a distinctive vantage point that only kids can provide. Or kids can spoof any aspect of popular culture, from rock concerts to late-night infomercials. Try using video to sell goods such as triangles and pentagons (shapes), or antimony and titanium (elements).

Anachronism. One avenue for parody is to use purposeful anachronism: having a CNN reporter interview Robert E. Lee, for instance, or showing television commercials for the fulcrum or any variety of historical products. Faux interviews are one kind of anachronism; combine them with role-playing elements and you have a visit to your school by Georgia O'Keefe and Frank Lloyd Wright.

Documentary. One of the great features of video is how you can use it to manipulate time. People can be interviewed before and after key events. Events themselves can be shown in slow motion (a moment in a lab experiment; a horse running at a gallup) or sped up (to illustrate an insect's behavior or life cycle, or a fort being built over a period of hours) to make whatever points are relevant. Time-lapse videography requires the use of a tripod and remote control (see "The Lockdown Shot," earlier in this chapter); if events occur over longer periods of time, using short video snippets connected with cutaway shots also works well (as in the interview with the artist about the mural).

Some camcorders have a feature that allows them to be set up to record a few frames at a time, every 15 seconds or so—a crude sort of animation that is easy to create.

Documentary projects allow students to shoot whatever interests them. They add scripted narration to explain the importance of the images being viewed, or to explain how to do something, such as preparing chicken cordon bleu or building a model plane.

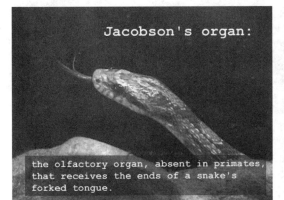

Jacobson's organ: the olfactory organ, absent in primates, that receives the ends of a snake's forked tongue.

The mouse is a mammal. How are people the same as mice?

Visual reports. Images from library books or stock Web video or even programs recorded from television can be re-edited into a kid-appropriate context. These videos can be modeled on Ken Burns's documentaries—breathing life into still images, charts and old photographs—or they can be more idiosyncratic, juxtaposing historical images with current video of places, people, statues, or museums.

Students can act out fables, folktales, or original stories. Video can even add depth to their understanding of important social documents, such as the Preamble to the Constitution or the Pledge of Allegiance.

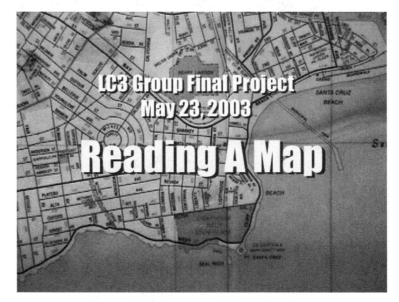

Personal topical narratives. Variations on a private video journal make good class projects. Students can record themselves discussing their subjects—my father's job; how I take care of my sister; my rock collection; how I prepare dinner; my favorite song; what freedom means to me—and then insert appropriate cutaways that help illustrate the journals.

Another variation is to have kids interview each other and ask questions about topical issues: What would you do if you were President? What is unique about your background?

Real-World Examples

You can view dozens of fine student videos at Apple's Web site (www.apple.com/education/ilife). Even though most of the projects weren't created with Final Cut (it's an iLife site, so the videos come from iMovie and iPhoto), they demonstrate the ways in which kids are experimenting with media.

You Made It!

Final Cut Express is a post-production tool of video and audio features that range in importance, depending on the amount of time you want to devote to post-producing videos.

Hopefully, this book has delivered a foundation for video literacy—arguably as important a set of skills for future generations as typing skills have been for us. With a solid understanding of editing tools, you know how to edit not only in Final Cut Express but also in Final Cut Pro—and in virtually *any other editing product, either in existence now or yet to be created.* That's a bold statement, but I believe it's true. Editing skills are transferable among products; you only need to learn what Product X calls its tools. In some other program they may have odd names or be accessed through tiny buttons, but if the software edits, I assure you that the basic functions are in it somewhere. You didn't learn how to edit with just Final Cut Express, you learned how to edit, *period*.

Now go get some video of your own, and see what you can do.

Appendix

Technical Issues

You can edit video without being much of a gearhead. And because you're a Mac owner, you can run a computer without being too much of a geek, either. Apple has made its hardware and software so simple and transparent that you could go through your editing career with extraordinarily paltry knowledge and still enjoy plenty of satisfaction. I put this technical info at the back of the book just so that no one gets spooked before they understand how fun editing can be. With some appreciation for editing, you're in a far better place to devote some time to technical topics. You can skip this technical stuff if you want, but it may make the rest of your editing experiences better in the long run.

Here are my top recommendations for technical subjects to learn a little more about, which should extend your ability to use computers and converse in "video":

- Storage
- Bandwidth

- FireWire
- Timecode

Storage

Whether you're talking about your computer's hard drive, a Zip disk, or a DVD, all digital storage media have certain characteristics that define their usability. Because digital video makes for relatively large data files that need to be moved around a lot, two of the most important characteristics of a storage device used with editing systems are data transfer rate and storage capacity.

Data transfer rate measures how quickly data can be moved onto or off of the disk. It's the result of a number of processes. Data transfer rate is important because for video to play, you need to move a great deal of data off the digital storage device very quickly. If you can't move it quickly, you need to make the digital data size of each frame smaller so that you can pump out the frames at 30 fps (frames per second). There are, of course, various ways to accomplish this (decrease the frame rate, make the size of each frame smaller, and so on), but each choice will compromise image quality to some degree.

Storage capacity simply refers to how much data can be stored on the disk. This quantity is expressed in terms of bytes: megabytes (MB) or gigabytes (GB).

After gigabytes there are even larger units of measurement: 1,024 gigabytes is a terabyte *(TB), 1,024 TB is a* petabyte *(PB), and 1,024 petabytes is an* exabyte *(EB). An exabyte is a quintillion bytes.*

New technologies keep increasing the quantity of data that disks can store. Today it's not uncommon for a Mac to come with a 60 or 100 GB drive (with the tower version containing room for three more drives inside the chassis); and with external FireWire devices, you can store even more data. Although a super-large drive seems like a blessing (and it is), there are some video performance limitations related to this big ol' drive.

In professional systems, it's considered good form to have your application software on one hard drive and your video media on another. In even more demanding situations, professionals often separate the video media from the audio, keeping them on separate hard drives. The goal is to ensure that video and audio can be accessed quickly, with minimal opportunity for playback problems. Separating media files from the applications and system files further protects you from risks to your Mac, should the digital media files get corrupted somehow and result in a full hard-drive repair or replacement. You wouldn't want to wipe out your whole system simply because a media file was ruined or you felt the need to reformat a drive.

Many professionals cannot divorce themselves from the need to maintain these separations. Apple even recommends them for best system performance. The ideal Mac configuration includes a small hard disk with the operating system, applications, and other files that might be on the computer (say, less than 10 GB and probably under 5 GB), and then one or more large drives for the video media files.

If you have only one hard disk in your Mac and don't expect to purchase another anytime soon, the next best thing is to fake it. Using the Disk Utility application that comes with your Mac OS, you can establish partitions on a single drive, so that the Mac thinks it has a number of drives. This creates a little safety margin in case of problems, (although you can resolve more performance issues if you have separate drives). Putting the media files and the rest of the OS and apps all on one drive can result in dropped frames during playback—an irritation that many choose to accept and others endure, unsure of why it's happening. If you're pushed to your limit by incessant "dropped frames during playback" warnings, you can uncheck this setting in the Preferences > General window:

☐ Report dropped frames during playback

If your video is balking when it tries to play video, you may have to attend to a hard disk issue. In the meantime, you can deselect this setting in the Preferences to allow Final Cut to drop frames in order to play smoothly. (And this has nothing to do with "drop frame timecode.")

Bandwidth

No talk of computers goes on very long without the word *band-width* coming up. This is true whether the discussion is about professional post-production, personal digital video, or the Internet. Bandwidth affects the speed of data transfers.

Every time you see a cable connecting two computer components (such as a camera and computer, a hard drive and the base tower, or two computers on the Internet), think bandwidth: How big is the pipe connecting these things?

People often use the bucket-drainpipe analogy when describing bandwidth: If digital data is water in a bucket (which represents your hard disk), and there is a hole with a pipe at the bottom that allows you to fill a glass when you want to, bandwidth is the diameter of the pipe. If you have big pipe (a lot of bandwidth), it doesn't take long to fill the glass. If you have a tiny straw for a pipe, water is going to dribble out and take a long time to fill the glass—even if the bucket is huge. Bandwidth is all about the diameter of the pipe.

Bandwidth, like velocity, is measured in terms of movement over time. For a cable, this is usually described as the number of *bits per second (bps)*. For a storage device, like a disk or drive, the bandwidth is described in *bytes* per second, abbreviated *Bps* (there are 8 bits to a byte). This is also sometimes referred to as a drive's *data transfer rate*.

Be careful of the difference between bytes per second (Bps) and bits per second (bps). Many publications and product spec sheets confuse the two. When comparing media formats (like miniDV or uncompressed video), you need to make sure that all your bandwidths are in the same units.

For more information on these and many other technical and historical aspects of digital editing, I recommend that you check out my book Nonlinear: A Field Guide to Digital Video and Film Editing (Triad, 2000) *or visit www.nonlinear.info on the Web. Shameless self-promotion notwithstanding, the book is mildly amusing and widely considered the bible on such topics.*

FireWire

In the mid-1990s, Apple pioneered a new kind of low-cost digital interface that would integrate the worlds of computers and video. Engineers representing different companies and industries gathered to develop an independent standard that would meet the demands of modern digital video and audio.

FireWire

The result was officially called *IEEE 1394* (standard number 1394 of the Institute of Electrical and Electronics Engineers), but it was trademarked under the name *FireWire* by Apple (the name recognized by most consumers) and branded as *i.Link* by Sony. By the late 1990s, professionals and consumers alike were using cameras, computers, and peripheral devices incorporating this standard. FireWire, i.Link, and IEEE 1394 are all essentially the same and are characterized by the following:

- A flexible digital interface standard, which addresses the constant signal degradation that occurs in repeated digital-to-analog conversions; it can connect computer to device, or skip the computer entirely and connect device to device

- Easy-to-use thin cables that have no need for terminators, device IDs, or screws

- A hot-swappable format, unlike SCSI, so devices can be added and removed while the computer is on and active

- Pretty dern fast, supporting data rates of 100 Mbps, 200 Mbps, and 400 Mbps

One key to FireWire's success is that by connecting computer to camera, editing software can control the camera directly. This delivers functionality previously only seen with professional editing systems using expensive machine controllers and timecode readers. But even better than that, FireWire delivers true *plug-and-play* experiences: You plug in a simple cable; the software "sees" the camera (or video deck or hard drive) and controls it as required. The development of FireWire was revolutionary.

The 4-pin FireWire plug on a digital camcorder and the i.Link logo.

Video, when stored digitally, creates enormous files. One minute of full broadcast-quality video would constitute a file of around 1.2 GB and would require a bandwidth of 160 Mbps to play. By contrast, the DV format (found in your miniDV and Digital8 cameras) compresses this signal, with nominal image degradation. The DV file takes up only 220 MB per minute and requires a bandwidth of 25 Mbps.

What all this means is that DV-format video fits nicely in most personal computers and easily plays through FireWire cables (25 Mbps is far smaller than the 100 Mbps data rate supported by even the most basic FireWire cable).

Timecode Basics

Timecode is a numbering system used on videotape to identify and locate frames. DV cameras automatically generate this timecode and record it onto blank cassettes at the same time they record pictures. Consumer cameras don't give you a great deal of control over timecode, but the control you have is sufficient, and mastery of timecode is important.

Timecode came from work done with missile tracking for the U.S. Department of Defense and landed in the world of video in the early 1970s. It's an eight-digit number that uniquely identifies each video frame. Timecode counts like a traditional clock, except for the final pair of digits, which are frames—each one 1/30 second long.

DROP-FRAME VS. NON–DROP-FRAME TIMECODE

People who work with video often want timecode to do two things: uniquely identify each frame and give accurate indications of running time (duration). You know that video plays at 30 fps. Videotape timecodes, therefore, count from frame :00 to frame :29 before rolling over to the next second.

Unfortunately, videotape doesn't really run at 30 fps; it runs precisely at 29.97 fps. So although you can use a timecode number to accurately identify every single video frame with a unique number, this "time" measurement isn't measuring the *real* elapsed time.

Say you've edited a sequence, and you begin recording it on a timecoded videotape, starting at 00:00:00:00. If the sequence ends exactly at 00:29:00:00, you might think your show is precisely 29 minutes long. *This is not correct*. Since your videotape is actually playing slightly slower than real time (0.1 percent slower, to be exact), your actual program duration is almost 2 full seconds longer!

Clearly, regular old timecode doesn't keep track of durations very accurately—at least not accurately enough for professional needs.

Regular old timecode—with a single number for every frame and which counts from frame :00 to frame :29, before rolling over to :00 again (but that is temporally inaccurate) is also called *non–drop-frame* timecode (NDF), because it never drops any numbers while it's counting.

The only way to make timecode keep close to the real elapsed time is to leave out certain numbers. If you skip some numbers (remember that this doesn't affect the video pictures at all; it is only a counting system), your duration calculations can be *extremely close* to the actual elapsed time of any video segment.

Timecode that skips certain timecode numbers is called *drop-frame* timecode (DF). The way it skips numbers is very precise: **It drops the :00 and :01 frame number every minute, except for every tenth minute.**

Notice that with DV footage and drop-frame timecode, numbers are skipped in consecutive frames (;00, ;01), but the frame images of video themselves are unaffected. This kind of timecode keeps better track of the actual elapsed time of video shots.

With drop-frame timecode, source and record times reflect real time, and thus can be used to determine durations. (To calculate shot durations using timecodes, subtract the "in point" timecode from the "out point" timecode. This math can be difficult; you might want to use a special timecode calculator designed for the purpose. Final Cut does this for you automatically.) For the most part, all consumer digital video cameras automatically generate drop-frame timecode—this way, you can easily rely on your duration fields to give you accurate time.

You can tell at a glance if a display of timecode is giving you drop-frame or non–drop-frame numbers: non–drop-frame timecode uses colons (:) between each pair of digits. Drop-frame timecode uses a semicolon (;) between the seconds and frames.

If you look at the timecode in the windows of Final Cut while you've been working, you'll notice that it's presenting all drop-frame timecode. It's not that Final Cut can't handle non–drop-frame timecode—it can. It's that consumer DV cameras *only* generate DF timecode.

NTSC VIDEO

As you continue to work with video, you will often see the initials *NTSC*. What is NTSC video and why do you care? The short answer is that it's the video format of television in the United States (adopted by Japan, among others). *NTSC* stands for *National Television Standards Committee,* and the video it standardized has 525 lines of resolution, playing at 30 fps (well, 29.97 actually). Engineers joke that *NTSC* stands for *Never the Same Color* because there are a number of technical issues with the U.S. standard that make color fidelity difficult to maintain from one device to another.

There are other standards of video. In France, *SECAM* is used. Most of Europe uses *PAL video,* which comes up often in discussions about video, even in the United States. PAL has 625 lines of resolution playing at 25 fps. Regular American television sets can't play PAL video, but if you've got an appropriate monitor, PAL provides users with a slightly higher image quality. Also, because PAL is closer to the frame rate of film (24 fps), it's often used as a better video format for independent filmmakers who shoot in video but plan an eventual transfer to film.

Answers to Chapter 1 Scavenger Hunt

(pages 47-48)

1. Large one-frame circle   0:27;09

2. Small one-frame square: 0:44;11

3. Duration between marks: 0:00;01

4. Large one-frame square: 1:37;23

5. Large one-frame triangle: 1:17;22

6. Last frame of small three-frame square: 0:49;10

7. Middle frame of small three-frame triangle: 1:07;11

8. Small one-frame circle: 1:27;28

Index

4-/6-pin connectors, 3, 4, 306

A

Add Keyframe button, 197
Additive Dissolve transition, 194
Adjust Line Segment pointer, 77
Adobe Photoshop, 104, 200, 265
Advanced menu, 250
advertisement videos, 294–295
AIFF files, 249, 251
ambience, 123–124, 284, 285
anachronism, purposeful, 296
analog connectors, 7, 8–9
Analog in/out plugs, 7
analog material, 222, 234
animation, 196, 203, 297
annotations, script, 55–56
answers, scavenger hunt, 309
Apple, 11, 299, 305
Applications folder, 11
Arrange menu, 214
arrow cursor, 83
arrow keys, 38–39, 41
arrow tool, 90
Aschbacher, James Carl, 286
aspect ratio, 199, 265
assistant editors, 218, 252
audio. *See also* sound
    filter effects in, 203
    scrubbing, 31
    stealing, 207
audio clips icon, 15
audio cross fades, 162–165
audio levels, adjusting, 77–78,
    160–165
audio mix. *See* sound mix

Audio Render Files folder, 231, 233
Audio slice, 58
audio tracks. *See* sound tracks
Audio Transitions folder, 163
Audio/Video plugs, 7
AV cables, 8–9

B

back light, 287
backtiming, 120
backups, 96, 234
bandwidth, 304
Batch option, Capture window,
    241
beat, 60
bins, 238, 246–248
bits per second, 304
black-and-white, converting color
    image to, 201
black leader, 255
blue frames, 220
Blur effect, 208
Bps/bps, 304
broken timecode, 219–221,
    242–245
Browser
    contrasted with iMovie Clip
      pane, 21
    devoting entire display to, 213
    displaying contents of, 13–14
    and Final Cut Express work-
      flow, 20
    illustrated, 13
    importing video clips into, 27
    purpose of, 13
    resizing, 212
    tabs in, 58

bumping, 221
burn-in window, 45, 46
burning DVDs, 266, 279
business videos, 289–295
bytes, 302, 304

C

cables
    AV, 8–9
    coaxial, 10–11
    FireWire, 3–4
    S-Video, 10
    SCSI, 4
camcorder, 2, 221. *See also* camera
camera
    connecting Mac to, 3–4
    connecting TV to, 6–11
    connecting VCR to, 10–11
    and timecode, 306
    using tripod with, 204, 260,
      282, 287
Canvas
    contrasted with iMovie moni-
      tor, 22
    contrasted with Timeline, 19
    contrasted with Viewer, 17–18
    Current Timecode field, 46
    and Final Cut Express work-
      flow, 20
    illustrated, 13
    purpose of, 17–18
    tabs in, 58
    and traditional editing setup,
      16
    video controls, 29

Capture Bin, 238
Capture mode, 23
Capture Scratch folder, 219, 231, 233, 245
Capture window, 235–239, 240
capturing video, 234–243
  accessing special tool for, 235
  contrasted with importing, 28
  description of process, 234
  options, 240–243
CD-R, backing up files on, 271
CD-ROM, distributing video on, 258, 259–260, 261
CDs, importing music from, 248–252
center-point dissolves, 189
Checker Wipe transition, 194
checkerboard, 166, 169
Chocoluv Tutorial, 50, 53
chocoluv.pdf, 50
chrominance, 201
clap/clapboards, 34, 35
Clip option, Capture window, 240–241
Clip Overlays control, 77–78, 160
Clip pane, iMovie, 21
clip speed, iMovie, 23
clips. *See also* shots; video clips
  defined, 27, 51
  dividing into subclips, 242, 246–247
  dragging, 61
  head *vs.* tail of, 32
  icons for, 14–15
  identifying beginning of, 71
  importing, 27–28
  long *vs.* short, 32
  marking, 127
  moving with Slide tool, 130–133
  naming, 245–247
  offline, 229
  relinking to media files, 229
  saving, 245–247
  searching for, 246
Clock Wipe transition, 194
Close Tab command, 58
close-up shots, 52
coaxial cable, 10–11
codecs, 259, 260
colon, 75
color bars, 255
color quality, 309
Command-Y, 164

Command-Z, 89
commercials, 294, 295
community videos, 293
compilation videos, 276–279
component video, 7
composite video, 7
compositing, 150, 197–200
compression, 258–264, 259, 266
Compression Settings dialog, 261
computer display, 5, 6. *See also* video monitor
conceptual folders, 238
contextual menus, 94
continuous timecode, 219–221
Control key, 94
controls. *See* video controls
Controls tab, 167–170, 183
Convert Selection from AIFF command, 250
countdown, 255
coverage, 53–58, 288
cross dissolves, 189–190, 192
cross fades, 162–165
CU, 52
cue/play tools, 23
culling, 93, 275–276
Current Timecode field, 46
cutaway shots, 52, 53, 117, 120
cuts-only sequences, 184
cutting, xii, 28, 97, 101
cutting block, xii

D

dailies, 54
Dailies Reel, 53–56, 63
data code, 237
data files, 228–229
data points, edit, 116
data transfer rate, 302, 304, 305
dB, 78, 161
De-interlace filter, 265
decibels, 78, 161
deleting, 90–94
  contrasted with trimming, 90
  with Lift edits, 90–92, 129–130
  with Razor Blade tool, 90
  with Ripple delete, 93–94
demonstration videos, 294
department videos, 291
Desktop, putting folders/projects on, 25, 26
destructive editing, 21
DF timecode, 307, 308

dialogue, 55, 59, 107. *See also* scripts
Diffuse effect, 201
Digital I/O plugs, 8
digital storage media, 302–303
Digital Video Book, The Little, 281
digitizing video, 234
Dip to Color transition, 194
disk space
  cost considerations, 227
  for edit bay, 2
  managing, 226–229
  recommended, xvii
  technical issues, 302–303
  viewing amount of available, 23
disk space indicator, iMovie, 23
Disk Utility application, 303
display. *See* computer display
dissolves, 185–195
  additive, 194
  center-point, 189
  cross, 189–190, 192
  dither, 194
  fade-in/fade-out, 185–189
  non-additive, 194
  ripple, 195
Dither Dissolve transition, 194
documentary-style projects, 242, 297
dollies, 287
down/up arrow keys, 39
drag hand, 157
dragging, 36, 61
drop-frame timecode, 75, 307–308
drop shadows, 178–182
"dropped frames during playback" message, 303
dubbing, 11, 244, 255
Duplicate command, 96
DV resolution, 227
DVD
  archiving videos on, 268
  burning, 266, 279
  compression considerations, 266
  copying files to, 266
  loading files from this book's, 25–27
  video clips provided on this book's, xviii
DVD Studio Pro, 266

E

EB, 302
ECU, 55
edit bay, 2–3
edit decisions, 15
Edit Overlay menu, 61
edit points, 79
editing
    adjusting interface to facilitate,
        211–216
    approaches to learning, xiv–xv,
        49–50, 218
    contrasted with culling, 93
    creating multiple versions
        while, 95–97
    defined, x
    destructive vs. nondestructive,
        21, 62
    essential skill required for, 28
    with Final Cut Express vs.
        iMovie, xiii–xiv, 21–23, 62
    with keyboard, 36–40
    with mouse, 29–36
    one- vs. two-hand, 36, 41
    popularity of, x
    purpose of, xi
    recommended book on, 304
    selectivity in, xiii
    technical issues associated
        with, 301–309
    three- vs. four-point, 116–117
    undoing, 89
    watching dailies prior to, 54
    workflow, 20
editors, 159, 218, 252
effects
    adding to Favorites folder, 195
    animating, 196, 203
    filter, 200–203, 265
    real-time vs. rendered, 173
    rendering, 233
    sound, 150–151
    speed, 204–207
    transition, 184–195
Effects folder, 195
Effects tab, 184
Effects window, 214
End Search feature, 221
entertainment videos, 292–293
ES, 52
establishing shots, 52, 279
EWS, 52

exabytes, 302
Export Size Settings dialog, 262
exporting
    Final Cut Movie, 267
    QuickTime movie, 258–264
    QuickTime still image, 264–266
Extend edits, 115
~Extras folder, 26
eyeball viewer, 137
eyeballs, 105

F

fades, 185–189, 278
fast forward/reverse, 29
Favorites folder, 195, 270
FCE Book Materials DVD, xviii, 25
FCE Project Files folder, 26, 53
field videos, 292
File menu, 235
files
    backing up, 96, 234, 270–271
    data vs. media, 228–229
    organizing, 219
fill light, 287
fillers, 124
film
    hunks of, 51
    marking In/Out points in, 43
    mechanical tools for editing,
        xii, 49
film-style editing, 67
filmstrip graphics, 41
filter effects, 200–203, 265
Filters slice, 58
Final Cut
    learning to use, xvi–xviii
    "light" version. See Final Cut
        Express
    locking picture cuts in, 151
    playing multiple tracks in, 150
    playing video in, 5
    Pro version. See Final Cut Pro
Final Cut Express. See also Final
    Cut
    complexity in, 49
    contrasted with iMovie,
        xiii–xiv, 21–23, 62
    getting ready to use, 1–11
    and hard-disk storage, 227
    hardware requirements, xvii,
        173
    interface, 11–20, 210–216

and keyframes, 196–197, 203
launching, 11–13
as "light" version of Final Cut
    Pro, ix, xv–xvi
mastering video controls for,
    28–48
quitting, 25
rearranging screen elements
    for, 12–13
resolution considerations, 227
title tools, 167
undo levels, 95
ways of using, ix
workflow, 20
Final Cut Pro. See also Final Cut
    Batch option, 241
    and hard-disk storage, 227
    importing music from CDs
        with, 250
    and keyframes, 196–197, 203
    "light" version of, ix, xv–xvi
    resolution considerations, 227
    title tools, 167, 168
    track controls, 105
    undo levels, 95
FireWire
    cables, 2, 3–4, 305
    connectors, 3, 306
    hard drives, 227
    standards, 305–306
flash frames, 191
folders. See also specific folders
    conceptual, 238
    creating, 238
    putting on Desktop, 26
fonts, 168, 176
footage, tutorial, xvii–xviii
four-point edits, 116–117
fps, 307, 309
frames
    blue, 220
    finding first/last, 32
    marking, 41–43
    measuring time by counting,
        75
    moving between, 38–39
    small white circle in, 34
frames per second, 307, 309
FreeHand, Macromedia, 104
fun videos, 287–289

G

gaffer, 287
gain, adjusting, 78, 161
Gain Adjust dialog, 161
gaps, timecode, 220, 274
Gaussian Blur effect, 208
GB, 302
Generator button/menu, 124–125, 165, 175
gigabytes, 302
grayscale, converting color image to, 201
green bars, 82, 110
green light, 105
grip, 287

H

hand pointer, 157
hard-disk storage
    cost considerations, 227
    for edit bay, 2
    managing, 226–229
    recommended, xvii
    technical issues, 302–303
    viewing amount of available, 23
hardware requirements, xvii, 173
head/tail terminology, 32
headphones, 2, 7
hiding edits, 107
HOFs, 51
holistic video, xii, 159
Hollywood
    assistant editors, 218
    editors, 218
    film-editing tools, xii, 49
    sound editors, 159
hot swapping, 4, 305

I

I key, 42
iBook, xvii
IC Memory, 221
iDVD, 266–270
IEEE 1394, 305
iLife, 299
i.Link, 305, 306
images. *See also* picture tracks
    compositing, 199
    converting to grayscale, 201
    exporting, 264–266
    icons for, 15

iMovie
    contrasted with Final Cut Express, xiii–xiv, 21–23, 62
    culling tapes with, 276
    interface, 21–23
    limitations of, xiii–xiv
    moving shots with, 137
    and timecode, 219
Import command, 27
importing
    contrasted with capturing, 28, 248
    music from CDs, 248–252
    setting preferences for, 249
In icon, 42
In/Out points
    determining elapsed time between, 46
    marking, 42–43
    Source *vs.* Master, 116
In point overlay, 64, 71
In Shift value, 89
inbetweening, 196
"Initializing Capture" message, 237
Insert button, 61
insert edits, 70. *See also* inserts
Insert Tracks command, 152
inserts, 115–128
    defined, 61, 65–66
    moving with Slide tool, 130–133
    non-rippling, 115, 117–128. *See also* Overwrite edits
    and nondestructive editing, 62
    in picture only, 117–121
    ripple, 66–67
    rolling, 67
    in sound only, 122–128
    and synchronization, 67
    telling Final Cut Express where to put, 69
    and three- *vs.* four-point edits, 116–117
    trimming, 129
installation support, 11
interface
    Final Cut Express, 11–20, 210–216
    iMovie, 21–23
Internet, delivering videos over, 258, 259, 260, 261

interviews, 121, 286, 296, 299
iPhoto, 295
iTunes, 248–251

J

J-cut, 108
J-K-L keys, 37–38, 41, 42
Jaws Wipe transition, 194
jog control, 33
jog wheel, 33, 36
journals, video, 298
JPEG files, 264

K

K key, 37–38
key light, 287
keyboard, editing with, 36–40
keyframes, 196–197, 203
keys, 199, 200
Keystone Cops effect, 204
Knowledge Base, 11

L

L-cut, 108
L key, 37–38
labeling videotapes, 218, 219, 253
LANC logo, 8
launching program, 11–13
layers
    compared with tracks, 104–105
    opacity of, 198, 199
    stacking up, 197, 209
leader, 255
left/right arrow keys, 38–39
level overlays, 77
levels, adjusting audio, 77–78, 160–165
libraries, iMovie, 23
Lift edits, 90–92, 129–130
lighting, 287
lined script, 56
Linking control, 106
Little Digital Video Book, The, 281
Lock Track control, 103
lockdown shots, 283, 297
log book, 2
log sheets, 223–224
logging information, 238, 246
Loop option, 256
luminance, 201

M

M tape, 253
Macintosh
    as component of edit bay, 2
    connecting to DV camera, 3–4
    hard drives, 302–303
    hardware requirements, xvii, 173
    ideal configuration, 303
Macromedia FreeHand, 104
macros, 130
magnifying glass icon, 74
Make Subclip command, 246
Making Movies with Mike folder, 26
Mark Clip button, 127
Mark In/Out buttons, 42–43, 83
Mark In/Out icons, 71
Mark menu, 45
marking frames, 41–43
Master data points, 116
master material, 222
Master Settings dialog, 254
master tapes, 253–257
    labeling, 253
    Print to Video settings for, 254–255
    purpose of, 253
    recording, 256–257
    titleless, 257
Match Frame button, 72
mattes, 199, 200
MB, 302
media files, 228–229, 238, 252
medium shots, 52
megabytes, 302
memory, xvii, 221
menus, contextual, 94
metadata, 228, 238, 246
microphones, 284, 287
mix. See sound mix
Modify menu, 246
monitor. See video monitor
motion effects, 23, 204–207
Motion slice, 58
Motion tab, 180, 181, 183
mouse, editing with, 29–36
.mov files, 263
Movie Settings dialog, 259, 262, 263
movies. See also video
    compression considerations, 258–260
    exporting, 258–264, 267
    QuickTime, 258–264

MPEG-2, 266
MPEG-4, 259, 260
MS, 52
music
    importing from CDs, 248–252
    replacing production sound with, 285
music tracks, 152–159. See also sound tracks
music videos, 121

N

naming
    clips, 245–247
    projects, 25, 230
    reels, 223
    scenes, 225
    sequences, 57
    shots, 225
    versions, 95–97
narration, 285, 286
navigation tools, 39, 72
NDF timecode, 307
New Project command, 230
Next Edit button, 82
"No Communication" message, 236
Non-Additive Dissolve transition, 194
non-drop-frame timecode, 307–308
non-playspeed, 29, 31
non-ripple
    deletes, 129–130
    inserts, 115, 117–128. See also Overwrite edits
    trims, 86–89, 109–111
nondestructive editing, 21, 62
Nonlinear: A Field Guide to Digital Video and Film Editing, 304
Now option, Capture window, 240, 241–243, 246
NTSC video, 260, 309

O

O key, 42
offline clips, 229
offsets, drop-shadow, 182
opacity, layer, 198, 199
organizing
    multi-track material, 153
    video projects, 218–219, 230–234

Out icon, 42
Out point overlay, 71
Out points. See In/Out points
Out Shift value, 89
output options
    distributing on DVD, 266–270
    exporting movies, 258–264
    exporting still images, 264–266
    recording to master tape, 253–257
overlaps, 107–115
    downside to, 109
    purpose of, 108
    with Roll edit, 109–111, 109–115
Overwrite edits, 115–128
    defined, 115
    in picture only, 117–121
    in sound only, 122–128
    and three- vs. four-point edits, 116–117, 120
    ways of using, 116, 121
Overwrite pointer, 138

P

PAL video, 260, 309
parody videos, 296
PB, 302
personal journals, 298
petabytes, 302
Photoshop, Adobe, 104, 200, 265
picture-in-picture feature, 198
picture tracks. See also tracks
    adding titles using new, 175–178
    locking, 122
    Overwrite edits in, 117–121
    real vs. non-real, 149
    rendering, 151
    splitting from sound, 101–102
    synchronizing with sound, 35, 67
pitch, 31, 38
pixels, 265
Play Around Edit Loop button, 81–82, 85
Play button, 30
playhead, 69, 117
playspeed, 29, 38
plug and play, 305
PNG files, 264
point of view, 52
pointer, 83
points, edit data, 116

Pond Ripple effect, 201
post-production activities, xi–xii,
    159–160, 217–218, 252, 279
poster frames, 54
postlap, 108
POV, 52
PowerBook, xvii
preferences
    dropped frames, 303
    import, 249
    scratch-disk, 231–234
prelap, 108
Previous Edit button, 82
Print to Video settings, 254–255
production, xi, xii, 218. *See also*
    shooting
Project option, Capture window,
    240, 241
project videos, 292
projects
    accessing multiple, 58
    backing up, 96, 234, 270–271
    basic components of, 27
    creating, 230–234
    file-size considerations, 228
    home *vs.* work, 218–219
    ideas for, 279–299
    importing music into, 248–252
    managing, 218–234
    naming, 25, 230
    opening, 53
    organizing, 230–234
    saving, 24–25, 230
    scripted *vs.* unscripted,
        224–225, 279, 280
punch frame, 34, 35, 36
punch shapes, hunting for, 43–48

Q

QuickTime
    movies, 258–264
    players, 260
    still images, 264–266

R

RAM, xvii
Razor Blade tool, 90, 91, 93,
    143–144, 275
RCA miniplugs, 8–9
reaction shots, 116, 117
real-time effects, 173
REC lock slider, 253

Reconnect Media command, 229
recruiting videos, 293
red plugs, 8, 9
Redo command, 164
Reel, Dailies, 53–56, 63
reel numbers, 222–223, 239
Render All command, 182
Render Files folder, 231, 233
render indicator bar, 173
Render Selection command, 173
rendering
    "all" *vs.* "selection," 182
    effects, 173, 233
    picture tracks, 151
    shots, 173, 182
    titles, 175, 178
reports, visual, 298
resolution, 227
reverse shots, 52, 279
RF plugs, 10
right/left arrow keys, 38–39
Ripple delete, 93–94, 275
Ripple Dissolve transition, 195
Ripple Edit icon, 83
ripple inserts, 66–67, 70
ripple trims, 80–82
rippling, 66–67
role-playing videos, 296
Roll Edit icon/mode, 83, 87, 110
Roll edits, 109–115, 129
rolling inserts, 67
room tone, 123
root-level folders, 238
Rubin Cuts folder/project, 99, 109
ruler, 73, 86
rushes, 54

S

S-Video, 7, 8, 10
Save dialog, 24
Save Project As command, 24, 230
saving
    clips, 245–247
    projects, 24–25, 230
scan lines, 264–265
scavenger hunt, 40–48, 309
scenes
    defined, 51
    getting familiar with, 50–58
    naming, 225
    reviewing coverage for, 54–58
school videos, 295–299
Scratch Disks tab, 231–234

screen direction, 85
scripted projects, 224–225, 279,
    286–299
scripts
    annotating, 55–56, 288
    Chocolov Tutorial, 50
    purpose of, 55, 286
scroll arrows, 76, 77
scroll bar, 76
scrubber bar, 22, 31–32, 45, 48
scrubbing audio, 31
SCSI cables, 4
search tools, 246
SECAM, 309
selection bars, 82
semicolon, 75
Sequence menu, 152
sequences
    adjusting interface to facilitate
        building of, 209–216
    backing up, 96
    closing, 58
    creating, 15
    creating multiple versions of,
        95–97
    defined, 27
    deleting material from, 90–94
    duplicating, 96
    head *vs.* tail of, 32
    icons for, 16
    renaming, 57
    reviewing, 53–54
setups, 51, 54–55
shift-offset, 132
shooting. *See also* shots
    contrasted with post-produc-
        tion activities, xi–xii
    dealing with sound recorded
        during, 284–285
    lockdown shots, 283
    video sketches, 280–282
shots
    adjusting one-track, 128–136
    adjusting volume of, 77–78
    applying speed effects to,
        204–207
    defined, 51
    deleting material from, 90–94
    determining duration of, 46
    editing, 59–60
    head *vs.* tail of, 32
    lockdown, 283, 297
    logging, 246
    moving, 136–141

shots *(continued)*
  naming, 225
  organizing, 51
  primary ways of fixing, 78
  relationships between, 52
  rendering, 173
  reversing direction of, 204
  searching for, 246
  slipping, 133–136
  trimming, 79–89
  types of, 52
shuttle controls, 23, 30–31, 32
sketches, 280–282
Sketchwork project, 286
slates, 35, 225, 255
slices, 58
Slide Item tool, 130
slide shows, 276
Slide tool, 130–133
Slip tool, 133–136
slugs, 124–128
snapping, 91, 106, 177
Sorenson codec, 259, 260, 263
sound editors, 159
sound effects, 150–151
sound files, importing, 248–252
sound mix, 159–165
  defined, 159
  environment considerations,
    162
  goal of, 160
  and Hollywood filmmaking,
    159
  importance of, 160, 284
  poor man's, 162
sound tracks. *See also* tracks
  adding, 150–159
  editing, 284
  locking, 117
  Overwrite edits in, 122–128
  real *vs.* non-real, 149
  splitting from picture tracks,
    101–102
  synchronizing with picture
    tracks, 35, 67
Source data points, 116
source material
  adding to edited sequences, 61,
    65
  generating specialized, 125
  unedited, 54
source tapes, 222
source video, destructive *vs.* non-
  destructive editing of, 21, 62

spacebar, 37, 41
speaker icon, 15, 84
speakers, 2
special effects, 150, 214. *See also*
  effects
Speed dialog, 205–206
speed effects, 204–207
splicing, 65
split edit, 108
Split Video Clip at Playhead tool,
  276
splitting tracks, 101–102
spots, 294, 295
sprocket holes, 71
standards
  FireWire, 305–306
  NTSC *vs.* PAL, 309
static electricity, 4
stealing audio, 207
stereo pair indicators, 62
stereo-to-mono adapter, 9
still images, exporting, 264–266
storage media, 302–303
straight cuts, 97, 101
streaming video, 198, 258
student videos, 299
subclips, 242, 246–247
Swap edits, 137, 139–140, 277
sync
  automated tools for restoring,
    143
  and clapboards/slates, 35
  moving in/out of, 141–147
  and ripple *vs.* rolling edits, 67,
    141–142
  and splitting of tracks, 102
  tools to prevent loss of, 141
system requirements, xvii, 173

T

tabs, 23, 58, 63
tail/head terminology, 32
takes, 51
"tape threading" message, 236
tapes
  continuous timecode on,
    219–221
  culling, 275–276
  ejecting, 240
  entering information about,
    239–240
  finding last frame of video on,
    221

labeling, 218, 219, 222–223,
  253
loading, 239–240
logging, 223–224
looping, 256
master. *See* master tapes
numbering system used on,
  306
Target Track control, 104
TB, 302
technical issues, 301–309
  bandwidth, 304
  FireWire, 305–306
  NTSC *vs.* PAL standard, 309
  storage, 302–303
  timecode, 305–308
Technical Support, Apple, 11
television. *See* TV
terabytes, 302
text. *See also* titles
  changing font for, 168, 176
  generating, 166, 176
  moving, 183
three-point edits, 116–117, 120,
  122
TIFF files, 264
time, measuring, 75
time-lapse videography, 297
time scale, 73–74
timecode
  broken *vs.* continuous,
    219–221, 242–243
  drop- *vs.* non-drop-frame,
    307–308
  fixing broken, 244–245
  ignoring, 219
  onscreen *vs.* burned-in, 45, 46
  recording, 47–48
  technical issues, 306–308
  using tape with broken, 244
Timecode Duration field, 46
Timeline
  adjusting shot volume in,
    77–78
  avoiding scrolling of, 211
  contrasted with Canvas, 19
  features, 73–78
  Final Cut Express *vs.* iMovie,
    22
  and Final Cut Express work-
    flow, 20
  illustrated, 13, 19
  inserting keyframes in, 197

managing complexity of, 128–129
purpose of, 18, 73
resizing, 211–212
scrolling, 76–77
specialized editing vocabulary in, 66
stacking elements in, 209
strengths of, 19
track controls, 102–107
trimming, 137
Tint effect, 201–202
titleless master tapes, 257
titles, 165–183
   adding drop shadows to, 178–182
   adding to existing track, 169–175
   adding to new picture track, 175–178
   animating, 196
   changing placement of, 183
   compression considerations, 260
   creating, 165–170, 208–209
   in Final Cut Pro, 167, 168
   improving readability of, 178, 182
   overlapping with pictures, 175
   rendering, 175
   selecting font for, 168
   and snapping feature, 177
   as source material, 165
   spot-checking, 178
track controls, Timeline, 102–107
Track Height control, 75–76, 211
track-insert logic, 154
Track Selection tools, 23
Track Visibility control, 103
tracks. See also picture tracks; sound tracks
   adding, 150–159
   adjusting thickness of, 75–76, 211
   compared with layers, 104–105
   controlling visibility of, 103
   linking/unlinking, 105–107
   locking, 103, 107
   splitting picture from sound, 101–102
   stacking, 209
   targeting for editing, 104
   turning on/off, 23

ways of using multiple, 149–151
trailer, 255
training videos, 121, 291
transition effects, 184–195
   adding to Favorites folder, 195
   compression considerations, 260
   defined, 184
   descriptions of specific, 185–190, 194–195
   folder, 184
   how Final Cut executes, 162
   how to add, 190–193
   purpose of, 184
transitions, adjusting, 79–80
Trim Edit window, 79–80, 82–83
trimming, 79–89
   contrasted with deleting, 90
   defined, 79
   non-ripple, 86–89
   ripple, 80–86
   Timeline, 137
tripods, 204, 260, 282, 287
troubleshooting
   choppy video, 30
   installation, 11
   Mac-camcorder connections, 236–237
tutorials, xvii–xviii, 24–28. See also Chocoluv Tutorial
TV
   as component of edit bay, 2, 16
   hooking up camera to, 6–11
   labeling of audio/video jacks on, 9
   S-Video inputs, 8
two-up display, 113

U

"Unable to initialize video deck" warning, 236
"Unable to locate external video device" warning, 11
"Unable to locate the capture device" warning, 236
undo levels, 95
undoing edits, 89
unedited source material, 54
unscripted projects, 224, 279, 280–286
up/down arrow keys, 39

V

VCR, connecting camera to, 10–11
VCR mode, 4, 5
versions, creating/naming, 95–97
VHS dubs, 11
video
   capturing, 234–243
   compilation, 276–279
   digitizing, 234
   distributing, 279
   for fun, 287–289
   logging, 246
   for school, 295–299
   streaming, 198, 258
   technical issues, 301–309
   for work, 289–295
video clips
   head vs. tail of, 32
   icon for, 15
   identifying beginning of, 71
   importing, 27–28
   long vs. short, 32
   moving backward/forward in, 28
video compositing. See compositing
video compression, 258–264
video controls, 28–48
   importance of mastering, 28–29
   keyboard method, 36–48
   mouse method, 29–36
   practicing use of, 33–36, 39–48
video editing. See also editing
   essential skill required for, 28
   with keyboard, 36–40
   with mouse, 29–36
   traditional display for, 13
video monitor, 5–11
   as component of edit bay, 2
   contrasted with computer display, 5, 6
   importance of, 5–6
   labeling of audio/video jacks on, 9
   using old TV set as, 6
video projects. See projects
video signals, 7
video sketches, 280–282
video streams, 198, 258
video tracks. See tracks
Video Transitions folder, 184
videocassette recorder, 5, 10–11. See also VCR

videotape recorder, 5
videotapes
    continuous timecode on,
        219–221
    culling, 275–276
    ejecting, 240
    entering information about,
        239–240
    finding last frame of video on,
        221
    labeling, 218, 219, 222–223,
        253
    loading, 239–240
    logging, 223–224
    looping, 256
    master. See master tapes
    numbering system used on,
        306
View Finder effect, 201
Viewer
    contrasted with Canvas, 17–18
    contrasted with iMovie moni-
        tor, 22
    Current Timecode field, 46
    and Final Cut Express work-
        flow, 20
    illustrated, 13
    purpose of, 17

tabs in, 58
and traditional editing setup,
    16
video controls, 29–30
visual reports, 298
vocabulary, shot, 52
Voice Over tool, 278, 285
volume, adjusting audio, 77–78,
    160–165
VTR, 5
"VTR OK" message, 237

W
warnings
    "dropped frames during play-
        back," 303
    "No Communication," 236
    "tape threading," 236
    "timecode break," 243
    "Unable to initialize video
        deck," 236
    "Unable to locate external
        video device," 11
    "Unable to locate the capture
        device," 236
white plugs, 8, 9
wide shots, 52

window-in-window feature, 198
Window menu, 214–215
windows
    activating, 20
    purpose/use of tabs in, 58
    rearranging elements in, 12–13
    resizing, 211
    workflow among, 20
wipes, 194
work videos, 289–295
workflow, 20
WS, 52

Y
Y/C video, 7
Y-cord, 9
yellow plugs, 8, 9
yin/yang metaphor, xii

Z
Zip disks, 271
Zoom control, 73–74
Zoom In/Out tools, 74
Zoom slider, 73, 76, 77